THE NATIONAL INSTITUTE OF
ECONOMIC AND SOCIAL RESEARCH

T0328194

Economic and Social Studies
XXIV

OCCUPATION AND PAY IN GREAT BRITAIN 1906-60

A

THE NATIONAL INSTITUTE OF ECONOMIC AND SOCIAL RESEARCH

The National Institute of Economic and Social Research is an independent, non-profit-making body, founded in 1938. It has as its aim the promotion of realistic research, particularly in the field of economics. It conducts research by its own research staff and in co-operation with the universities and other academic bodies. The results of the work done under the Institute's auspices are published in several series, and a list of its publications up to the present time will be found at the end of this volume.

OCCUPATION AND PAY IN GREAT BRITAIN 1906-60

BY

GUY ROUTH

CAMBRIDGE
AT THE UNIVERSITY PRESS
1965

CAMBRIDGE UNIVERSITY PRESS
Cambridge, New York, Melbourne, Madrid, Cape Town, Singapore,
São Paulo, Delhi, Dubai, Tokyo

Cambridge University Press
The Edinburgh Building, Cambridge CB2 8RU, UK

Published in the United States of America by Cambridge University Press, New York

www.cambridge.org
Information on this title: www.cambridge.org/9780521136976

© THE NATIONAL INSTITUTE OF ECONOMIC
AND SOCIAL RESEARCH 1965

First published 1965
This digitally printed version 2010

A catalogue record for this publication is available from the British Library

ISBN 978-0-521-06141-4 Hardback
ISBN 978-0-521-13697-6 Paperback

CONTENTS

Symbols used in tables   *page* vi

List of main tables in text   vii

Preface   ix

INTRODUCTION   1

I OCCUPATIONAL CLASS STRUCTURE
1 Occupational classification   3
2 Distribution by occupational class   6
3 Training time   8
4 International comparisons   11
5 Changes within occupational classes   14
6 The effects of industrial change   39
7 Changes between 1951 and 1959   42
8 Participation rates by age and sex   43
9 Men and women by industry and occupational class, 1951 and 1959   47

II OCCUPATIONAL PAY
1 Employee income distribution 1911/12 and 1958/9   51
2 Pay of occupations and occupational classes   60
3 Class averages for manual workers   101
4 Comparison of occupational class averages   103

III THE TIME AND CIRCUMSTANCES OF PAY CHANGES
1 1906 to 1924   109
2 1924 to 1934   119
3 1935 to 1955   123
4 1956 to 1960   128
5 Periods of change   132

IV INTERPRETATIONS
1 The origin of pay structure   135
2 The driving force of competition   144
3 An explanatory hypothesis   147

APPENDICES

A Occupational composition of the occupational classes *page* 155
B Occupational groups by industry, England and Wales, 1951   158
C Derivation of data on increases in certain professions between
   1951 and 1960   163
D Income distribution, 1911/12 and 1958/9 (table 24)   165
E Employee income after tax (table 25)   169
F Dispersion of manual earnings   170
G Derivation of professional earnings data (table 30)   172
H Derivation of managers' and administrators' earnings   176

Index   177

SYMBOLS USED IN TABLES

..   not available or not applicable

—   nil or negligible

N.D. not distinguished

LIST OF MAIN TABLES IN TEXT

1 Occupational class, sex and industrial status of the gainfully occupied population in Great Britain, 1911, 1921, 1931, 1951 *page* 4
2 Indices of growth of occupational classes, 1911–59 7
3 Percentage of occupied population in Professional, technical and related group and Administrative, executive, managerial and clerical group, nine countries (circa 1950) and USSR (1959) 12
4 Percentage of occupied population in occupational groups, United States (1910–50) and Great Britain (1911–51) 13
5 Higher professions (constituents of class 1A), census years, 1911–51 15
6 Lower professions (constituents of class 1B), census years, 1921–51 17
7 Employers and proprietors (constituents of class 2A), census years, 1911–51 20
8 Managers and administrators (constituents of class 2B), census years, 1911–51 23
9 Staff per employer and manager in various industrial groups, census years, 1911–51 23
10 Clerical workers (constituents of class 3), census years, 1911–51 25
11 Number of foremen and number of manual employees per foreman in various occupational groups, census years, 1911–51 28
12 Skilled manual workers (major constituents of class 5: employees and self-employed), census years, 1911–51 29
13 Distribution of women within class 5 (Skilled workers), chief occupational groups including self-employed, census years, 1911–51 32
14 Semi-skilled workers (major divisions of class 6), census years, 1911–51 34
15(a) Semi-skilled workers in mining and quarrying and in various manufacturing occupations (excluding self-employed), census years, 1911–51 34
  (b) Semi-skilled workers in various occupations in transport and communication, census years, 1911–51 35
16 Unskilled workers (major constituents of class 7: employees only, unless otherwise stated), census years, 1911–51 38
17 Occupational class distribution by industry, England and Wales, 1951 39
18 Distribution of occupied population (including employers, self-employed and unemployed) by industry, census years, 1911–51 and 1959 40
19 Indices of changes in the proportions of each occupational class due to changes in the relative size of Industry Orders (A), all changes (B) and changes within Industry Orders (C), census years, 1911–51 and 1959 42
20 Males and females aged 14 or 15 and over, with numbers and percentages at work, census years, 1911–51 and 1960 44
21 Participation rate of married and unmarried (including widowed and divorced) women in four age-groups, 1931 and 1951 46
22 Female employees in civil employment as a percentage of all females by quinquennial age-groups, 1951 and 1959 47
23 Employment of men and women in Industry Orders, 1951 and 1959 48
24 Distribution of annual income before tax, Great Britain (all employees) 52
25 Distribution of annual income after tax, Great Britain (all employees) 54
26 Employee income distribution after tax, 1911/12 and 1958/9 55
27 Dispersion of manual earnings, 1906, 1938 and 1960 57
28 Dispersion of manual earnings, 1906, 1938 and 1960 (unweighted averages for eight industrial groups) 58
29 Professional earnings, 1913/14, 1922/3 and 1955/6 62
30 Average professional earnings (occupational class 1A), 1913/14, 1922/4, 1935/7, 1955/6 and 1960 64
31 Professional pay in the Civil Service, 1913/14, 1922/4, 1935/7, 1955/6 and 1960 66

32   Lower-professional salaries for men in the Civil Service, 1913, 1924, 1936,
     1955 and 1960   *page* 68
33   Pay in the lower professions (constituents of class 1B), 1913, 1924, 1936, 1955
     and 1960   69
34   Salaries of administrators and managers in the Civil Service (men) (occupa-
     tional class 2B), 1913, 1924, 1936, 1955 and 1960 (London rates)   70
35   Salaries of five managerial occupations, July 1960, with changes between
     1956 and 1960   76
36   Managers' pay, 1913/14, 1924/5, 1938, 1955/6 and 1960   78
37   Clerks' pay (occupational class 3), 1911/13, 1924, 1935, 1955 and 1960 79
38   Earnings of skilled men (occupational class 5), 1906, 1924, 1935, 1955 and
     1960   88
39   Earnings of skilled women manual workers (occupational class 5), 1906,
     1924, 1935, 1955 and 1960   90
40   Earnings or rates for semi-skilled men (occupational class 6), 1906, 1924,
     1935, 1955 and 1960   92
41   Average pay for semi-skilled men (occupational class 6), 1906, 1924, 1935,
     1955 and 1960   93
42   Earnings of semi-skilled women (occupational class 6), 1906, 1924, 1935,
     1955 and 1960   95
43   Earnings or rates for unskilled men (occupational class 7), 1906 and 1924   97
44   Earnings or rates for unskilled men (occupational class 7), 1924, 1935,
     1955 and 1960   98
45   Average earnings of unskilled women, all women manual workers (selected
     industries) and the manual average (selected industries)   101
46   Median earnings for occupational classes 4 and 5, 6 and 7 in various
     industries, 1906 and 1960   102
47   Average earnings, seven occupational classes, 1913/14, 1922/24, 1935/6,
     1955/6 and 1960   104
48   Occupational class averages as percentages of the average for all occupational
     classes, men and women, 1913/14, 1922/4, 1935/6, 1955/6 and 1960   107
49   Indices of wage rates and the cost of living and percentage unemployment,
     United Kingdom, 1906–60   110
50   Estimated increase in average salary of Schedule E tax-payers with new
     arrivals excluded each year, 1915/16 to 1920/1   113
51   Number of workpeople reported as affected by changes in weekly full-time
     rates of wages and aggregate amount of such changes in the years 1920–4   115
52   Salaries in public companies in various industries, 1920/1 to 1924/5   117
53   Professional incomes in 1921/2 and 1922/3   118
54   Indices of pay movements (for non-manual workers), 1924–34   121
55   Engineering industry: interrelationship of earnings in various occupations,
     1950–60   129
56   Unemployment and unfilled vacancies from employment exchange records,
     average for 1958, 1959 and 1960, June and December each year   130
57   Percentage distribution of draughtsmen by fathers' occupational class, 1960,
     and distribution of occupied men by occupational class, 1931   142
58   Occupational classes of draughtsmen's children   143

PREFACE

The project from which this book has come was designed originally by Mr W. A. B. Hopkin when he was Director of the National Institute of Economic and Social Research. With funds from the Nuffield Foundation, the Institute appointed me to begin research in September 1957, and I was joined soon after by Miss Beryl Swift and later by Miss Pam Peachey.

Our brief was to investigate the changing economic fortunes of the principal 'Common Interest Groups' of which society is composed. Source of income was suggested as the criterion by which common interest should be defined and since, for the economically active population, occupation is the main determinant of income, it followed that our concern should be with the fortunes of people following similar occupations. For most occupations there are professional institutions, associations or trade unions whose function is to protect and promote the interests of the group that they represent. Here, we have tried to measure the growth or decline in numbers of these groups and in their relative income between the years immediately preceding the first world war and 1960. The income data cover the major groups of employees and, in addition, some of those in independent practice in the professions, but other self-employed people, proprietors and employers, are omitted. Ideally, we should have included these too, as well as those whose income is derived from property, but an extension of our research into these fields would have yielded dubious results for much labour and we did not even attempt it.

In the event, we found the shifts in occupational distribution much smaller than we had anticipated. General characteristics in 1951 (and in 1959, as far as we could judge) were similar to those of 1911: the bulk of the labour force was still engaged in manual work, while the higher professional class remained numerically insignificant. Managers and working proprietors were an almost constant proportion of the total and though skilled manual workers fell as a proportion, they remained almost constant in numbers. Of the seven classes into which we divided the labour force, only clerical workers rose substantially both in numbers and as a proportion of the whole. As another measure of the extent of qualitative change in the labour force, we estimated time spent in vocational training, over and above minimum school-leaving requirements: this rose from 16·1 years per hundred persons employed in 1911 to 18·3 years in 1959. The rise occasioned considerable effort, but registered as little more than an additional week per occupied person.

Judged by their social and political correlates, these occupational changes have been small; but the *technical* effect of even a small change in proportions may be very great. The work of doctors, engineers and scientists is of profound importance; it is their presence that distinguishes the present from previous epochs. Yet, in 1951, the Census showed only 62,000 doctors, 138,000 engineers, surveyors and architects, and 49,000 scientists. In 1911, however, there were only 36,000 doctors, 25,000 engineers and 5,000 scientists. Their numbers have almost quadrupled, though the increase represents only three-quarters of one per cent of the labour force.

In pay structure, again, the most impressive finding was the rigidity of the inter-class and inter-occupational relationships. According to our calculations, the average for semi-skilled men was 86 per cent of the all-class average in 1913 and 85 per cent in 1960; for unskilled men, the percentage was the same in both years. The women's average was 63 per cent of the all-class average in 1913 and 64 per cent in 1960.

For manual workers in manufacturing and building, there were moderate changes in the dispersion of earnings, as measured by the relationship between median and quartiles, between 1906, 1938 and 1960; but much of this change is eliminated when adjustments are made for the changed proportions of skilled, semi-skilled and unskilled manual workers. For men in manufacturing, the semi-skilled median is 75·7 per cent of the average for foremen and skilled workers in 1906 and 73·3 per cent in 1960; for unskilled men it is 61·9 per cent in both years.

Over the whole range of occupations, however, there have been some striking changes: specifically, in the reduced relative pay of professional workers, both higher and lower, and of male clerical workers. There has been some reduction, too, in the relative pay of skilled manual-working men. These changes have led some people to believe in an inherent tendency for inequalities of pay to diminish with economic advance. When one traces the course of relative pay over time, however, the interesting fact emerges that these reductions have not occurred gradually, as a result of a general tendency, but suddenly, within short periods and owing to an extraordinary conjuncture of circumstances. In intervening periods, egalitarian tendencies have disappeared or been reversed. It is the medieval doctrine of the Just Wage that asserts itself, while the neo-classic doctrine of marginal productivity or even the broader classical doctrine of demand and supply are but dimly discerned.

In the course of our investigations we consulted many individuals and organizations. With few exceptions, they answered our questions with patience and candour[1]. Particular thanks must go to the Ministry of Labour, whose

[1]The most notable exception being the national newspapers, who declined to reveal the pay of their editors, now or in days gone by.

officials were generous with advice and information, and the Committee of London Clearing Bankers, who conducted a special inquiry to give us information that could be compared with pre-war data.

Individuals to whom particular thanks are due for general guidance or help on special problems are Professors E. H. Phelps Brown, B. C. Roberts, Alec Nove and Joan Robinson; Mr Bernard Benjamin of the General Register Office; Mr G. Paine of the Inland Revenue; Mr V. Peschanski of the Institute of World Economy, Moscow; Mr Joseph S. Zeisel of the United States Department of Labor; and my one-time fellow-students of the London School of Economics, Dr Stefan Nedzynski (now Assistant General Secretary of the International Confederation of Free Trade Unions) and Mr J. Simmons (now of the Israel Institute of Productivity). Still more particularly, I should like to thank Lady Wootton, who read and commented on various drafts of the present book and greatly encouraged our efforts; Mr Ernest Kettlety who, as Education Officer of the Institute of Personnel Management, collaborated with me in organizing a series of conferences on pay and employment; Mr Christopher Saunders, at that time Director of the National Institute of Economic and Social Research, and Mrs Anne Jackson, the Institute's Executive Secretary. To Mr Saunders, my debt is profound. He worked through my pages with immense patience; his suggestions have made the book much more intelligible than it would otherwise have been. Miss Jane Harington, the Institute's Librarian, had the task of preparing the manuscript for the press—in the course of which it was greatly improved. The secretarial work was performed with calm efficiency by Miss Ivy Aird.

The labour of collecting and interpreting the data was shared with Miss Swift and Miss Peachey; this was a truly co-operative effort, though the final responsibility for the presentation and interpretation, with all their imperfections, is my own.

Finally, I must thank the Nuffield Foundation who so generously financed this enterprise and Mr W. A. B. Hopkin on whose initiative it was begun.

GUY ROUTH

University of Sussex,

April 1965

INTRODUCTION

For the fifty years between leaving school and retirement, man's central activity is work. His work creates the wealth of society and entitles him to a share of that wealth; and the sort of work that he does is a major determinant of the size of his share. On this basic economic relationship of production and distribution, a complex of other relationships exists, for occupation is itself an important (though by no means the only) determinant of differences in morbidity, mortality, fertility, social outlook and political allegiance, while the occupation of the father, again, partly determines the occupations of his children and, in turn, his children's children[1]. It is to be expected, then, that those who follow a particular occupation should have common interests and a common destiny and should be drawn together to protect and promote those interests.

The British Medical Association was established in 1832, the National Union of Teachers in 1870[2], and somewhere in between there grew the associations of skilled craftsmen that formed the basis of the modern trade union movement. In the 1890's there followed the large-scale organization of unskilled workers, on the one hand, and non-manual workers on the other. Later, we shall consider the roles of these organizations in determining changes in pay, but here we may note that, in origin, they were associations of people following the same occupations (or closely related occupations) and that, even today when trade unions sometimes attempt to embrace all the occupations in a particular industry, rates of pay are fixed by occupation, with other features, such as personal qualities, industry or place, as secondary considerations.

This book is concerned with the changing size of occupational classes and with their concomitant pay structure in Great Britain in the years 1906 to 1960[3]. Comparisons of occupational structure in a country at different times (or different countries at the same time) are significant indicators of social differences because each occupation consists of a bundle of attributes: literacy, theoretical knowledge or manual skill; earning and productive capacity; fertility, mortality and social outlook.

Occupational patterns change with technical advance and capital accumulation, which require a growth of investment in people no less than in machines.

---

[1]Since 1801, when the first population census was held in Great Britain, questions have been included to enable those gainfully employed to be classified by occupation and/or industry. The Registrar General began his decennial investigations into occupational mortality in 1851 and into occupational fertility in 1911.

[2]The British Medical Association assumed its present title in 1856; the National Union of Teachers in 1889.

[3]We should have liked to extend our investigation to the United Kingdom by including Northern Ireland, but the difficulties were insuperable. The population census of 1911 covered all Ireland; none was held there in 1921.

Rising living standards themselves call new services into being, thus causing further occupational change. Technical advance requires a more highly educated work force; and this itself speeds the rate of advance.

Pay structure, too, is indicative of a country's stage of development, a large rural and small urban population going with great inequalities of pay between unskilled labourers and craftsmen and between manual workers in general and professional, administrative and clerical workers. Later, with diversification of the labour force and the spread of literacy, the gulf is narrowed, though what happens in subsequent stages of development is more obscure. Some writers claim to have discovered an inherent tendency for inequalities to disappear as industrial societies mature; others dispute their claims.

The basic assumption of economic theory is that changes in one or more of the variables demand, supply and price will produce such changes in the other or others as to restore (or tend to restore) the equilibrium of the system. But Adam Smith, Mill, Cairnes, Wicksteed and Marshall all gave prominence to warnings of the institutional and psychological impediments to the achievement of this ideal. In latter-day economics, these aspects have tended to be obscured by a controversy about the role of trade unions in the pay-fixing process, some attributing to them almost unlimited power to raise pay whilst others regard them as simple underwriters of market decisions that would have been arrived at anyway. Concurrently, the question of social stratification has become a major preoccupation of sociologists, whose findings have great relevance to the understanding of the labour market.

The questions thus raised are fundamental to an understanding of the society in which we live. To answer them, even tentatively, we need to know a good deal about the changing quantity and price of the occupational units of which the labour market is composed and the demand-supply relationships with which they are associated. In what follows, the quantity aspect (occupational class structure) is considered in chapter I; price (or pay structure) in chapter II; the time and circumstance of pay changes in chapter III. Finally, in chapter IV we consider the nature of the society that has given rise to these relationships and changes and the relevance to it of the dominant theories of economics and sociology.

CHAPTER I

OCCUPATIONAL CLASS STRUCTURE

1. OCCUPATIONAL CLASSIFICATION

Occupation is what a worker does; industry is defined by the final product. The occupations of fitter, clerk, typographer and packer, for example, are followed in a multitude of different industries. Though the Ministry of Labour gives us monthly estimates of the industrial distribution of the occupied population, it is only once in ten years, in the census of population, that we are shown its distribution by occupation[1].

In the report of the 1951 Census, the occupied population was classified into 584 groups, according to 'the kind of work done and the nature of the operation performed'. Each heading describes what can be roughly distinguished as a group of jobs, closely enough related to be performed by people of the same sort of skill, using similar materials and techniques in the same sort of environment. The advantage of this method of classification is its flexibility; the parts are small enough to be manoeuvrable but not so small as to overwhelm with detail. Specifically, they are susceptible to classification into larger groups, whose limits are defined by the purpose of the particular study.

For present purposes, we have posted the 584 occupations of the population census to seven classes, two of which have been subdivided:

Class	1A.	Higher professional
	B.	Lower professional
	2A.	Employers and proprietors
	B.	Managers and administrators
	3.	Clerical workers
	4.	Foremen, inspectors, supervisors
	Manual workers	
	5.	Skilled
	6.	Semi-skilled
	7.	Unskilled

For purposes of comparison, the census occupational tables for England and Wales and Scotland for 1911, 1921 and 1931 have been recast for the present study in accordance with the 1951 classification. We shall refer to these groups as *occupational classes* to distinguish them from the social classes and socio-economic groups used in the census. They are essentially an adaption of these

[1]From May 1963 the Ministry of Labour has produced an annual occupational analysis of employees in manufacturing industry.

Table 1. Occupational class, sex and industrial status of the gainfully occupied population in Great Britain, 1911, 1921, 1931, 1951: numbers in thousands

		All				Males				Females			
		1911	1921	1931	1951	1911	1921	1931	1951	1911	1921	1931	1951
1. Professional													
A. Higher	Employers	..	25	38	34	..	25	37	33	..	—	—	1
	Own account	..	36	44	44	..	35	41	40	..	2	3	4
	Employees	184	134	158	356	173	126	144	326	11	8	15	31
	All	184	195	240	434	173	186	222	399	11	10	18	36
	Per cent	1·00	1·01	1·14	1·93	1·34	1·36	1·50	2·56	0·20	0·18	0·29	0·52
B. Lower	Employers	..	18	15	10	..	14	8	7	..	4	7	3
	Own account	..	62	70	42	..	20	22	22	..	42	48	20
	Employees	560	600	643	1,007	208	242	270	463	352	357	373	544
	All	560	680	728	1,059	208	276	300	492	352	403	428	567
	Per cent	3·05	3·52	3·46	4·70	1·61	2·02	2·03	3·16	6·49	7·07	6·83	8·18
2. Employers, administrators, managers													
A. Employers and proprietors	Employers	763	692	727	457	661	613	646	400	102	79	82	56
	Own account	469	626	682	661	339	435	483	494	130	191	196	167
	All	1,232	1,318	1,409	1,118	1,000	1,048	1,129	894	232	270	278	223
	Per cent	6·71	6·82	6·70	4·97	7·74	7·69	7·65	5·74	4·28	4·74	4·44	3·22
B. Managers and administrators	Own account	21	29	30	31	20	27	28	27	2	2	2	3
	Employees	608	675	740	1,215	486	557	642	1,029	123	118	98	186
	All	629	704	770	1,246	506	584	670	1,056	125	120	100	189
	Per cent	3·43	3·64	3·66	5·53	3·91	4·28	4·54	6·78	2·30	2·11	1·60	2·73

3. Clerical workers												
Own account	—	1	2	3	—	1	2	2	—	—	—	1
Employees	887	1,299	1,463	2,401	708	735	815	988	179	564	648	1,413
All	887	1,300	1,465	2,404	708	736	817	990	179	564	648	1,414
Per cent	4·84	6·72	6·97	10·68	5·48	5·40	5·53	6·35	3·30	9·90	10·34	20·41
4. Foremen, inspectors, supervisors												
Employees	236	279	323	590	227	261	295	511	10	18	28	79
Per cent	1·29	1·44	1·54	2·62	1·75	1·91	2·00	3·28	0·18	0·32	0·45	1·14
Manual workers												
5. Skilled												
Own account	329	293	268	251	170	205	200	214	159	88	68	37
Employees	5,279	5,280	5,351	5,365	4,094	4,200	4,223	4,519	1,185	1,080	1,128	847
All	5,608	5,573	5,619	5,616	4,264	4,405	4,423	4,733	1,344	1,168	1,196	884
Per cent	30·56	28·83	26·72	24·95	32·99	32·30	29·96	30·36	24·78	20·50	19·09	12·75
6. Semi-skilled												
Own account	71	98	96	82	41	70	78	73	30	28	17	10
Employees	7,173	6,446	7,264	7,256	4,305	3,789	4,181	4,279	2,868	2,656	3,084	2,978
All	7,244	6,544	7,360	7,338	4,346	3,859	4,259	4,352	2,898	2,684	3,101	2,988
Per cent	39·48	33·85	35·00	32·60	33·63	28·30	28·85	27·92	53·42	47·11	49·51	43·12
7. Unskilled												
Own account	47	62	78	33	38	48	65	29	9	14	13	3
Employees	1,720	2,678	3,034	2,676	1,455	2,232	2,580	2,129	265	446	454	547
All	1,767	2,740	3,115	2,709	1,493	2,280	2,645	2,158	274	460	467	550
Per cent	9·63	14·17	14·81	12·03	11·55	16·72	17·92	13·84	5·05	8·07	7·45	7·94
All	18,347	19,333	21,029	22,514	12,925	13,636	14,761	15,584	5,425	5,697	6,264	6,930
Per cent	100·00	100·00	100·00	100·00	100·00	100·00	100·00	100·00	100·00	100·00	100·00	100·00

census groupings, with certain modifications in detail. Their composition is shown in Appendix A[1].

2. DISTRIBUTION BY OCCUPATIONAL CLASS

The world of 1911 seems remote when viewed from the modern age. We look back, over wars and revolutions, to a world of gaslight, music hall and hansom cab, which seems vastly different from our own. We should expect these differences to be reflected in the occupational groupings of the labour force, and yet the dominant fact, then and now, is the preponderance of the group of manual workers. The professional class has remained an insignificant proportion of the whole: a little over 4 per cent in 1911; a little under 8 per cent in 1959. Numbers and proportions for the four census years are shown in table 1. The proportions constituted by manual workers and classes 1 to 3 in these years and in 1959 were as follows[2]:

Percentages

		1911	1921	1931	1951	1959
1.	Professional	4·05	4·53	4·60	6·63	7·78
2.	Employers, managers	10·14	10·46	10·36	10·50	10·06
3.	Clerical	4·84	6·72	6·97	10·68	12·00
4-7.	Foremen and manual	80·97	78·29	78·07	72·19	70·16
		100·00	100·00	100·00	100·00	100·00

It is the clerks who have taken up most of the group yielded by the manual workers; the relative growth of the professionals has been more moderate, while the employers, proprietors, managers and administrators of class 2 have maintained a remarkable constancy. While the proportion of foremen, inspectors and supervisors (occupational class 4) has increased steadily, from 1·3 per cent in 1911 to 2·6 per cent in 1951, that of skilled manual workers has

[1]Since 1861, to the inconvenience of those who use them, the census reports for England and Wales, on the one hand, and Scotland, on the other, have been published separately, though taken on the same day; here the numbers have been added together.   There was no great difficulty in reconciling the classifications of 1921 and 1931 with 1951 for, despite some aberrations in 1931, they remained fairly consistent.   A particular obstacle relates to the status divisions of 1931, in which employers and managers were pooled under the heading 'managerial'; where other guides were not available, these were subdivided in the 1921 ratio.   For 1911, the task was much more hazardous.   In some cases, for example in the professions and the building industry, the occupational demarcation was similar; in others, such as mining and railways, information was available from current reports; for process workers in manufacturing industry, where the occupational classification was still heavily laced with industrial elements, numbers were divided according to the occupational ratios shown for the relevant industry in the Board of Trade *Report of an Enquiry . . . into Earnings and Hours of Labour of Workpeople in the United Kingdom in 1906*, 8 parts (H.M. Stationery Office, 1909-13).   Whatever uncertainty may be inherent in occupational information derived from households, it is thus greatly magnified in much of the material relating to 1911.   Where the 1951 categories were not matched and have had to be estimated for the earlier years on inadequate information, numbers in the tables have been put in brackets.

[2]The 1959 distribution makes allowance only for changes since 1951 in industrial distribution and, for manufacturing industries, changed proportions of manual and non-manual workers.   Its derivation is explained on page 43.

shown a steady fall. So has that of semi-skilled workers, with the exception of the period 1921-31. By contrast, the fall in the proportion of the unskilled began only after 1931.

What come through as small changes in the grand design are the result of quite substantial changes in the parts, for a change of one per cent in relative share in 1951, for example, would have required the transfer of 225,000 people from one class to another. These changes are measured in table 2 which shows, for each class, its relative increase from one census year to the next.

Table 2. *Indices of growth of occupational classes, 1911-59*

Occupational class	'000s in 1911	Percentage of previous census year				Percentage of 1911
		1921	1931	1951	1959	1959
1A. Higher professional	184	*106*	*123*	*181*	*126*	*297*
B. Lower professional	560	*121*	*107*	*145*	*126*	*238*
2A. Employers and proprietors	1,232	*107*	*107*	*79*		
B. Managers and administrators	629	*112*	*109*	*162*	*103*	*131*
3. Clerical workers	887	*147*	*113*	*164*	*121*	*327*
4. Foremen, inspectors, supervisors	236	*118*	*116*	*183*	*109*	*272*
5. Skilled workers	5,608	*99*	*101*	*100*	*107*	*106*
6. Semi-skilled workers	7,244	*90*	*112*	*100*	*102*	*104*
7. Unskilled workers	1,767	*155*	*114*	*87*	*104*	*159*
	18,348	*106*	*108*	*107*	*104*	*132*

The higher professional class is small, but its numbers increased almost threefold between 1911 and 1959. Lower professionals, clerks and foremen also increased substantially more than the labour force, while skilled and semi-skilled manual workers increased substantially less.

Not only are there great differences in the rate of increase of various classes; these rates have varied considerably over time. This is best shown by comparing the average annual compound percentage rates of increase in the different periods:

	1911–21	1921–31	1931–51	1951–9
1A. Higher professional	0·5	2·1	3·0	3·0
1B. Lower professional	1·9	0·7	1·9	3·0
3. Clerks	3·9	1·2	2·5	2·4
Total occupied population	0·5	0·8	0·3	0·4

The class changes are the net result of various effects: the rise or fall of the occupations of which each class is composed, which themselves are part result of changes in industrial distribution. These will be considered later in this chapter, together with the changes in participation rate by age and sex. But before that is done, two things will help to bring the data of table 1 into focus: a consideration of the training time required to produce the occupants of each class and a comparison of occupational distribution in Britain with that in various other countries.

3. TRAINING TIME

One way of gauging the significance of the occupational class divisions is to estimate the average time required beyond the minimum school-leaving age to train a worker for entry into each class. A first approximation is to find how much full-time formal education is normally obtained by those in occupations characteristic of each class.

In 1951, the census schedule asked, for the first time, for those in or seeking employment, the age at which full-time education had come to an end[1]. In unskilled occupations (Order XXVI, England and Wales) in the age-group 25 to 44, those who had left under 15 constituted 92·4 per cent of the men and 93·9 per cent of the women. The average terminal age was 14·2 years for men and 14·1 for women[2]. As we ascend the occupational hierarchy, average terminal ages advance as follows:

	Males	Females
Road transport workers	14·2	—
Salesman, shop assistants	14·5	14·3
Fitters, machine erectors (inc. mates)	14·3	—
Engineering foremen	14·4	—
Clerks, typists, etc.	15·4	15·3
Managers in industrial undertakings[a]	15·6	—
Professional engineers, architects[a]	17·3	—
Teachers[a]	19·1	19·6

[a]Assuming that those who left at 20 or over, left, on average, at 21. An assumption of an average leaving age of 22 for this group would raise the average fractionally.

The differences are surprisingly small: only fifteen weeks between the average for the unskilled man and the engineering foreman, and less than a year between the foreman and the clerk. The professional engineer and architect have two years more than the average clerk and the teacher one and three-quarter years more than the engineer. But in part this merely shows the difference between those occupations where a great deal of study may take place in part-time study and on the job, and those where the occupant is produced by an educational establishment 'ready-to-work'. Clergymen and

[1]See chapter VI of the *Census 1951, England and Wales: General Report* (H.M. Stationery Office, 1958), and tables 42 to 48 of the *General Tables* (H.M. Stationery Office, 1957).

[2]Terminal ages are tabulated in five groups: under 15, 15, 16, 17-19, 20 and over. In calculating the averages, we have assumed that those who left school under 15 left at 14, those who left in the span 17-19 left on average at 18, and those who left at 20 or over (0·5 per cent of the men in this Order) are assumed to have left at 20.

medical practitioners belong to the latter category and 80 and 90 per cent respectively had, in 1951, ceased full-time education over the age of nineteen.

There is little significant difference in the average terminal age in occupational classes 4 to 7 (foremen, skilled, semi-skilled and unskilled manual workers), in all of which four-fifths or more of those employed left school under the age of fifteen[1].

The amount of full-time formal education, however, tells only part of the story. We must also look at training requirements on the job. For semi-skilled work this varies considerably. In some cases, the approach may be through unskilled work: on the railways, firemen are recruited from cleaners, drivers from firemen, and most of the requisite knowledge is acquired in those capacities. A bus driver or conductor, postman or ticket examiner may be working efficiently after a few weeks. In manufacturing industry, it may take longer before sufficient dexterity and knowledge has been acquired for the value of production to outweigh the cost of wages plus that of spoilt goods. In retail distribution and catering, authority acquired through knowledge and experience are needed for the handling of customers. In farming, knowledge may be absorbed from childhood and be enriched by experience from year to year. The range of training time is thus wide, its boundaries ill-defined.

The standard for the skilled worker (occupational class 5) is the time-served craftsman, though apprenticeship is by no means the only path to this level of skill[2]. Engineering and building apprentices are indentured for five years; those in printing, for six. In 1958, a sub-committee of the National Joint Advisory Council reported, 'There are some occupations for which five years may not be too long; but we feel that with the adoption of up-to-date methods of training there are others in which the present period could be reduced'[3].

However, in assessing the time-cost of training, we must deduct not only time unnecessarily spent, but the time-value of goods produced or services performed. We shall follow Dr Liepmann in concluding that the break-even point comes after two years of training[4].

The full-time education of foremen (occupational class 4) hardly differs from that of craftsmen. In fact, they are generally recruited from the ranks of the skilled workers who are promoted not because of any additional formal

[1]There are some notable exceptions. In the case of shop assistants in chemists' and photographic shops, only 49 per cent of the men and 66 per cent of the women had left school under the age of 15; for telephone operators (female) the percentage was 66 and for foremen electricians, 73.

[2]In engineering, in southern England, craft jobs are often filled by promotion of the semi-skilled; in metal manufacture and textiles, too, skilled work is reached by promotion.

[3]Ministry of Labour and National Service, *Training for Skill* (H.M. Stationery Office, 1958), p. 23.

[4]Kate Liepmann, *Apprenticeship* (London, Routledge and Kegan Paul, 1960), p. 81.

training but by virtue of personality and experience[1]. Accordingly, we attribute two years' training time to foremen: the same as for skilled workers.

The clerk has on average about one year's full-time education in excess of the craftsman. Thereafter, he begins to pay his way within a fairly short time. He will be promoted as he gathers experience and will be taught new routines as he comes to them so that, like the foreman, he will continue to increase his value as a productive agent for many years. Some office jobs, like shorthand and typing, can be learnt outside the office and the average terminal education age for women secretary-shorthand typists (all age-groups) in 1951 was ten months in excess of that for other female clerks or a year and ten months more than that of engineering fitters. It seems reasonable, then, to attribute a two-year training period to clerks too.

For classes 2A and 2B (Employers, proprietors, managers and administrators) formal evaluation is much more difficult because of the diverse modes of entry and the variety of qualifications needed (or judged superfluous). However, there are many occupations in class 2B for which formal qualifications are required (for example, chartered secretaries, bank and insurance managers, administrative and executive officers in the Civil Service) and these entail, in addition to experience in the field, a full-time (or part-time equivalent) training of four or five years. We therefore adopt four and a half years as the standard for this class.

A similar corpus of knowledge is required of those in the lower professions. Draughtsmen are drawn from the ranks of boys who have completed a craft apprenticeship or who have some General Certificate of Education passes. Most draughtsmen acquire an Ordinary or Higher National Certificate or their equivalent in relevant subjects. Chiropodists need four GCE ordinary level passes, followed by a three-year full-time training; teachers, a university degree or a two- or three-year training at a teachers' training college; occupational therapists, a three- or three-and-a-half-year post-GCE study period and two years' apprenticeship. We adopt five years as the standard training time for this class.

The higher professions require post-GCE full-time courses of between four and six years or, in certain cases, their part-time equivalent combined with practical experience. Chartered accountants must be articled for five years and pass the examinations of the Institute. Engineers may qualify by a three- or four-year university course or the more arduous method of part-time study, leading to membership of a professional institute. After the minimum school-leaving age, then, class 1A occupations require on average about seven years of full-time study or the part-time equivalent.

The effect on learning time of changes in occupational distribution may now be summarized by multiplying the class percentages shown in table 1 by the

[1]See National Institute of Industrial Psychology, *The Foreman: a Study of Supervision in British Industry* (London, Staples Press, 1951), pp. 128-9.

learning time suggested above for the relevant class.   The result gives learning time per hundred occupied in each year and is as follows:

	Years
1911	16·1
1921	16·2
1931	16·0
1951	17·7
1959	18·3

For every hundred members of the labour force there was an investment of 16·1 years of training in 1911 and 18·3 years in 1959.   The rise has occasioned considerable effort, though it registers as little more than an additional week per occupied person.   The calculation regards occupational class 7 (Unskilled workers) as requiring no training and takes no account of changes in the minimum school-leaving age nor of the social benefits that this may have produced.

4.   INTERNATIONAL COMPARISONS

It is illuminating to compare the broad occupational structure of Britain with some other countries.   For this purpose, we use the *International Standard Classification of Occupations*[1] Major Group 0 (Professional, technical and related workers) and Major Groups 1 and 2 (Administrative, executive and managerial workers and Clerical workers).   Even this broad analysis restricts comparison to a few countries and excludes, for example, France and the German Federal Republic, for which occupational distributions are not available.

The proportions for ten countries are shown in table 3.   There is clearly a correlation between the level of industrial development and the proportion of the labour force in these two non-manual groups.   At the one end are countries where great blocks of the population are occupied in own-account or family subsistence farming and what might be called the 'subsistence trading' that is a feature of backward economies; at the other end, countries where farming itself is a branch of capitalist enterprise.   The finer gradations are the result of a multiplicity of causes including the real wealth of the community and its industrial distribution[2].

The USSR shows an extraordinary contrast with its high proportion of professionals and low proportion of managers and clerks.   While we estimate that clerical workers in Britain constituted twelve per cent of the occupied population in 1959, Soviet reports show 2·8 per cent for the USSR.   Professor Alec Nove has commented on this phenomenon: '. . . there are remarkably few

[1]International Labour Office (Geneva, 1958).
[2]Greater wealth requires a larger financial sector to service it, while as we demonstrate for Great Britain in Appendix B, there is a considerable difference in the occupational class composition of different industries.

Table 3. *Percentage of occupied population in Professional, technical and related group and Administrative, executive, managerial and clerical group, nine countries (circa 1950) and USSR (1959)*

		Professional[a]	Administrative[b]	Total
United States	(1950)	7·9	20·7	28·6
Canada	(1951)	7·1	20·3	27·4
Australia[c]	(1947)	5·1	18·3	23·4
Great Britain	(1951)	6·3	16·8	23·1
Sweden	(1950)	7·0	13·2	20·2
USSR	(1959)	10·1	5·8	15·9
Japan[c]	(1950)	4·6	10·5	15·1
Spain	(1950)	3·3	7·3	10·6
Brazil[c]	(1950)	2·3	6·4	8·7
India[d]	(1951)	1·6	0·3	1·9

[a]Professional, etc., workers exclude officers in the armed services, navigating officers and pilots, but otherwise accord with occupational class 1.
[b]Administrative, etc., workers exclude farmers and farm managers, own-account shopkeepers and most other working proprietors.
[c]Excludes unemployed.
[d]Excludes dependants, even though earning.
Sources: Great Britain, *Census 1951*; USSR *Vestnik Statistiki*, no. 12, 1960; other countries, United Nations *Demographic Yearbook, 1956* (New York, 1956), table 13, p. 388.

clerks in the Soviet civil service, and this, one suspects, is generally true of their way of doing business. Far fewer letters, far smaller offices . . . Much more seems to be decided by more senior staff, and by word of mouth, by personal dealings or at meetings'[1].

Some of the forms that national differences may take are shown in the more detailed comparison of Great Britain and the United States in table 4. For this purpose, we have reclassified the British data to accord with the 'social-economic groups' used by Alba M. Edwards in his official study for the United States[2]. American usage is in marked contrast to the British in some respects: the 'clerical and kindred' group includes not only office workers but also radio operators, laboratory assistants, caretakers, messengers, baggagemen, postmen, telegraphists and telephonists; the 'skilled workers' group is restricted much more closely to the traditional crafts but includes bus conductors who are

[1]*Occupational Patterns in the USSR and Great Britain: Some Comparisons and Contrasts*, Manchester Statistical Society, paper read 10 January 1962, p. 11.
[2]United States Bureau of the Census, *Comparative Occupation Statistics for the United States, 1870 to 1940*, 16th Census of the United States, 1940, Population (Washington, Government Printing Office, 1943), part III. The series is extended to 1950 in *The American Workers' Fact Book* (Washington, United States Department of Labor, 1956), pp. 20 and 22. Sales workers have here been separated from 'clerical and kindred' by using the figures for the former given in the United States Bureau of the Census, *Historical Statistics of the United States, Colonial Times to 1957* (Washington, Government Printing Office, 1960), pp. 75–8. The same source was used for the separation of wholesale and retail dealers from 'other proprietors, etc.' for 1950.

graded as semi-skilled in the British scheme. 'Conductors (railroad)' are given a still more elevated status and classified with 'other proprietors and managers'.

Table 4. *Percentage of occupied population in occupational groups, United States (1910-50) and Great Britain (1911-51)*

		US GB	1910 1911	1920 1921	1930 1931	1940	1950 1951
1. Professional and semi-professional		US GB	4·4 4·1	5·0 4·3	6·1 4·4	6·5 ..	7·5 6·1
2. Proprietors, managers, officials		US GB	23·0 10·4	22·3 10·7	19·9 10·6	17·8 ..	16·3 10·6
of whom	Farmers	US GB	16·5 1·6	15·5 1·8	12·4 1·6	10·1 ..	7·5 0·9
	Wholesale and retail dealers	US GB	3·3 2·7	3·4 2·4	3·7 2·8	3·9 ..	3·2 2·0
	Others	US GB	3·2 6·1	3·4 6·5	3·8 6·2	3·7 ..	5·6 7·7
3. Clerical and kindred		US GB	5·2 7·3	8·8 8·8	10·0 9·2	10·6 ..	13·3 12·7
4. Sales		US GB	5·0 5·7	5·0 4·7	6·3 6·1	6·6 ..	6·9 5·4
5. Skilled workers and foremen		US GB	11·7 13·9	13·5 15·7	12·9 15·0	11·7 ..	13·8 16·8
6. Servant classes		US GB	6·8 10·4	5·4 8·4	6·9 9·4	8·0 ..	7·4 6·1
7. Farm labourers		US GB	14·5 6·5	9·4 5·2	8·6 4·4	7·1 ..	4·6 3·2
8. Semi-skilled and unskilled workers, not elsewhere classified		US GB	29·4 41·7	30·7 42·2	29·3 40·9	31·7 ..	30·2 39·1

Source: See text, p. 12, and footnote 2.

In part, the differences shown in table 4 are geographically determined: the United States draws its food from within its own borders, while Britain gets the bulk of its supply from other countries. This has the effect of raising the relative number of farmers and farm labourers in the United States and thus lowering the proportion of all other classes. In 1910, farm employment absorbed 31 per cent of the labour force in the United States, compared with 8·1 per cent in Britain. In 1950, the relevant percentages were 12·1 and 4·1. If the comparison is confined to non-farm employment, the professional and clerical groups compare thus:

		United States %	Great Britain %
Professional	1910 or 1911	5·8	4·4
	1950 or 1951	8·4	6·35
Clerical	1910 or 1911	6·8	7·9
	1950 or 1951	14·9	13·2

The apparent excess of semi-skilled and unskilled workers in Britain is reduced to some extent by the elimination of farm labour from the comparison: 38·5 per cent in the United States in 1910, compared to 45·1 per cent in Britain, and 33·9 to 40·7 per cent for 1950 or 1951.

In general, the similarities are more striking than the differences, and it seems surprising that the superior wealth and industrial advancement of the United States has not resulted in a much greater difference in the proportion of white-collar workers.

In the case of non-administrative office workers (or *clerks* in the British sense) the proportions are extraordinarily similar[1]:

United States	%	Great Britain	%
1910	4·0	1911	4·8
1920	6·6	1921	6·7
1930	7·3	1931	7·0
1940	8·2	..	..
1950	10·4	1951	10·7

This suggests a certain inevitability about certain aspects of occupational distribution, dependent on technique and social advance, that overrides national boundaries. However, the relative size of the occupational classes is the result of many influences. Of immediate interest in assessing the significance of their growth or decline is a consideration of variations in the numbers in the occupations of which each class is composed and it is to this that we shall now turn.

5. CHANGES WITHIN THE OCCUPATIONAL CLASSES

(a) Class 1A (Higher professions)

In 1911, the dominant group amongst the higher professions was constituted by the 53,000 ministers of religion. Then came the 36,000 doctors and dentists and then the 26,000 lawyers. Professional engineers, numbering ten thousand, were a smaller group than naval and army officers, writers or chartered accountants. There were less than five thousand scientists. Then those in the technological professions increased with extraordinary rapidity: in table 5 their size and growth is shown alongside that of the other major groups in class 1A. This group, comprising engineers, architects, surveyors and scientists, increased at a compound annual rate of 4·75 per cent between 1911 and 1921;

[1]The data include cashiers and book-keepers; stenographers, typists and secretaries; office machine operators; shipping and receiving clerks; bank tellers; dispatchers and starters, vehicle; clerical and kindred not elsewhere classified.

Table 5. *Higher professions (constituents of class 1A), census years, 1911-51*

	1911	1921		1931		1951		
	'000s	'000s	% of 1911	'000s	% of 1921	'000s	% of 1931	% of 1911
Church	53	45	85	48	107	49	102	92
Medicine	36	38	106	46	121	62	135	172
Law	26	22	85	23	105	27	117	104
Engineering[a]	25	35	140	51	146	138	271	552
Writing[b]	15	14	93	21	150	26	124	173
Armed forces[c]	14	19	136	16	84	46	288	329
Accounting	11	9	82	16	174	37	231	336
Science[d]	5	13	260	20	154	49	245	980
Total	184	195	106	240	123	434	181	236
All occupational classes	18,347	19,333	106	21,029	108	22,514	107	123

[a]Includes surveyors, architects and ship-designers.
[b]Includes editors and journalists.
[c]Commissioned officers.
[d]Includes statisticians and economists.

4 per cent between 1921 and 1931 and 5 per cent between 1931 and 1951. The major increase for mechanical and electrical engineers was in the decade to 1931, in which their numbers rose from two thousand to twelve thousand. This, of course, was a period of rapid growth in the electrical and motor industries.

Thus the constitution of the higher professional class was markedly different in 1951 from what it had been in 1911. Between 1951 and 1960, the change continued at accelerated pace: the annual rate of increase of engineers we estimate at about 7 per cent and that of scientists at about 7·5 per cent. Doctors increased by rather more than 2 per cent per year, while the number of dentists increased not at all[1].

We cannot say with any certainty how class 1A as a whole had grown by 1960. The Ministry of Labour does give us the distribution of the employed population by industry, however, as well as the proportion of non-manual workers (those in our occupational classes 1 to 3) in manufacturing industries and the effect of these changes (other things being equal) would have been to raise the numbers in class 1A from 434,000 in 1951 to 545,000 in 1960, that is from 1·9 to 2·3 per cent of the work force[2].

[1]The calculations are described in Appendix C.
[2]The effect of industrial change is analysed in §6, pp. 39-42 below.

Industrial status

In 1931, 34 per cent of the class were employers or self-employed; by 1951, the proportion had fallen to 18 per cent.   Indeed, the percentage of non-employees is reduced to 13 for 1951 if medical practitioners are regarded as employees of the National Health Service[1].   Lawyers, architects, accountants and writers presented the largest proportions of employers or self-employed outside medicine, but it was only in the legal profession in 1951 that employees remained in the minority:

Percentages

		Employers	Self-employed	Employees
Lawyers	1931	59	18	22
	1951	39	18	42
Architects	1931	27	26	47
	1951	13	12	75
Accountants	1931	39	12	49
	1951	21	10	79
Authors, editors, journalists	1931	4	26	70
	1951	1	21	78

Distribution by sex

Women have formed only a small proportion of the higher professions: 6 per cent in 1911, 8 per cent in 1951.   Even if engineers and officers in the armed services are excluded, women formed only 10 per cent of the remainder in 1931 and 11 per cent in 1951.   The professions where they were most strongly represented were:

	1951	
	Nos.	%
Doctors and dentists	7,613	*15·5*
Scientists	4,938	*10·0*
Authors, editors, journalists	4,988	*23·9*

Compared with 1931, there had been a great increase in the number of women solicitors, dentists, architects and accountants, but in none of these professions did they number as many as a thousand.

(b) *Class 1B (Lower professions)*

Nurses and teachers constituted more than half of this class in 1951.   The rise in their numbers has been proceeding steadily since the latter half of the nineteenth century: the number of nurses doubled between 1881 and 1911 and increased two and a half times between 1911 and 1951.   The number of teachers (including university teachers) rose one and a half times between 1881 and 1911 and one and a quarter times between 1911 and 1951.

But there are other occupations in this class whose rise has been of such

---

[1]They are taxed under Schedule D, but are *defacto* employees engaged on task work. Dentists, by contrast, are paid by the piece.

Table 6. *Lower professions (constituents of class 1B), census years, 1921-51*

		1921 '000s	1931 '000s	1931 % of 1921	1951 '000s	1951 % of 1931	% of 1921
Nurses	M	2	4	200	29	725	1,450
	F	113	141	125	237	168	210
Others in medicine[a]	M	17	19	112	41	216	241
	F	4	8	200	29	362·5	725
Teachers[b]	M	77	89	116	133	149	173
	F	210	206	98	207	100	99
Draughtsmen[c]	M	34	53	156	120	226	353
	F	4	6	150	14	233	350
Laboratory technicians	M	4	9	225	51	566	1,275
	F	1	2	200	18	900	1,800
Librarians	M	1	3	300	5	166	500
	F	1	4	400	11	275	1,100
Social welfare workers	M	1	5	500	10	200	1,000
	F	2	4	200	14	350	700
Navigating and engineering officers, aircrew	M	37	36	97	30	83	∖81
	F	—	—	—	—	—	—
Arts[d]	M	42	49	117	39	80	93
	F	40	42	105	27	64	67·5
Others[e]	M	59	30	51	35	117	59
	F	25	9	36	8	89	32
All in Class 1B	M	276	300	109	492	164	178
	F	404	427	106	567	133	140
Total		680	728	108	1,059	145	156
All occupational classes		19,333	21,029	108	22,514	107	116

[a]Includes veterinary surgeons, pharmacists and opticians.
[b]Excludes music teachers.
[c]Includes industrial designers.
[d]Includes painters, producers, actors, musicians and music teachers.
[e]Includes articled students in 1921 and 1931.

recent origin that they were of insufficient importance for separate listing in 1911: draughtsmen were included with clerks; laboratory assistants with physicists, metallurgists and others as 'persons engaged in scientific pursuits'. Nor were librarians or social welfare workers separately distinguished and aviators (or pilots, aeroplane) were classified with acrobats and professors of legerdemain under the subhead 'Performer, showman: exhibition, games–service'.

Most of the occupations included rose in numbers between 1911 and 1921; in the few cases where a decline was registered (engineering officers on board ship, painters and sculptors, musicians and music teachers) it was small. As far as can be estimated, the class total rose from about 560,000 to 680,000. Table 6 shows the major changes between 1921 and 1951.

Most of the groups have been growing fast, but a few have been in decline. In some cases, we can bring our information up to 1960 (though using somewhat different definitions)[1]:

	1951 '000s	1960 '000s	1960 % of 1951
Nurses and midwives, National Health Service			
Whole-time	154·7	185·7	*120*
Part-time	29·2	50·0	*171*
Total	183·9	235·7	*128*
Other medical auxiliaries, hospital service			
Whole-time	16·2	21·6	*134*
Teachers, full-time			
University	8·6	11·8	*134*
Other	272·9	350·0	*128*
Total	281·5	361·8	*129*
Laboratory technicians[a]	39·0	67·0	*172*
Draughtsmen and design technicians[a]	89·0	198·0	*222*

[a]In chemical, metal and engineering industries only.

Rates of increase remain extraordinarily high. For nurses, the compound rate of increase has fallen fractionally as compared with the period 1921-31, from 2·9 to 2·8 per cent per year. The medical auxiliaries in the hospital service form less than a quarter of those listed as 'others in medicine' in table 6, but it is unlikely that their rate of increase has been less than that of the whole group. It seems, then, that the rate of increase, though still high, has fallen below that for the period 1931-51: from 4·9 to 3·2 per cent per year. The rate of increase in the number of teachers, by contrast, has greatly increased: from 0·8 per cent per year from 1931-51, to 2·8 per cent per year from 1951-60.

Rates of increase for laboratory technicians and draughtsmen have been extraordinary:

	Increase % per year	
	1931–51	1951–60
Laboratory technicians	9·5	6·2
Draughtsmen	4·2	9·2

For 1951-60, the rate of increase is that for the group *chemicals, metals and engineering* (where one would expect it to be at its maximum) whose total labour force went up by 11 per cent between 1951 and 1960. But even if there had been no increase at all outside these industries, the compound increases would have been 5 per cent for laboratory technicians and 6·8 per cent for draughtsmen[2].

[1]The calculations are described in Appendix C.
[2]Of course, this is subject to any exaggeration implicit in the Ministry of Labour's sample described in Appendix C.

Industrial status

For most occupations in this class, employees predominate. Where they do not, the drift to employee status, noted above, is revealed in the comparison of 1951 with 1931, with actors and musicians moving against the trend.

		Total '000s	Percentage of total Employers	Own account
Subordinate medical service[a]	1931	33·8	*10·6*	*16·7*
	1951	66·8	*6·9*	*13·7*
Music teachers	1931	24·6	*7·6*	*82·2*
	1951	13·0	*0·6*	*59·6*
Painters, sculptors	1931	16·9	*4·0*	*47·3*
	1951	17·6	*2·8*	*36·8*
Actors and entertainers	1931	18·8	*1·0*	*13·1*
	1951	16·0	*0·8*	*17·8*
Musicians	1931	27·9	*1·2*	*18·3*
	1951	16·0	*1·3*	*26·8*

[a]So styled in 1921 and 1931.   Includes pharmacists, opticians, masseurs, physiotherapists, chiropodists.

Distribution by sex

Numbers of males and females in the main occupational groups have been shown in table 6. As with the higher professions, so here sex barriers have tended to disappear over the years. Not only are women now established in what were almost exclusively male professions, but the reverse has taken place too: in 1951, more than 10 per cent of nurses were men, while men accounted for the entire increase in the number of teachers between 1911 and 1951. But the number of women teachers, that had hardly varied between 1911 and 1951, began increasing after the latter year. Between 1951 and 1960 in England and Wales, the number of women teachers rose by 21,000 (22 per cent) and the number of men teachers by 36,000 (37 per cent).

There are very few professions where barriers to entry on grounds of sex are at present applicable.

(c)   Class 2A (*Employers and proprietors*)

All employers are included in this class, except those in occupational class 1, but only those self-employed proprietors for whose occupation the control of property is decisive[1]. Thus farmers, shopkeepers and boarding-house

[1]But the distinction between an employer and a manager is a distinction rather in law than in economics, for an employer becomes a manager as soon as his business is incorporated, and, however interesting the distinction may be, we cannot, from the census material, distinguish between a manager who depends for his position in a business on his ownership of shares and one who does not.

In the 1961 classification, employers with 25 or more employees are distinguished from those with fewer, but for previous years there was no means of knowing how many employees an employer employed.

Table 7. *Employers and proprietors (constituents of class 2A),*
census years, 1911-51

	1911 '000s	1921 '000s	1921 % of 1911	1931 '000s	1931 % of 1921	1951 '000s	1951 % of 1931	1951 % of 1911
Farmers								
Employers	172	167	97	163	98	123	75	72
Own account	73	135	185	114	84	179	157	245
Total	245	302	123	277	92	302	109	123
Mining and manufacturing								
Employers	173	178	103	167	94	55	33	32
Building and decorating								
Employers	70	42	60	58	138	38	66	54
Road transport								
Employers	13	15	115	19	127	9	47	69
Own account	21	37	176	40	108	38	95	181
Total	34	52	153	59	113	47	80	138
Distributive trade								
Employers	220	182	83	217	119	128	59	58
Own account	275	286	104	362	127	312	86	113
Total	495	468	95	579	124	440	76	89
Personal service[a]								
Employers	79	58	73	58	100	54	93	68
Catering[b]								
Own account	70	132	189	125	95	111	89	159
Others in class 2A								
Employers	36	50	139	45	90	50	111	139
Own account	30	36	120	41	114	21	51	70
Total	66	86	130	86	100	71	83	109
All class 2A								
Employers	763	692	91	727	106	457	63	60
Own account	469	626	133	682	109	661	97	141
Total	1,232	1,318	107	1,409	107	1,118	79	91
All occupational classes	18,347	19,333	106	21,029	108	22,514	107	123

[a]Includes catering employers.
[b]Includes restaurants, boarding houses, hotels and public houses.

proprietors are included, while window-cleaners, building craftsmen and
tailors working on their own account are not.

The industrial distribution of those in class 2A is summarized in table 7.

Until 1931, the class grew at about the same pace as the occupied population;
after that, as we have noticed, its 21 per cent decline to 1951 is balanced by an
increase in the number of managers.   But the movement between the various
industrial sectors was very uneven.   In 1951, nearly three-quarters of the total
were in farming or the distributive trade.

In mining and manufacturing, there were still 55,000 employers in 1951, but this was less than a third of those who had been so engaged up to 1931.

We may follow the changes in the proportion of unincorporated and incorporated businesses since 1951 by reference to the *Reports* of the Commissioners of Inland Revenue[1]. In 1951 and in 1959, unincorporated businesses formed the following percentages of all businesses:

	1951	1959
All[a]	90·4	88·2
Agriculture and horticulture	99·0	99·5
Shipbuilding and non-electrical engineering	49·7	49·2
Vehicles	79·3	73·2
Clothing	85·1	74·0
Chemicals and allied	30·1	26·7
Food	81·4	76·1
Road transport	90·6	86·5
Distributive trades	91·7	89·1
Other services[b]	94·1	93·1

[a]All unincorporated businesses assessed under Schedule D. Includes professional persons working on their own account.

[b]Includes *inter alia* catering, laundries, dry cleaning, garages, hairdressing, domestic service and photography.

The trend towards incorporation noted between 1931 and 1951 continues, though only to a minor extent in the great preserves of the self-employed: the distributive trades and the miscellaneous group of 'other services'. In agriculture, the proportion of incorporated enterprises has actually fallen.

We cannot deduce from the tax figures how many individuals were involved, for the unit here is 'incomes' and a partnership is listed only once, however many partners it may have. Excluding professional services, entertainment and sport, other services and undertakings abroad, the number of assessments on individuals and partnerships decreased from 1,227,000 in 1950/1 to 1,154,000 in 1958/9. The number of individuals has fallen, but the number of partnerships in all Schedule D trade groups has increased by 54,000, that is, a minimum of 108,000 individuals. This indicates a fall of about 2 per cent in a period in which the occupied population rose by 4 per cent.

Distribution by sex

It is only as boarding-house keepers that women have been in the majority; within this occupation there was a male resurgence between 1931 and 1951, when the number of men boarding-house proprietors almost doubled to 8,000, while the number of women was halved to 29,000.

However, women have formed a high and stable proportion of the employers

[1]See *95th Report*, Cmd 8726 (H.M. Stationery Office, 1953) and *103rd Report*, Cmnd 1258 (1961), table 39 *et seq.*

C

in personal service and catering (32 per cent in 1951) and in the distributive trades (28 per cent in 1951). It is surprising to find 26,000 women amongst the employers and proprietors in farming in 1911: just over 10 per cent of the total. Their numbers had fallen to 20,000 in 1951 and their proportion to a little under 7 per cent. As employers in manufacturing it is only in the clothing industry that they are found in any significant number, and there they represent about a fifth of the total.

(d)   Class 2B (Managers and administrators)

In census terminology, a manager is an employee (not describing himself as a foreman, supervisor or inspector) managing any number of people[1]. The range of authority is obviously very wide. There were over 200,000 manufacturing establishments in Britain in 1959, of which about 150,000 had less than eleven employees[2]. Some of these must have been one-man workshops, perhaps occasionally employing a worker or two; the rest would have been in the charge of some 55,000 employers and something over 200,000 managers. A great many would have been in the 402 establishments with 2,000 or more employees, in charge of small departments or themselves in charge of a number of subordinate managers.

Table 8 shows class 2B classified by industrial sector for the census years.

In part, the figures merely express the relative rise or decline of the various sectors or the propensity of firms towards incorporation. We must go further if we are to measure organic changes. It would be interesting if we could classify the managers by number of subordinates, but the data are not available. We can, however, compare the number of employed persons per employer or manager in various industrial groups for the various years, and this is done in table 9[3].

Table 9 does not support the popular view that the proportion of managers increases as production methods advance. Even in the case of the first industrial group (mining and the treatment of non-metallic mining products) the apparent increase is due to the fall in the relative importance of mining and quarrying, which in 1951 had a ratio of 153 employed to each manager[4].

---

[1]There is no precise distinction between a manager and an administrator; the exercise of authority is an attribute of both. But while the manager exercises it over subordinate employees, the administrator may be vested with power, by law or regulation, to exercise it over members of the public.

[2]*Ministry of Labour Gazette*, vol. 67, no. 9, September 1959, p. 331.

[3]By dividing the industrial totals by the number of employers and managers listed in the census *Occupation Tables* for the relevant industry. Of course, the two classifications do not match, even though the managers are divided industrially. A manager listed in engineering in the *Occupation Tables* may be managing a department counted as being, for example, in the chemical industry in the *Industry Tables* if it is within a chemical firm. Nonetheless, this method gives a rough guide to the proportion of managers to all employed.

[4]That is, to each manager employed in Code 620 in Industry Order II. See table 7 of the 1951 *Industry Tables*.

Table 8. *Managers and administrators (constituents of class 2B),*
census years, 1911-51

	1911	1921		1931		1951		
	'000s	'000s	% of 1911	'000s	% of 1921	'000s	% of 1931	% of 1911
Land and agriculture[a]	(7)	16	(229)	18	113	18	100	(257)
Public service[b]	(34)	(62)	(182)	52	(84)	124	238	(364)
Office managers	N.D.	18	..	35	194	61	174	..
Mining and manufacturing	63	93	148	80	86	214	268	340
Building and contracting	N.D.	5	..	7	140	33	471	..
Transport[c]	(29)	46	(159)	48	104	67	140	(231)
Brokers, agents[d]								
Own account	21	26		27		22		
Employees	137	132		190		209		
Total	158	158	100	217	137	231	106	146
Retail and wholesale businesses	(115)	121	(105)	132	109	258	195	(224)
Finance	(27)	38	(141)	57	150	58	102	(215)
Catering[e]	146	90	62	64	71	84	131	58
Others in class 2B	50	115	230	140	122	98	70	196
All in class 2B	629	704	112	770	109	1,246	162	198
All occupational classes	18,347	19,333	106	21,029	108	22,514	107	123

N.D. = not distinguished.
Numbers in brackets include estimates for, or exclude, some categories not distinguished in the year concerned.

[a] In 1911, farm managers only.
[b] For 1911 and 1921, estimated from the *Report of the Committee on pay, etc. of State Servants* (Anderson Committee) (London, H.M. Stationery Office, 1923); and Royal Commission on the Civil Service (1929-31), *Appendix to Part I of Minutes of Evidence: Introductory Memoranda relating to the Civil Service; submitted by the Treasury* (London, H.M. Stationery Office, 1929).
[c] Including garage managers and shipbrokers.
[d] Including buyers, sales managers, advertising agents, estate agents, auctioneers and commercial travellers. Does not include stockbrokers.
[e] Restaurants, boarding houses, hotels, public houses.

Table 9. *Staff per employer and manager in various industrial groups,*
census years, 1911-51

	1911	1921	1931	1951
Mining and non-metallic mining products	96	100	102	82
Chemical and allied	18	32	31	33
Metals, engineering and allied	28	34	36	35
Textiles, leather, and textile and leather goods	29	27	33	33
All the above (weighted average)	33	36	40	38

Status of managers

The census tables for 1951 for the first time classified managers into three status groups, as follows:

	All		General managers directors, etc.		Branch or primary dept. managers		Office or subsidiary dept. managers	
	'000s	%	'000s	%	'000s	%	'000s	%
Men	665	82·4	167	89·7	413	78·5	85	89·4
Women	142	17·6	19	10·3	113	21·5	10	10·6
All	807	100·00	186	100·00	526	100·00	95	100·00

Distribution by sex

Of the whole of class 2B, women formed 20 per cent in 1911, 17 per cent in 1921, 13 per cent in 1931 and 15 per cent in 1951. The proportion was lowest in manufacturing industry (even in the textile and clothing trades, with a high proportion of female employees, they were outnumbered by nine to one) and highest in the Post Office and catering trades.

Women formed the following percentages of all managers and administrators in the sectors listed:

	1931	1951
Public service[a]	5·8	15·4
Secretaries and registrars of companies, institutes and charities	11·3	32·0
Textiles, textile goods, leather and leather goods	9·7	11·2
Other transport[b]	46·9	42·4
Retail and wholesale businesses	16·1	20·7
Bank managers, inspectors	0·3	0·7
Insurance managers, underwriters	4·4	1·9
Restaurants	57·9	67·5
Hotels and public houses	29·2	46·0

[a]Administrative and executive officers and 'other officials (not clerks)' and Civil Service higher clerical officers. Excludes that part of Post Office allocated to 'other transport'.
[b]Other than road, rail, sea and air. Mainly Post Office.

(e)   Class 3 (Clerical workers)

In 1911, the Census recognized only one category of clerk. Indeed, while 'commercial or business clerks' were distinguished, those in the public service, finance and railways were lumped together with 'officials'[1]. Those were the days when 'female typewriters' were still a novelty and correspondence was done in the copyist's beautiful hand.

In 1921, costing and estimating clerks were distinguished and in 1931, typists. In 1951, there was a further subdivision into shorthand typists, typists, other office machine operators and book-keepers[2].

[1]They have been separated by estimates based on official reports and railway returns.
[2]But in the more austere classification of 1961, the division between typists and shorthand typists is abandoned and clerks, book-keepers and office machine operators are pooled as in 1931. Professionally qualified accountants have throughout been classified separately.

Table 10.   Clerical workers (constituents of class 3), census years, 1911-51

	1911 '000s	1921 '000s	1921 % of 1911	1931 '000s	1931 % of 1921	1951 '000s	1951 % of 1931	% of 1911
Insurance agents and canvassers								
Male	54	40	74	59	147·5	58	98	107
Female	1	4	400	2	50	5	250	500
Total	55	44	80	61	139	63	103	115
Others								
Male	654	697	107	758	109	932	123	143
Female	179	560	313	646	115	1,409	218	787
Total	832	1,257	151	1,404	112	2,341	167	281
of which Typists								
Male	..	..	..	5	..	16	302	..
Female	..	..	..	239	..	543	227	..
Total	..	..	..	244	..	559	229	..
All								
Male	708	737	104	817	111	990	121	140
Female	179	564	315	648	115	1,414	218	790
Total	887	1,300	147	1,465	113	2,404	164	271
All occupational classes	18,347	19,333	106	21,029	108	22,514	107	123

Table 10 shows the numbers in this class in each census year. The rise in the number of typists and shorthand typists may be indicative of the increase in letter- and report-writing relative to other clerical work; it is more likely simply a sign of greater specialization.

We know from the census reports that the number of costing and estimating clerks increased from 22,000 in 1921 to 31,000 in 1931 and (from general observation) that costing and estimating is done in a much more elaborate way today than it was thirty years ago.

The 1951 tables distinguish the following:

	'000s	Per cent
Shorthand typists	430	18·3
Typists	129	5·5
Other office machine operators	79	3·4
Book-keepers	484	20·7
Others	1,219	52·1
	2,341	100·00

We cannot estimate changes in the number of clerks since 1951 with any pretensions to accuracy. From the change in the size of industries and the proportion of non-manual workers in manufacturing we estimated that there would have been an increase of 21 per cent between 1951 and 1959[1], so that the

[1] See table 2.

clerks would have then constituted 12 per cent of the occupied population.

We do know, however, from the Ministry of Labour's sample survey[1], that in the chemical and allied and metal-making and metal-working industries managerial, administrative and clerical workers constituted 17·9 per cent of the work force in 1959. In 1951, they constituted 15·4 per cent[2]. If we apply to the total for these industries the 17·9 per cent shown in the sample, the two years would compare thus:

	1951	1960
Managerial, administrative and clerical		
Per cent	*15·4*	*17·9*
Number (in thousands)	685	883
Total employed (in thousands)	4,451	4,935

This is an increase of 29 per cent for the managers and clerks in this group of industries compared with an increase of 11 per cent for the whole work force.

Distribution by sex

The substitution of women for men first took place on a large scale during the first world war. Between 1911 and 1921, the number of male clerks increased a little more slowly than the occupied population, while the number of female clerks increased more than three times. By 1951, women had a comfortable majority, constituting nearly 60 per cent of the class. But 54 per cent of the 483,000 book-keepers, estimating and costing clerks were men and 3·5 per cent of the 429,000 shorthand typists.

We may learn something of the change in sex composition since 1951 from the *Clerical Salaries Analysis*[3]. Average percentages for 1950-52 and for 1960 were as follows:

	1950-2	1960
Men	36	35
Women	64	65

However, the sample does not include insurance, banking and finance nor the public service, and here the change has been more substantial. In the Civil Service, women formed 45·5 per cent of the clerical and sub-clerical classes in 1951, and 48 per cent in 1960. Of all those employed in insurance, banking and finance in 1951, women constituted 38·3 per cent, and in 1960 43·2 per cent.

It is probable that between 1951 and 1960, clerks will have increased rather more than by the 21 per cent given in table 2, and that the proportion of women will have increased from 58·8 to something over 60 per cent.

[1]*Ministry of Labour Gazette*, vol. 68, no. 12, December 1960, p. 464. See Appendix C.
[2]See Appendix B.
[3]Published every two years by the Institute of Office Management, London.

The *Clerical Salaries Analysis* for 1960 distinguishes women shorthand and audio-typists, copy typists and machine operators from other clerks. The percentage distribution compares as follows with that for 1951:

	1951	1960
Shorthand (and audio-) typists	29	23
Copy typists	9	14
Machine operators	6	17
Other clerks	56	46
	100	100

The proportion of copy typists is higher in the 1960 figures: it may well be that a greater division of labour has been effected as a result of the general short supply of shorthand typists. But the most striking feature is the very high proportion of machine operators in 1960. The ratio of shorthand typists to 'other clerks' is almost the same in both years.

(f) Class 4 (*Foremen, supervisors, inspectors*)

Foremen were distinguished from other workers in 1921, 1931 and 1951 and were posted to orders or sub-orders according to the occupations of the workers whom they supervised. Thus, in 1951, foremen supervising chemical workers were classified under Order V, Sub-order 2, 'Workers in chemical and allied trades'. Of the 9,512 foremen so enumerated in England and Wales in 1951, 7,476 were in Industry Order IV (Chemical and allied trades), and the rest spread over a number of other industries.

The relevant coding instruction says, 'Persons returned as foremen, over-looker, or any synonymous term should be assigned to the "foreman, overlooker" or other similarly entitled group within the appropriate Order, as indicated by the statement of employer's business, or the kind of work or activity'[1]. The census schedule called for the foreman's department to be stated as well as the employer's name and business, but of course there is no guarantee (nor much likelihood) that a foreman will be in charge exclusively of those in the occupations with which he is bracketed. For example, the foreman of 1951 Code 100 (Chemicals) might be in charge of maintenance fitters, storemen, time-clerks and cleaners as well as chemical process workers.

In 1911, foremen were not distinguished in the census and reference was made to the 1906 earnings census to determine the proportion of foremen to other operatives in various industries. This has the advantage of reliance on a return from employers instead of heads of households, but the disadvantage of failing to distinguish between, for example, foremen of engineering workers in the engineering industry and foremen of non-engineering workers in the

---

[1]*Census 1951: Classification of Occupations* (London, H.M. Stationery Office, 1956), p. x.

Table 11. *Number of foremen and number of manual employees per foreman in various occupational groups, census years, 1911-51*

	1911		1921		1931		1951	
	'000s	Em-ployees	'000s	Em-ployees	'000s	Em-ployees	'000s	Em-ployees
Farm bailiffs, foremen	29	32	28	29	22	31	19	29
Coalmining overmen, etc.	34	29	46	24	40	24	42	14
Non-metallic mining products	3	55	3	57	4	55	7	32
Chemical and allied	4	24	5	15	5	18	12	15
Metal-making and metal-working	31	54	49	42	63	34	263	12
Textiles	45	30	40	26	38	38	26	27
Building and contracting	32	13	24	25	37	19	64	16
All above	178	32	195	30	209	28	433	15
All in class 4	236		279		323		590	

engineering industry. It is probable that, with a lower degree of vertical integration, the overlap was less extensive in 1911 than in later years, but these qualifications should be borne in mind when table 11 is considered.

This shows the number of foremen in various occupational groups and the average number of manual process workers per foreman in each group. This is calculated by dividing the number of workers listed for the group in the occupational tables by the number of foremen shown for that occupational group.

Table 11 indicates a tendency towards closer supervision since 1931 that is in keeping with modern principles of management, though a foreman is in charge of goods and machines as well as men and part of the increase in the ratio of supervisors to supervised is no doubt due to the increased productivity of the latter. The effect of mechanization, standardization and mass production is seen in the emergence of a class of engineering 'inspectors, viewers, testers', which was distinguished first in 1951 (except for electrical work, for which it was recognized in 1921). There were 126,000 in this category in 1951.

The proportion of forewomen in the class total has increased greatly. In 1911, it was possible to distinguish only 9,700: 4·1 per cent of the class total. In 1921, the proportion was 6·6 per cent; in 1931, 8·6 per cent and in 1951, 13·3 per cent.

(g) Class 5 (Skilled manual workers)

Skilled workers are specialists and, *ipso facto*, can be classified into a multitude of occupations. There are no less than 224 identified in occupational class 5, and a number of these are themselves composed of groups of occupations. In

Table 12. *Skilled manual workers (major constituents of class 5: employees and self-employed), census years, 1911-51*

		1911 '000s	1921 '000s	% of 1911	1931 '000s	% of 1921	1951 '000s	% of 1931	% of 1911
Agricultural machine drivers and attendants		6	10	167	7	70	74	1,057	1,233
Coal hewers and getters		586	615	105	495	80	226	46	39
Non-metallic mining products	M	57	48	84	50	104	53	106	93
	F	15	28	187	29	104	36	124	240
	Total	72	76	106	79	104	89	113	124
Metal-makers and metal-workers		1,289	1,663	129	1,581	95	2,096	133	163
Textiles	M	351	194	55	184	95	123	67	35
	F	654	526	80	533	101	322	60	49
	Total	1,005	720	72	717	100	445	62	44
Leather and textile goods	M	290	229	79	249	109	181	73	62
	F	483	328	68	293	89	198	68	41
	Total	773	557	72	542	97	379	70	49
Wood, cane and cork		472	445	94	483	109	461	95	98
Paper and printing	M	168	139	83	165	119	199	121	118
	F	66	82	124	95	116	80	84	121
	Total	234	221	94	260	118	279	107	119
Other manufactures		226	245	108	259	106	274	106	121
Building, contracting, decorating		436	388	89	485	125	582	120	133
Railway transport		103	140	136	129	92	145	112	141
Sea transport		(59)	79	(134)	75	95	52	69	(88)
Police (other ranks)		55	64	116	68	106	80	118	145
Hairdressers and manicurists	M	39	34	87	46	135	35	76	90
	F	5	6	120	34	567	48	141	960
	Total	44	40	91	80	200	83	104	189
Warehousemen		N.D.	110	..	119	108	110	92	..
Stationary engine drivers, etc.[a]		111	107	96	103	94	138	135	124
Others		137	93	68	137	147	103	75	75
All class 5	M	4,264	4,405	103	4,423	100	4,732	107	111
	F	1,344	1,168	87	1,196	102	884	74	66
	Total	5,608	5,573	99	5,619	101	5,616	100	100
All occupational classes		18,347	19,333	106	21,029	108	22,514	107	123

N.D. = not distinguished
( ) = not completely distinguished.

[a]Including crane drivers, drivers of civil engineering plant, switchboard attendants **and** battery chargers.

metal-making and metal-working, no less than sixty-seven skilled occupations are distinguished.

Table 12 shows this class subdivided according to the material worked in, the product made or the service given[1]. The sexes are distinguished only where women form a significant part of the work force.

There have been very wide variations in the fortunes of the various groups and the stability of the class total is the outcome of conflicting tendencies in the parts. The rise in the number of agricultural machine drivers and attendants and the decline in the number of coalface workers are symptomatic of the same thing: the increased application of engineering to productive processes. Hence the increase in skilled metal-makers and metal-workers between 1931 and 1951 almost exactly balanced the fall in the number of skilled workers in textiles, leather, and textile and leather goods.

In part, the changes have been due to contrasting rates of growth or decline in the various industries: the textile industry in 1951 employed 73 per cent of its working force of 1911, chemicals 369 per cent, engineering and shipbuilding 205 per cent, vehicle manufacture 347 per cent; in part, to the changing use of their labour outside their 'home' industries; in part to changes in the skill mix. The ratio of skilled workers to all manual workers in various occupational groups has been as follows[2]:

	1911	1921	1931	1951
Coalminers	59·4	56·7	51·2	38·5
Workers in:				
Non-metallic mining products	44·2	44·4	35·9	39·1
Metal-making and metal-using	77·9	77·7	71·7	66·3
Textiles	74·8	67·7	67·4	62·0
Building, contracting, decorating	66·7	57·8	62·8	50·4
Weighted average of above	70·6	68·0	64·1	58·9

Of course, not all the changes in skill coefficients registered above are due to changing techniques. Shifts within industries or sub-industries would also have influenced the coefficients. For example, the rise in the number of skilled maintenance workers necessitated by increased mechanization tends to raise the proportion of skilled metal workers, while the rise in the number of machine minders in the engineering industry tends to lower it.

Industrial status

The total number of self-employed craftsmen has remained remarkably stable in an age of growing concentration, falling from 329,000 in 1911 to 251,000 in

[1]This is not an industrial classification, for all skilled metal-makers and metal-workers, for example, are included under that head without regard to the industry in which they are employed.

[2]Not, N.B., in various industries, for of course the skilled, semi-skilled and unskilled workers in each occupational group are spread through many industries. The self-employed have been excluded from the calculation.

1951 (table 1). But they have formed a falling proportion of the class: 5·9 per cent in 1911 and 4·5 per cent in 1951. Amongst the 251,000 self-employed, the major groups in 1951 were as follows:

	No.	Per cent of total in occupation
Blacksmiths	4,777	*9*
Motor mechanics	9,292	*6*
Plumbers	9,772	*10*
Watchmakers	5,603	*4*
Electricians	6,631	*3*
Shoemakers	19,039	*48*
Bakers	10,964	*11*
Carpenters and cabinet-makers	14,437	*5*
Building workers[a]	44,175	*14*
Painters and decorators[b]	25,218	*9*
Hairdressers	26,690	*32*
Photographers	4,108	*18*
	180,706	

[a]Excluding painters and decorators.
[b]Including signwriters.

Other self-employed workers were scattered through the occupations in small numbers.

Few of the women were self-employed. In 1911, 136,000 (86 per cent) of the women in class 5 working on their own account were dressmakers. By 1921, the number of dressmakers had fallen to 66,000; by 1931, to 44,000; by 1951, to 13,000.

Distribution by sex

While the number of skilled men increased by 11 per cent between 1911 and 1951, the number of women fell by 34 per cent, for as table 12 shows, the women have been concentrated in the textile and clothing industries whose labour force has been much reduced.

In the case of the men, the outstanding feature has been the shift to the metal-using trades. The central grade, variously known as fitter, mechanic or mill-wright, had in it about 325,000 men in 1911. By 1921, the number had increased by nearly a third to 429,000. Then followed a fall bringing the number to 400,000 in 1931, then a further substantial increase to 511,000 in 1951. With the fall in the number of coalface workers, this was then second in size only to agricultural workers as an occupational unit.

Machine-tool setters have grown with even greater rapidity. There were 12,000 when they were distinguished for the first time in 1931. In 1951, there were 112,000.

The weight of the major groups has varied as follows:

| | Percentage of all men in class 5 | | | |
	1911	1921	1931	1951
Metal-makers and metal-workers	23	30	28	36
Textile workers	18	13	13	8
Leather and leather and textile goods	14	10	10	6·5
Coalface workers	10	11	9	4
Woodworkers	8	8	10	8
Building craftsmen	8	7	9	10
Others	19	21	21	27·5
	100	100	100	100

The distribution of women in class 5 is shown in table 13. Nothing has emerged to compensate for the decline of the skilled spinners and weavers and dressmakers, who made up 72 per cent of the women in class 5 in 1911. Even in engineering and printing, where substantial numbers are employed, there has been a decline since 1931. The rise in the number of hairdressers presents the one buoyant feature.

Table 13. *Distribution of women within class 5 (Skilled workers), chief occupational groups including self-employed, census years, 1911-51*

| | 1911 | 1921 | | 1931 | | 1951 | | |
	'000s	'000s	% of 1911	'000s	% of 1921	'000s	% of 1931	% of 1911
Pottery	14	24	171	24	100	28	117	200
Metal and engineering	47	83	177	94	113	76	81	162
Textiles	654	526	80	533	101	322	60	49
Boots and shoes	45	38	84	47	124	47	100	104
Clothing cutters	13	6	46	12	200	15	125	115
Dresses and other light clothing	317	162	51	126	78	59	47	19
Millinery	56	48	86	34	71	6	18	11
Other hats and caps	5	16	320	14	88	6	43	120
Upholstery	10	8	80	12	150	14	117	140
Bakers and pastry-cooks	N.D.	22	..	29	132	26	90	..
Sugar confectionery	7	18	257	16	89	6	38	86
Paper and printing, photography	66	82	124	95	116	80	84	121
French polishers	7	7	100	10	143	4	40	57
Hairdressers, manicurists	5	6	120	34	567	48	141	960
Others	98	122	124	116	95	147	127	149
All women in class 5	1,344	1,168	87	1,196	102	884	74	66
All occupational classes	18,347	19,333	106	21,029	108	22,514	107	123

N.D. = not distinguished.

(h)   *Class 6 (Semi-skilled manual workers)*

Table 14 gives a preliminary survey of class 6, by dividing it into seven sections.

Except for packers and storekeepers, and the armed services, none of the groups has kept pace with the occupied population over the forty years to 1951. Here included are the two great reservoirs upon which other industries have been able to draw: agriculture and domestic service. Between 1921 and 1931, with a consistently high level of unemployment, the decline in the number of agricultural labourers was reduced (though not for women thus engaged) and in catering, domestic and personal service, it was strongly reversed. But by 1951, the trend of 1911-21 had again asserted itself. Oddly enough, the number of women agricultural workers in 1951 was 80 per cent above 1931, while in the distributive trades a substantial reduction in the number of men had been offset by a substantial rise in the number of women.

In domestic service, a big reduction in employment in private households has been partly offset by an increase in the catering trade.

Indoor domestic servants (thousands)

	1911	1921	1931	1951
Private				
Male	45	31	37	9
Female	1,403	1,072	1,262	343
Total	1,448	1,103	1,299	352
Other				
Male	13	33	48	62
Female	67	199	210	454
	80	232	258	516
All	1,528	1,335	1,557	868

In tables 15(a) and 15(b) details are given for mining and manufacturing, transport and communication. Until 1931, occupations in manufacturing barely retained their proportion in the semi-skilled class; after 1931, their numbers increased so that in 1951 they constituted 17·9 per cent of the class compared with 14·6 per cent in 1911. Movements in various industries have been contrasting, especially between 1931 and 1951 when the chemical and metal groups were strongly expansionary while textiles and clothing declined or were stationary.

The transport group, too, has increased its share of the class: from 12 per cent in 1911 to over 18 per cent in 1951. Table 15(b) tells the economic history of this age: horse and railway, tram and barge disappear before the inexorable motor. There has been a minor revolution, too, in the Post Office group: telegraphists have been reduced from 25,000 in 1921 to 15,000 in 1951; telephonists have increased from 26,000 to 87,000.

Table 14. *Semi-skilled workers (major divisions of class 6), census years, 1911-51*

	1911 '000s	1921 '000s	1921 % of 1911	1931 '000s	1931 % of 1921	1951 '000s	1951 % of 1931	% of 1911
Agricultural labourers, foresters, fishermen	1,288	1,094	85	1,011	92	795	79	62
Including Males	1,188	1,013	85	962	95	707	73	60
Females	100	81	81	49	60	88	180	88
Mining and manufacturing industry	1,606	1,513	94	1,599	106	1,828	114	114
Transport and communication	965	861	89	990	115	1,094	111	113
Distributive trades	930	839	90	1,163	139	1,111	96	119
Including Males	588	414	70	660	159	459	70	78
Females	342	425	124	503	118	652	130	191
Armed services, other ranks	196	221	113	173	78	531	307	271
Catering, domestic and personal service	2,003	1,742	87	2,109	121	1,468	60	63
Including Males	225	203	90	296	146	283	96	126
Females	1,778	1,539	87	1,813	118	1,185	65	67
Packers and storekeepers	(170)	202	(119)	243	120	386	159	(227)
Others in class 6	86	71	83	71	100	126	177	139
All class 6	7,244	6,543	90	7,359	112	7,339	100	101
Including Males	4,346	3,859	89	4,259	110	4,352	102	100
Females	2,898	2,684	93	3,101	116	2,978	96	103
All occupational classes	18,347	19,333	106	21,029	108	22,514	107	123

Table 15(a). *Semi-skilled workers in mining and quarrying and in various manufacturing occupations (excluding self-employed), census years, 1911-51*

	1911 '000s	1921 '000s	1921 % of 1911	1931 '000s	1931 % of 1921	1951 '000s	1951 % of 1931	% of 1911
Non-metallic mining products and chemicals	109	62	57	66	106	123	186	112
Metal-making and metal-using	237	224	95	257	115	510	198	215
Textiles	198	201	102	233	116	161	69	81
Clothing and other textile goods	371	335	90	365	109	375	103	100
Food, drink, tobacco	115	93	81	78	84	96	123	83
All the above	1,030	915	89	999	109	1,265	127	123
Mining and quarrying	501	525	105	539	103	399	74	80
All class 6	7,244	6,543	90	7,359	112	7,339	100	101

Table 15(b). *Semi-skilled workers in various occupations in transport and communication, census years, 1911-51*

	1911	1921		1931		1951		
	'000s	'000s	% of 1911	'000s	% of 1921	'000s	% of 1931	% of 1911
Platelayers, paviours, tunnel-miners	111	62	56	62	100	59	95	53
Railway firemen, ticket collectors, etc.[a]	98	99	101	78	78	80	103	82
Vehicle drivers:								
Horse-drawn	404	220	54	139	63	15	11	4
Trams and trolley-buses	17	23	135	23	100	13	57	76
Motor	50	169	338	380	225	547	144	1,094
Bus and tram conductors	21	31	148	67	216	97	148	461
Water transport[b]	69	61	88	58	95	36	62	52
P.O. manipulative, etc.[c]	118	124	105	139	112	210	151	178
All the above	888	789	89	946	120	1,057	112	119
All class 6	7,244	6,543	90	7,359	112	7,339	100	101

Note: Table 15 compares those sections of each industrial group, excluding the self-employed, that can be identified for all four years. Totals are not exhaustive of semi-skilled workers in mining and manufacturing or transport and communication.

[a]Includes running-shed workers and a miscellany of workers in Code 649 'Other railway transport workers'.

[b]Firemen, trimmers, bargemen, boatmen, tugmen, lock-keepers, etc.

[c]Postmen, sorters, telephonists, telegraphists and Code 709 'Other workers in transport and communications'.

We can deduce something about movements between 1951 and 1960 by looking at industrial totals.

Numbers of employees (thousands)

		1951	1960	1960 as % of 1951
Agriculture and horticulture	M	673	492	73
	F	103	90	87
	Total	776	582	75
Coalmining	M	767	685	89
Distributive trades	M	1,106	1,355	123
	F	1,032	1,453	141
	Total	2,138	2,808	131
Catering, hotels, etc.	M	187	172[a]	92
	F	492	502[a]	102
	Total	679	674	99
Private domestic service	M	45	27	60
	F	366	252	69
	Total	411	279	68

[a]May 1959. *Standard Industrial Classification* (1948).

On average, employment in the above groups rose by five per cent between 1951 and 1960, while the whole employee population rose by seven per cent. But the industrial totals include all those who are employed in the relevant industry, regardless of occupation, and it is likely that the semi-skilled have formed a declining proportion of those totals. In particular, in retail distribution, where employment has increased so substantially since 1951, cashiers in self-service stores have taken over work formerly done by shop-assistants.

Distribution by sex

The proportion of women in class 6 has remained remarkably constant: 40 per cent in 1911, rising to 42 per cent in 1931 and falling to 41 per cent in 1951. In part this was due to the fact that the numbers of agricultural labourers and of domestic servants (the largest men's and women's occupations of 1911) have been drastically reduced, the former by 500,000 between 1911 and 1951, the latter by 700,000.

In the catering, domestic and laundry services, the working force has always been largely female. But proportions have been reversed for shop-assistants as they have for office workers: in 1911, there were sixty-two male shop-assistants to every thirty-eight female; in 1951, there were sixty-seven females to every thirty-three males.

Since 1951, the number of women has continued to increase faster (or decline slower) than that of men in catering, distribution and agriculture, but in chemicals and engineering, where their proportions increased significantly between 1931 and 1951, there does not appear to have been much further change. This is indicated by the proportion of women in the very large sample of manual workers for whom information is obtained in the Ministry of Labour's earnings inquiries[1]. These include not all but a very high proportion of the manual workers in the industries concerned. In pharmaceuticals and toilet preparations, the percentage of women rose from 55·6 per cent in October 1951 to 58·6 per cent in October 1960, but in chemicals and dyes fell from 14·5 to 10·1 per cent. In engineering and electrical goods, in the same period, there was a fractional increase, from 29·2 to 29·4 per cent.

(i)   Class 7 (Unskilled workers)

There was a big increase in the number of unskilled workers from 1911 to 1921, from 10 to 14 per cent of the occupied population (table 1). Most of this was in engineering and other manufacturing industries that expanded during the war. This continued, at a lower rate, up to 1931, after which the

[1]Published in the *Ministry of Labour Gazette*.

numbers and proportions of unskilled workers fell, despite a further substantial increase in their numbers in metals and engineering.

Unskilled work cannot be classified occupationally in the accepted sense, though there are a few unskilled occupations that are distinguished. The numbers in these and in certain industrial divisions are shown in table 16.

The most important changes, resulting in the net loss between 1931 and 1951, were as follows:

| | | *Nos. in thousands* | | |
		1931	1951	1951 as % of 1931
Dock labourers		120	81	*67·5*
Messengers	M	186	47	*25*
	F	21	3	*14*
	Total	207	50	*24*
Porters		69	45	*65*
Charwomen	M	5	14	*280*
	F	158	238	*151*
	Total	163	252	*155*
Chemical and allied	M	57	61	*107*
	F	9	13	*144*
	Total	66	74	*112*
Metal-working, engineering, electrical and allied	M	316	467	*148*
	F	33	61	*185*
	Total	349	528	*151*
Miscellaneous	M	989	432	*44*
	F	132	126	*95*
	Total	1,121	558	*50*

Technical changes are again in evidence: the fall in the number of dock labourers; a stable level in the chemical and allied industry despite a great rise in output; the replacement of messengers by the telephone. The miscellaneous group, on the other hand, and the street traders listed in table 16, probably owe their reduction to the change from high unemployment to full employment and the expanded opportunities for acquiring skill that this has brought about.

Distribution by sex

Labouring jobs, depending on strength without skill, are mainly performed by men; charing and office cleaning is mainly done by women and occupies a third of the women in class 7. But women have been used to replace men in some class 7 occupations in time of war and owing to the scarcity of male labour they tended to remain there after 1945. There were 1,000 women working

D

Table 16.   *Unskilled workers (major constituents of class 7: employees only, unless otherwise stated), census years, 1911-51*

	1911 '000s	1921 '000s	% of 1911	1931 '000s	% of 1921	1951 '000s	% of 1931	% of 1911
Building and civil engineering	197	252	*128*	352	*140*	493	*140*	*250*
Transport[a]	455	500	*110*	552	*110*	318	*58*	*70*
Charwomen, office cleaners	137	132	*96*	163	*123*	252	*155*	*184*
Street sellers[b]								
Employees	31	15		37		10		
Own account	46	52		73		29		
Total	77	67	*87*	110	*164*	39	*35*	*51*
Warehouse and store-keepers' assistants	N.D.	58	..	66	*114*	82	*124*	..
Boiler firemen and stokers	N.D.	63	..	56	*89*	80	*143*	..
Non-metallic mining products and chemicals		110		161		183		
Metals and engineering		238		349		529		
Textiles (not textile goods)		140		112		110		
All other commercial and industrial undertakings[c]		1,127		1,121		559		
Total, 4 preceding groups	844	1,615	*191*	1,743	*108*	1,381	*79*	*164*
Others in class 7	57	53	*92*	73	*138*	64	*88*	*112*
All class 7 including own account	1,767	2,740	*155*	3,115	*114*	2,709	*87*	*153*
All occupational classes	18,347	19,333	*106*	21,029	*108*	22,514	*107*	*123*

N.D. = not distinguished.

[a] Porters (railway and hotel, etc.), lorry drivers' mates, dock labourers, messengers, lift-attendants.
[b] Costermongers, hawkers, newspaper sellers.
[c] 1951 Census Code 950.

as labourers in the building industry in 1951, over two thousand as railway porters. The number of unskilled women workers in the chemical and allied industries increased by a third between 1931 and 1951, and doubled in metals and engineering:

		Nos. in thousands	
		1931	1951
Chemical and allied trades	M	57·0	60·8
	F	9·5	12·7
	Total	66·5	73·5
Metal-working, engineering, electrical and allied trades	M	315·8	467·5
	F	32·8	61·2
	Total	348·6	528·7

6. THE EFFECTS OF INDUSTRIAL CHANGE

There are two proximate causes for changes in occupational distribution: technical changes within industries leading to changes in skill coefficients, and differences in the relative rate of growth of industries.

Table 17 shows the percentages in which, in 1951, the occupational classes were combined in the twenty-four Industrial Orders of the industrial classification[1].

Table 17. *Occupational class distribution by industry, England and Wales, 1951*

Order	Industry	Occupational Class								
		1A	1B	2	3	4	5	6	7	All
I	Agriculture, etc.	0·03	0·09	28·61	0·72	1·83	7·67	60·81	0·24	100
II	Mining	0·65	0·39	0·91	3·13	5·65	39·52	47·64	2·11	100
III	Ceramics, etc.	0·51	1·35	4·05	6·76	2·97	37·93	19·39	27·04	100
IV	Chemicals	3·83	4·96	7·03	16·02	3·58	15·33	27·00	22·24	100
V	Metal manufacture	1·23	1·86	2·74	8·86	5·37	38·48	18·56	22·89	100
VI	Engineering and shipbuilding	1·63	4·01	4·13	11·37	6·49	41·17	18·98	12·20	100
VII	Vehicles	0·88	2·50	4·77	9·88	6·18	47·74	16·85	11·19	100
VIII	Metal goods	0·40	0·48	4·86	8·67	5·26	37·17	28·71	14·45	100
IX	Precision instruments	0·92	2·34	5·96	10·96	4·80	52·52	15·18	7·32	100
X	Textiles	0·33	0·77	3·22	5·14	3·07	50·49	23·19	13·79	100
XI	Leather, etc.	0·38	0·49	6·86	6·05	2·86	66·21	4·48	12·67	100
XII	Clothing	0·04	0·17	4·34	4·79	2·03	36·63	48·10	3·90	100
XIII	Food, drink and tobacco	0·56	0·72	6·94	10·77	3·33	25·97	30·80	20·90	100
XIV	Manufactures of wood and cork	0·13	0·69	4·98	5·63	3·02	63·48	8·77	13·31	100
XV	Paper and printing	3·52	1·30	6·87	12·43	2·78	44·85	13·91	14·33	100
XVI	Other manufactured goods	0·86	2·70	6·42	11·10	3·47	42·08	15·02	18·35	100
XVII	Building and contracting	1·22	0·40	3·88	3·91	3·78	57·64	4·36	24·80	100
XVIII	Gas, electricity and water	3·66	1·63	4·88	15·57	2·33	27·61	18·24	26·08	100
XIX	Transport and communication	0·33	1·75	4·53	13·05	3·49	19·63	41·81	15·41	100
XX	Distributive trades	0·15	1·04	30·13	12·35	0·50	5·55	43·43	6·85	100
XXI	Finance	1·31	0·16	18·97	66·83	0·22	2·28	3·88	6·34	100
XXII	Public administration	5·00	2·97	7·90	18·25	1·18	10·25	39·63	14·83	100
XXIII	Professional services	12·73	44·95	2·88	13·92	0·14	2·66	17·95	4·77	100
XXIV	Miscellaneous services	0·36	3·00	13·06	4·66	0·12	8·45	65·06	5·29	100
	All	1·96	4·67	9·95	10·85	2·69	25·37	32·84	11·67	100

[1]This analysis is made possible by the introduction of a complete industry–occupation cross tabulation for England and Wales in 1951 (table 7 of the *Census 1951, England and Wales: Industry Tables*, H.M. Stationery Office, 1957). For previous years, and for Scotland in 1951, there are only tables, similar in scope to table 8 of the 1951 *England and Wales Industry Tables*, showing the numbers in the more important occupations in each industry. Census Industry Table 7 shows no status divisions, however, so that the numbers derived from it do not represent quite the same allocation of employers and self-employed as the tables that have appeared in this study. The discrepancy has been partly overcome by the combination of classes 2A and 2B. There is also an occasional deficiency in the numbers on which the percentages have been based, due to the omission of sub-orders and groups when no figure of 10 or more would appear in the line to which they referred.

Table 18. *Distribution of occupied population (including employers, self-employed and unemployed) by industry, census years, 1911-51 and 1959*

	1911 '000s	1911 Per cent	1921 '000s	1921 Per cent	1931 '000s	1931 Per cent	1951 '000s	1951 Per cent	1959 '000s	1959 Per cent
I Agriculture, etc	1,499	8·4	1,372	7·3	1,257	6·1	1,142	5·0	969	4·1
II Mining, etc.	1,128	6·3	1,305	6·9	1,166	5·7	861	3·8	844	3·6
III Ceramics, glass, etc.	201	1·1	214	1·1	265	1·3	318	1·4	326	1·4
IV Chemicals	147	0·8	215	1·1	239	1·2	442	2·0	543	2·3
V Metal manufacture	509	2·8	562	3·0	524	2·6	579	2·6	558	2·3
VI Engineering and shipbuilding	878	4·9	1,203	6·4	1,090	5·3	1,801	8·0	2,121	8·9
VII Vehicles	291	1·6	375	2·0	402	2·0	1,009	4·5	1,246	5·2
VIII Metal goods n.e.s. IX Precision instruments, jewellery, etc.	321	1·8	424	2·2	450	2·2	636	2·8	676	2·8
X Textiles	1,359	7·6	1,305	6·9	1,338	6·5	997	4·4	865	3·6
XI Leather, etc.	93	0·5	87	0·5	92	0·4	79	0·4	67	0·3
XII Clothing	1,159	6·5	873	4·6	880	4·3	729	3·2	646	2·7
XIII Food, drink and tobacco	554	3·1	623	3·3	709	3·5	756	3·4	920	3·9
XIV Wood	276	1·5	304	1·6	321	1·6	333	1·5	310	1·3
XV Paper and printing	334	1·9	403	2·1	497	2·4	520	2·3	589	2·5
XVI Other manufactures	96	0·5	205	1·1	235	1·1	267	1·2	288	1·2
XVII Building	950	5·3	795	4·2	1,122	5·5	1,431	6·4	1,543	6·5
XVIII Gas, electricity and water	116	0·6	179	0·9	246	1·2	361	1·6	380	1·6
XIX Transport and communication	1,416	7·9	1,570	8·3	1,671	8·2	1,734	7·7	1,700	7·2
XX Distributive trades	2,133	11·9	2,239	11·9	2,697	13·2	2,712	12·1	2,988	12·6
XXI Finance	199	1·1	311	1·6	366	1·8	439	2·0	543	2·3
XXII Public administration and defence	701	3·9	1,007	5·3	999[a]	4·9	1,726	7·7	1,898	8·0
XXIII Professional services	798	4·4	886	4·7	1,067	5·2	1,543	6·9	1,984	8·3
XXIV Miscellaneous services	2,783	15·5	2,398	12·7	2,865	14·0	2,086	9·3	1,763	7·4
Total	17,941	100·0	18,855	100·0	20,498	100·0	22,501	100·0	23,767	100·0

[a]Local authority 'institutions' distinguished in 1931, and posted to 'Professional services'. In 1921, only nurses, attendants and medical occupations extracted from XXII and posted XXIII.

It is apparent that the proportions vary widely from industry to industry and that differential rates of growth between industries will, of themselves, affect the class structure of the labour force. Table 18 shows the industrial distribution of those occupied in the four census years and in 1959[1].

[1]The *Ministry of Labour Gazette* publishes monthly estimates for the occupied population, including employers and the self-employed, in broad industrial categories. For table 18, the Ministry has supplied a breakdown by Industrial Order as at March 1959. Numbers unemployed have been added. Estimates for end-June each year appear in the Central Statistical Office *Annual Abstract of Statistics* (H.M. Stationery Office).

We may now combine tables 17 and 18 in order to show the effect on occupational patterns of the changing fortunes of individual industries. If the distribution of occupations within each industry had been throughout the same as in 1951, occupational class distribution in each year would have been as follows:

Percentages

	1A	1B	2	3	4	5	6	7	All
1911	1·29	3·39	10·88	8·62	2·45	24·95	38·36	10·04	100
1921	1·46	3·61	10·52	9·52	2·61	25·11	36·72	10·46	100
1931	1·52	3·81	10·72	9·74	2·47	24·68	36·30	10·76	100
1951	1·96	4·67	9·95	10·85	2·69	25·37	32·84	11·67	100
1959	2·18	5·35	9·81	11·36	2·74	25·29	31·42	11·85	100

Changes in industrial distribution have worked strongly in favour of the use of more professional workers and clerks, have been almost neutral as far as skilled manual workers are concerned, have tended to reduce substantially the proportion of the semi-skilled and to increase slightly the proportion of the unskilled. These changes, however, were small in 1921 to 1931, but considerable between 1931 and 1951; they continued throughout the 1950's.

Our findings may now be summarized by comparing an index of changes in the proportions of the occupational classes (as shown in table 1) with an index calculated from proportions shown above. The results are shown in table 19. Line A shows the extent to which the proportion of each would have changed from one census year to the next (or from 1951 to 1959) if the only changes had been in the relative sizes of the twenty-four Industry Orders.

Line B shows the extent to which the proportion of each class *did* change as a result of all changes—both of the relative size of the Industry Orders and of the proportions in which the classes were blended within these orders.

Line C, which shows line B as a percentage of line A, isolates the effect of changes *within* each Industry Order.

To illustrate, the proportion of the occupied population in class 1A increased by one per cent between 1911 and 1921. If no other factor had been at work, the change in the relative size of the Industry Orders would have increased it by 13 per cent. We then deduce that changes in the proportion of this class *within* industries had moved against it and would (in isolation) have *reduced* its share in the labour force by 11 per cent. But between 1911 and 1951, changes in the relative size of industries and changes within industries each operated to raise the proportion of higher professionals, the one by 52 per cent, the other by 27 per cent, so that the proportion of higher professionals (or their number in each 100 of the occupied population) almost doubled.

For both lower and higher professionals, the growth of industries has been more potent than their proportions within each industry; for clerical workers and foremen, the reverse has been true—it is their increased proportions within

Table 19.   *Indices of changes in the proportions of each occupational class due to changes in the relative size of Industry Orders (A), all changes (B) and changes within Industry Orders (C), census years, 1911-51 and 1959*

		1921	1931	1951	1959	1911–51
		Previous census year = *100*				*Cumulative change*
1A. Higher professional	A	113	104	129	111	152
	B	101	113	169	..	193
	C	89	109	131	..	127
1B. Lower professional	A	106	106	123	115	138
	B	115	98	136	..	154
	C	108	92	111	..	112
2. Employers, proprietors,	A	97	102	93	99	92
administrators, managers	B	103	99	101	..	103
	C	106	97	108	..	112
3. Clerical workers	A	110	102	111	105	125
	B	139	104	153	..	221
	C	126	102	138	..	177
4. Foremen, inspectors	A	107	95	109	102	111
	B	112	107	170	..	203
	C	105	113	156	..	183
5. Skilled manual workers	A	101	99	103	100	103
	B	94	93	93	..	81
	C	93	94	90	..	79
6. Semi-skilled manual	A	96	99	90	96	86
workers	B	86	103	93	..	83
	C	90	104	103	..	97
7. Unskilled manual	A	104	103	108	102	116
workers	B	147	105	81	..	125
	C	141	102	75	..	108

industries that have given the strongest impetus to their growth.   For skilled workers, changes in the relative size of industries have been almost neutral, while their proportion within industries has tended gently but consistently downward; for the unskilled, both influences were upward until 1931, after which their proportions within industries fell sharply.

To put it another way, changes in the relative size of class 2 (Employers, managers, etc.), clerks, foremen and skilled manual workers represent in the main the changed proportions with which they are blended with other workers within industries; with the other classes, the change in the relative size of industries has been the major influence.

7.   CHANGES BETWEEN 1951 AND 1959

We have estimated occupational class distribution as it would have been in 1959 if coefficients within industries had been the same in that year as in 1951.

We may make one further adjustment, allowing for the changing proportion between manual and non-manual workers in manufacturing industry[1].

Our projection of the class proportions of April 1951 for manufacturing industry, allowing only for the change in relative size of industries, gives an answer of 18·35 as the percentage of classes 1, 2 and 3 (excluding employers) in those industries in October 1959. The Ministry of Labour inquiry for that month, however, shows that 21·3 per cent of the employees in manufacturing were non-manual (the equivalent of our classes 1, 2 and 3)[2]. Thus, to give effect to the drift from manual to non-manual occupations, we must multiply the proportions in manufacturing in classes 1, 2 and 3 by 1·16 (that is 21·3 divided by 18·35) and reduce the proportions of the other classes accordingly. This affects the 1959 distribution as follows:

Percentages

	1A	1B	2	3	4	5	6	7	All
1. Industry changes only	2·18	5·35	9·8	11·36	2·74	25·29	31·42	11·85	100
2. 1, plus changes in manual/non-manual ratio in manufacturing	2·26	5·52	10·06	12·00	2·66	24·72	31·12	11·66	100

Line 2 makes no allowance for shifts from manual to clerical and administrative employment in industries outside manufacturing which, particularly in the distributive trade, must have been quite considerable. A shift of three per cent from manual to non-manual in the distributive trade would have added 0·4 per cent to the non-manual proportion for all occupied, thus raising it to 30·2 per cent of the total. Changes in the other industry orders would have probably increased the proportion to not less than 31 per cent, compared with 27·4 per cent in 1951. The proportion is itself rising, then, at a compound rate of about 1½ per cent per annum. At this rate, it would take forty years, from 1951, before manual and non-manual workers formed equal proportions of the occupied population.

8. PARTICIPATION RATES BY AGE AND SEX

Table 20 compares the numbers and proportions of males and females aged over fourteen or fifteen and at work in the census years and in 1960[3].

[1]In October of each year, the Ministry of Labour collects information regarding the number of administrative, technical and clerical employees, on the one hand, and operatives, on the other, in manufacturing industry. For October 1950, the non-manual percentage was 16·5, for October 1951, 17·0, so that when the population census was taken in April 1951, it was presumably somewhere within these limits. This is close to the 17·3 per cent for classes 1 to 3 that may be deduced for manufacturing industries in 1951 from the population census Industry Table 7. If employers are extracted, the proportion is reduced to 16·6 per cent, remarkably close to the Ministry of Labour figure.

[2]See *Ministry of Labour Gazette*, vol. 69, no. 1, January 1961, p. 9.

[3]The age divisions of the 1921 and 1931 tables do not enable the 14-year-olds to be distinguished from the 15-year-olds. The Census of 1911 counted those occupied from the age of ten, that for 1921 from the age of twelve, 1931 from the age of fourteen and 1951 from the age of fifteen. A comparison made on this basis gives a participation rate of 56·9 per cent for 1911, rising to 60·1 per cent in 1931.

Table 20. *Males and females aged 14 or 15 and over, with numbers, in thousands, and percentages at work, census years, 1911–51 and 1960*

	1911[a]			1921[b]			1931[b]			1951[a]			1960[a]		
	M	F	Total	M	F	Total	M	F	Total	M	F	Total	M	F	Total
At or above 14 or 15	13,451	14,793	28,244	14,826	16,827	31,653	16,341	18,320	34,661	17,862	20,045	37,907	18,532	20,627	39,159
At or seeking work	12,581	5,224	17,805	13,612	5,673	19,285	14,801	6,273	21,074	15,649	6,961	22,610	16,239	8,197	24,436
Per cent M and F of total	70·7	29·3	100·0	70·6	29·4	100·0	70·2	29·8	100·0	69·2	30·8	100·0	66·5	33·5	100·0
Participation rate (%)	93·5	35·3	63·0	91·8	33·7	60·9	90·6	34·2	60·1	87·6	34·0	59·6	87·6	39·7	62·4

[a] Aged 15 and over.
[b] Aged 14 and over.

The participation rate for males aged fifteen or over fell from 93·5 per cent in 1911 to 87·6 per cent in 1951 and there it remained in 1960. The female rate remained curiously static until 1951, but between 1951 and 1960 rose from 34·0 to 39·7 per cent. This is reflected in the proportions that each sex constituted of the occupied population: ratios that hardly changed between 1911 and 1951 and then changed significantly.

For males, the difference in participation rate between 1931 and 1951 is the net result of two contradictory tendencies: an increase in full-time education reduced the rate for those under twenty-five; improved health increased the rate for those over thirty-four[1]. We are not given details for the fifteen-year-olds in 1931, but most boys of that age would have been at or seeking work, whereas, as a result of the raising of the school-leaving age from April 1947, only 64·5 per cent of them were in the labour force in April 1951[2].

The participation rate for males aged sixteen to sixty-four (inclusive) was identical in 1931 and 1951 (96·1 per cent). But of the boys aged sixteen and seventeen 88·7 per cent were at work in 1931; 84·6 per cent in 1951. For males aged eighteen to twenty-four inclusive, the percentages were 96·5 and 94·4[3]. Then the rates are about equal in both years until, between thirty-five and sixty-four, the rates for 1951 are higher. In the older ranges, the rates for men compare as follows:

					Percentages
	55–9	60–4	65–9	70–4	75 and over
1931	93·9	87·2	64·9	41·7	22·8
1951	95·0	87·5	47·2	27·4	12·6

Though the male participation rate did not change between 1951 and 1960, there was a further shift as between young and old, with a fall for boys aged fifteen to nineteen inclusive from 83·5 per cent in May 1951 to 77 per cent in May 1959.

The participation rate for women is influenced not only by changes in education and health but also by changes in the ratio between the married and unmarried and the proportions engaged full-time in domestic work. The proportion of married women who are gainfully employed is, of course, much lower than that of single women, so that an increase in numbers married will tend to lower the overall participation rate even though participation rates for single and married, considered separately, may be rising.

Thus, though the overall female participation rate was constant from 1911 to 1951 (table 20), the age-specific rate for single and for married women was

[1] A reflection of the improvement in health is the rise in the expectation of life. In England and Wales in 1911 a boy aged fifteen could expect to reach an age of 63·6. By 1951, this had risen to 69·4.

[2] From April 1947, a child could not leave school until the end of the term in which he or she turned fifteen.

[3] There were 58,500 males aged 18-24 in full-time education in 1931 (2·2 per cent of the age-group) and 93,500 in 1951 (4·3 per cent of the age-group).

Table 21. *Participation rate of married and unmarried (including widowed and divorced) women in four age-groups, 1931 and 1951*

Nos. in thousands

		1931			1951		
		Total	Occupied	Per cent	Total	Occupied	Per cent
20–4[a]	Married	466·9	86·3	*18·5*	795·5	290·5	*36·5*
	Unmarried	1,150·5	969·2	*84·2*	896·5	815·7	*91·0*
25–9	Married	1,115·1	163·6	*14·5*	1,408·6	362·6	*25·7*
	Unmarried	815·4	664·3	*81·5*	439·5	385·0	*87·6*
30–4	Married	1,312·0	156·9	*11·9*	1,433·6	331·0	*23·1*
	Unmarried	497·3	380·0	*76·4*	309·8	252·5	*81·5*
45–54	Married	2,091·3	178·2	*8·5*	2,612·5	618·1	*23·6*
	Unmarried	832·0	435·1	*52·3*	857·6	576·4	*67·2*

[a]1931: 21–4.

rising, a rise that was just balanced by the higher proportion of marriages and the ageing of the female population. In particular, the overall rate was unchanged between 1931 and 1951, when the rate for married women, aged fifteen and over, rose from 10 to 22 per cent, while that for single, widowed or divorced women fell from 60 to 55 per cent. The effect of these cross-currents is demonstrated in table 21, where four age-groups are compared for 1931 and 1951.

The participation rate for married women in the 20–4 age-group rose from 18·5 to 36·5 per cent; that for unmarried women from 84 to 91 per cent, yet the rate for the age-group as a whole remained constant at 65 per cent. In the age-group 25–9, the rate for the group actually fell from 43 to 40 per cent and it is only after that that the increase by marital status is reflected in an increase for the age-group taken as a whole.

The *Ministry of Labour Gazette* for March 1958[1] remarks, 'The available age-analyses show that this expansion of the female working population was achieved largely by the attraction into employment of large numbers of women over 30 years of age. In 1950 (the first year for which a detailed age-analysis is available), the total number of women employees between the ages of 30 and 50 was 2,603,000, but by 1956 the number in the same group (i.e., aged 36–55) was 2,925,000, an increase of more than 300,000. As this was a net increase after replacement of wastage, the gross recruitment of women of those ages into employment during the six years must have been considerably greater than 300,000.'

The trend here observed continued into 1959, for in May of that year, the

---

[1]'The Employment of Women and Girls in Great Britain since the War', vol. 66, no. 3, p. 97. The article remarks on the great discrepancies between regions in the increase in the female labour force.

Table 22.   *Female employees in civil employment as a percentage of all females*
by quinquennial age-groups, 1951 and 1959

Nos. in thousands

1 Age-group	2 Total	1951 3 Employed	4 Employed Per cent	5 Total	1959 6 Employed	7 Employed Per cent	8 Col. 7 as % of col. 4
15–19	1,558	1,209	77·6	1,644	1,211	73·7	94·9
20– 4	1,692	1,137	67·2	1,609	1,045	64·9	96·9
25– 9	1,848	778	42·1	1,601	657	41·0	97·3
30– 4	1,744	632	36·2	1,691	624	36·9	101·9
35– 9	1,882	673	35·8	1,941	787	40·5	113·1
40– 4	1,897	729	38·4	1,602	713	44·5	116·5
45– 9	1,797	679	37·8	1,848	817	44·2	116·9
50– 4	1,674	554	33·1	1,806	754	41·7	126·0
55– 9	1,479	411	27·8	1,667	581	34·9	125·5
60– 4	1,331	182	13·7	1,463	281	19·2	140·1
65– 9	1,158	70	6·0	1,250	121	9·7	161·7
15–69	18,058	7,054	39·1	18,122	7,591	41·9	107·2

Sources: (i)   Total number of women: *Annual Abstract of Statistics*, no. 94, 1957 (H.M.
Stationery Office), p. 10.   1959: total number at 30 June 1959 from *Monthly*
Digest of Statistics, no. 173, May 1960, table 11, p. 11:

   (ii)   Employed women : *Ministry of Labour Gazette*, vol. 60, no. 6, June 1952,
p. 195, and *Ministry of Labour Gazette*, vol. 68, no. 6, June 1960, p. 230.
Estimated number of employees as at the end of May in each year. It
includes not only persons at work but also those who were unemployed and
those absent through sickness, holidays and other causes.   The estimates are
based on a sample and are therefore subject to error.   See references for a
discussion of the margin of error.

number of women employees aged 39 to 58 had increased to 2,949,000, so that
24,000 more had gone to work than had retired.

The tendency for more married women to work has continued.   In May
1951, about 43 per cent of female employees were married; in May 1959, about
52 per cent.   During this period, the number of married women rose by
750,000, but the number of married women employees rose by 1,000,000[1].

Table 22 compares the participation rate as employees of females in quinquennial age-groups in 1951 and 1959.   There has been a substantial fall in the
lower age-groups but an even more substantial countervailing rise in the upper
ones.   Thus, while the participation rate for women aged 30 to 34 (inclusive)
had hardly changed, for those aged 35 to 39 it had risen by 13 per cent, for those
in their forties by more than 16 per cent and for those in their fifties by more than
25 per cent.

9.   MEN AND WOMEN BY INDUSTRY AND OCCUPATIONAL CLASS, 1951 AND 1959

In table 23 we show changes in the industrial distribution of men and women
between 1951 (Census *Industry Tables*) and March 1959 (Ministry of Labour).

[1]*Ministry of Labour Gazette*, vol. 68, no. 6, June 1960, p. 231.

Table 23. *Employment of men and women in Industry Orders, 1951 and 1959*

Nos. in thousands

Industry Order	1951				1959				1959 as % of 1951
	Male	Female	Total	% Female of total	Male	Female	Total	% Female of total	
I Agriculture, etc	1,025	117	1,142	10·25	869	98	967	10·13	84·68
II Mining, etc.	847	14	861	1·63	818	24	842	2·85	97·79
III Ceramics, glass, etc.	244	74	318	23·27	255	79	334	23·65	105·03
IV Chemicals	325	117	442	26·47	396	150	546	27·47	123·53
V Metal manufacture	517	62	579	10·71	499	65	564	11·52	97·41
VI Engineering and shipbuilding	1,447	354	1,801	19·66	1,693	471	2,164	21·77	120·16
VII Vehicles	885	124	1,009	12·29	1,072	178	1,250	14·24	123·89
VIII Metal goods n.e.s.	323	159	482	32·99	351	177	528	33·52	109·54
IX Precision instruments, jewellery, etc.	105	49	154	31·82	103	57	160	35·63	103·90
X Textiles	443	554	997	55·57	388	479	867	55·25	86·96
XI Leather, etc.	51	28	79	35·44	49	32	81	39·51	102·53
XII Clothing	243	486	729	66·67	208	445	653	68·15	89·57
XIII Food, drink and tobacco	475	281	756	37·17	536	390	926	42·12	122·49
XIV Wood	279	54	333	16·22	254	63	317	19·87	95·20
XV Paper and printing	337	183	520	35·19	388	207	595	34·79	114·42
XVI Other manufactures	161	106	267	39·70	181	113	294	38·44	110·11
XVII Building	1,390	41	1,431	2·87	1,477	65	1,542	4·22	107·76
XVIII Gas, electricity and water	329	32	361	8·86	339	42	381	11·02	105·54
XIX Transport and communication	1,517	217	1,734	12·51	1,448	253	1,701	14·87	98·10
XX Distributive trades	1,545	1,167	2,712	43·03	1,606	1,424	3,030	47·00	111·73
XXI Finance	288	151	439	43·40	322	225	547	41·13	124·60
XXII Public administration and defence	1,452	274	1,726	15·87	1,514	390	1,904	20·48	110·31
XXIII Professional services	637	906	1,543	58·72	762	1,236	1,998	61·86	129·49
XXIV Miscellaneous services	710	1,376	2,086	65·96	583	1,235	1,818	67·93	87·15
Total	15,575	6,926	22,501	30·78	16,111	7,898	24,009	32·90	106·70

Notes: 1951: Census *Industry Tables*.
1959: estimates supplied by the Ministry of Labour. Total numbers in employment.

Not only has it been a period of considerable change in industrial deployment but, as we have seen, one in which female participation has increased substantially.

Clothing, textiles and 'miscellaneous services' (including domestic service) which traditionally employ a high proportion of women, declined substantially, but this was more than offset by an increase in the proportion of women in the work force of most industries and a considerable expansion of some other industries with a large female section, in particular food, drink and tobacco, finance and professional services.

These shifts in industrial distribution, if they had been the only changes involved, would have affected the women's share of each occupational class as follows:

Women as a percentage of each occupational class

	1A	1B	2	3	4	5	6	7	All
1951	8·0	53·2	18·5	58·2	13·7	15·8	40·5	20·9	30·9
1959	9·5	57·8	20·1	62·4	14·9	15·2	42·2	22·7	32·9

Note: The 1951 proportions are in Appendix B and differ slightly from those derived from table 1.

Applying these proportions to the class totals for 1959, we get the following percentage distribution for men and women:

		1A	1B	2	3	4	5	6	7	All
Men	1951	2·61	3·16	11·74	6·56	3·36	30·91	28·29	13·35	100
	1959	2·93	3·35	11·62	6·33	3·46	31·80	26·93	13·58	100
Women	1951	0·51	8·05	5·95	20·43	1·19	12·97	43·01	7·90	100
	1959	0·64	9·50	6·06	21·76	1·25	11·80	40·72	8·27	100
All	1951	1·96	4·67	9·95	10·85	2·69	25·37	32·84	11·67	100
	1959	2·18	5·35	9·81	11·36	2·74	25·29	31·42	11·85	100

Thus women are contributing more than men both to the expansion and enrichment of the work force. Full employment, wider occupational choice, improved educational opportunity, increased demand for professional skills, higher productivity and real incomes, shorter hours, earlier marriage, mechanization of housekeeping, have interacted to bring about a social change since 1951 that may be of outstanding importance for the future: that is, the return of married women to the work force. In some cases employers have made special efforts to make use of this reserve of labour, notably by the recruitment of part-time workers. But the unused potential is still very great.

CHAPTER II

OCCUPATIONAL PAY

1. EMPLOYEE INCOME DISTRIBUTION, 1911/12 AND 1958/9

(a) *Income before tax*

The units of the labour market are defined by occupation. Employers do not buy labour as such; they buy the service of fitters, bricklayers, clothing machinists, nurses, teachers or typists and it is by occupation that rates of pay are fixed. On the other hand, most of the data are collected and presented as if the market were industrially defined, the only occupational distinction being between manual and non-manual workers. This applies to the Ministry of Labour statistics of manual earnings subsequent to those of 1906 and to the recently inaugurated inquiry into the earnings of administrative, technical and clerical employees[1]. The Inland Revenue data, too, are given by range of income or by industry and not by occupation.

Thus, if we are to make use of this authoritative material, we must begin with aggregates that include all sorts of occupations and then analyse the changes that they display. These changes may be in response to three sorts of stimuli: there may be a general rise or fall in pay resulting from changes in the value of money, with relative occupational levels unchanged; there may be a change in the relative pay levels of different occupations; or there may be a change in the relative numbers employed in different occupations. This last may be the result of technical changes within industries or the relative growth or decline of particular industries.

As a preliminary view we show, in table 24, how employees were distributed in income ranges near the beginning and near the end of the period of study. It would be more satisfactory if the whole occupied population could be distinguished by level of earned income, but the nature of the data makes this impossible[2].

[1]See *Ministry of Labour Gazette*, vol. 69, no. 6, June 1961, p. 240.
[2]In the Inland Revenue *Reports* personal income is, of course, classified by income units, not persons, and includes income from all sources. Schedule D units are shown in ranges separately for individuals and for partnerships as well as for companies, etc. But the source of the income of the individuals and partners and its origin as earned or unearned income vary considerably from trade group to trade group and from case to case. One individual may own a shop but not work in it; a farmer may be an employer and work himself; a medical practitioner may earn his income entirely from his own labours. Data will be produced later relating to levels of professional Schedule D earnings. It is only in the tables relating to pay-as-you-earn income that the earned income of individuals is distinguished and it is from these that the 1958/9 data of table 24 are derived.

For 1958/9, table 24 uses tax data; for 1911/12, tax data embrace only the top 3 per cent of the employee population and other sources must be used for the remaining 97 per cent. Methods and sources are described in Appendix D (page 165).

Table 24.2 shows pay at the deciles, etc., for male, female and all employees, and table 24.3 shows these points in relation to the medians. For males and females together, there has been a widening of differentials up to the median (or fifth decile) and thereafter a narrowing. Between 1911/12 and 1958/9, pay at the median rose 8·6 times; at the third and ninth deciles, it rose 7·7 times; at the 99th centile, 7·1 times; at the 999th millile, 5·8 times.

But these movements in the totals are compounded of opposing movements in the parts: for men, there has been a general narrowing of differentials; for women, a general widening. Increases were as follows (1958/9 levels as multiples of those of 1911/12) :

	Men	Women
3rd decile	9·6	5·7
Median	8·5	6·3
9th decile	7·8	7·7
99th centile	7·1	8·9
999th millile	5·6	13·9

Table 24. *Distribution of annual income before tax, Great Britain (all employees)*
(numbers in thousands)

1. *Cumulative frequency distribution*

1911/12				1958/9			
Getting more than £	Male	Female	Total	Getting more than £	Male	Female	Total
0	11,665	4,993	16,658	0	14,820	7,614	22,434
10	11,621	4,884	16,505	189	14,718	5,896	20,614
20	10,984	4,553	15,537	199	14,639	5,665	20,304
40	9,807	3,097	12,904	249	14,086	4,279	18,365
60	6,879	667	7,546	299	13,570	3,039	16,609
80	4,355	175	4,530	399	12,376	1,437	13,813
100	2,602	65	2,667	499	10,155	729	10,884
120	1,185	9	1,194	599	7,070	396	7,466
140	641	2	643	799	2,842	131	2,973
160	451		451	999	1,176	54	1,230
200	277		277	1,499	367	13	380
300	125		125	1,999	183·7	5·3	189
400	72		72	2,999	68·4	1·6	70
500	44		44	4,999	17·9	0·1	18
600	30		30				
700	22		22				
800	17		17				
900	14		14				
1,000	9		9				
2,000	1·8		1·8				
3,000	0·75		0·75				
4,000	0·4		0·4				
5,000	0·2		0·2				

2. Deciles and highest centiles and milliles

	Male £	Female £	Both £		Male £	Female £	Both £
	1911/12				1958/9		
			Deciles				
1	28	22	25	1	320	..	205
2	43	35	38	2	430	(160)[a]	270
3	51	37	43	3	490	210	330
4	59	41	49	4	540	240	410
5 Median	67	43	56	5 Median	570	270	480
6	76	45	65	6	640	300	550
7	88	49	76	7	705	340	620
8	103	55	92	8	795	390	710
9	121	64	112	9	945	490	860
			Highest centile				
99	310	103	265	99	2,200	920	1,880
			Highest millile				
999	945	128	810	999	5,300	1,780	4,700

[a]By extrapolation.

3. Deciles and highest centiles and milliles as per cent of median

	Male %	Female %	Both %		Male %	Female %	Both %
	1911/12				1958/9		
			Deciles				
1	42	51	45	1	56	..	43
2	64	81	68	2	75	(59)	56
3	76	86	77	3	86	78	69
4	88	95	88	4	95	89	85
5	100	100	100	5	100	100	100
6	113	105	116	6	112	111	115
7	131	114	136	7	124	126	129
8	154	128	164	8	140	144	148
9	181	149	200	9	166	182	179
			Highest centile				
99	463	240	473	99	386	341	392
			Highest millile				
999	1,410	298	1,446	999	930	659	979

Thus, for women, the third decile was 86 per cent of the median in 1911/12 and 78 per cent in 1958/9; the ninth decile 149 per cent and 182 per cent. In the higher ranges, the rise in differentials was still more striking.

Table 24.1 demonstrates a feature of the pay structure present in both periods: the relative lowness of women's pay. In part, this is because women tend to work fewer hours than men and because there are more female part-time workers. Another cause, shown in table 1[1], is the disproportionately large number of women doing semi-skilled work and the disproportionately

[1]Chapter I, p. 4.

E

small numbers in the higher occupational classes. Later we shall be able to measure the effect of these factors against the tendency for women to be paid less than men even for performing the same job.

Meanwhile, we may note a steep decline in the percentage of women as we ascend through the pay ranges. Females formed the following percentages of the total in various income ranges:

More than £	1911/12 %	More than £	1958/9 %
0	30	0	34
20	29	199	28
40	24	299	18
60	9	399	10
80	4	599	5

However, the tail had grown longer by 1958/9: 4 per cent of those getting more than £999 and 3 per cent of those getting more than £1,999 were women.

Another manifestation of the rise in differentials in the female distribution is that, until the ninth decile, women's pay was lower in proportion to men's pay in 1958/9 than in 1911/12. At the median, it fell from 64 to 47 per cent of men's pay, at the ninth decile from 53 to 52 per cent. At the 99th centile, however, it had risen from 33 to 42 per cent and at the 999th millile from 13·5 to 34 per cent.

(b) *Income after tax*

We deal below with the occupational content of these changes, but before doing so it is important to get some idea of the effect of taxation on employee income distribution. Pay before tax is significant for the employer for it is this that determines his labour costs and measures the relative costs of different sorts of labour, but it is pay after tax that is significant for the employee for it is this that measures the financial compensation that he gets for his effort.

Table 25.   *Distribution of annual income after tax, Great Britain (all employees), deciles and highest centiles and milliles*

	1911/12			1958/9	
		Deciles			
	£	Per cent of median		£	Per cent of median
1	25	45	1	205	44
2	38	68	2	270	57
3	43	77	3	327	70
4	49	88	4	405	86
5	56	100	5	470	100
6	65	116	6	537	114
7	76	136	7	601	128
8	92	164	8	685	146
9	112	200	9	821	175
		Highest centile			
99	260	464	99	1,523	324
		Highest millile			
999	780	1,393	999	2,632	560

The dispersion of employee income was estimated as it would be after tax and the deciles, etc., calculated. These are shown in table 25[1].

We have already mentioned that only a small proportion of the population paid tax in 1911/12: it would have reduced an income of £265 by about £5 and one of £810 by £30, but even at the level of the highest decile, no tax would have been paid at all.

In 1958/9, tax would have reduced the median from £480 to £470 and the ninth decile from £860 to £821. For 90 per cent of employees, tax does not rise above 5 per cent and the redistributive effect is negligible. But the highest centile now becomes 3·2 times the median instead of 3·9 times, representing a tax deduction of 19 per cent, while the highest millile is reduced from 9·8 to 5·6 times the median, a tax deduction of 44 per cent.

(c) Changes in real income

One more comparison will help to get these changes into focus: the conversion of the nominal values into real terms. This we do by raising the 1911/12 figures in proportion to the rise in retail prices between 1911/12 and 1958/9[2].

Table 26. *Employee income distribution after tax, 1911/12 and 1958/9 in 1958/9 prices, deciles and highest centiles and milliles*

	1911/12			1958/9	
	£	*Deciles*		£	Per cent of 1911/12
1	108		1	205	*190*
2	164		2	270	*165*
3	186		3	327	*176*
4	212		4	405	*191*
5 Median	242		5 Median	470	*194*
6	281		6	537	*191*
7	328		7	601	*183*
8	397		8	685	*173*
9	484		9	821	*170*
		Highest centile			
99	1,123		99	1,523	*136*
		Highest millile			
999	3,370		999	2,632	*78*

On average, the deciles, reckoned in 1958/9 retail prices, were 80 per cent higher in that year than in 1911/12. The three lowest deciles show an average increase of 77 per cent; the three highest, 75 per cent; the three in the middle, 92 per cent.

[1] The method used is described in Appendix E. It would be as well to emphasize that table 25 is 'abstract art', for allowances are calculated and incomes taxed in income units, more than half of which consist of married couples, while the rate at which incomes are taxed rises with the increase in total income. Thus it is not possible (except marginally) to distinguish tax on earned income from that on unearned income.

[2] The index used is that published by the London and Cambridge Economic Service, with A. L. Bowley's index (*Wages and Income in the United Kingdom since 1860* (Cambridge, University Press, 1937), p. 121) for the years prior to 1914. With 1911/12=100, 1958/9=432.

The decline in the relative size of increase continues until at a post-tax level of about £2,300 (in 1958/9 prices), or 0·3 per cent from the top of the scale, the break-even point is reached. At the highest millile, 0·1 per cent from the top of the income scale, we register a fall in real income between 1911/12 and 1958/9, of 22 per cent.

From another viewpoint, the three middle deciles together in 1958/9 averaged 847 per cent of those of 1911/12, using current prices. But in £'s of constant value, the 1958/9 figure would be 192 per cent: in nominal terms, an increase of 747 per cent; in constant price terms, 92 per cent. One-eighth of the nominal increase represents an increase in purchasing power; seven-eighths, a fall in the value of money.

These comparisons do not show what has happened to the incomes in particular occupations. They do show what has happened to the income of a man whose *relative place in the whole income structure* has remained the same. For example, the man who in 1911/12 had the thousandth highest income (the 999th millile) received £945 before tax (table 24.2) and his income was 14·1 times that of the median man (table 24.3). In 1958/9, the thousandth man from the top got £5,300, but only 9·3 times the income of the median man. Even after tax, this thousandth man from the top in 1911/12, with £780, still got 13·9 times the median income (table 25); by 1958/9, he got £2,632, but only 5·6 times the median income. And his real income shrank over the period by 22 per cent (table 26).

(d) Dispersion of manual earnings, 1906, 1938 and 1960[1]

In table 24, we noted a general narrowing of differentials for men between 1958/9 and 1911/12, and for women a general widening. The Ministry of Labour manual earnings inquiries have on three occasions called for information about the dispersion of earnings (in 1906, 1938 and 1960) so that we may now see whether these opposing tendencies are reflected in the earnings data and, if so, how much of the process had taken place before the second world war[2].

The nearest we can get to a consistent comparison is between the distribution for a normal week in 1906 with that for a week of 44 to 48 hours in 1938; and

---

[1]There is no accepted rule for the separation of occupations into manual and non-manual. The Ministry of Labour publishes its (now) six-monthly earnings data in the *Ministry of Labour Gazette* as the 'earnings and working hours of manual workers', but in the questionnaire sent to employers calls for information relating to the 'earnings and hours of wage-earners' and explains, 'foremen, transport workers, warehousemen, etc., should be included, but managers, clerks, typists, commercial travellers, shop assistants and salaried persons generally should be excluded'.

[2]1906: *Report of an Enquiry by the Board of Trade into Earnings and Hours of Labour of Workpeople in the United Kingdom in 1906, loc. cit.* For 1938, data concerning dispersion were given by R. B. Ainsworth in a paper read to the Royal Statistical Society ('Earnings and Working Hours of Manual Wage-Earners in the United Kingdom in October 1938', *Journal of the Royal Statistical Society, Series A*, vol. 112, part 1, 1949, p. 35). For 1960, the results appeared in the *Ministry of Labour Gazette*, vol. 69, nos. 4 and 6, for April and June 1961, pp. 137 and 242. The comparability of the three reports is discussed in Appendix F.

for those who worked 44 hours or more in 1938 with the 'full-time' workers of 1960 (that is, including the effects of overtime). Table 27 shows these comparisons for the quartiles and medians in the three years.

Table 27. *Dispersion of manual earnings, 1906, 1938 and 1960*[a]

A. 1906 and 1938

	1906				1938			
	Men		Women		Men		Women	
		% of median		% of median		% of median		% of median
Lower quartile	20s. 9d.	78	10s. 7d.	79	55s. 6d.	83	27s. 0d.	80
Median	26s. 7d.	100	13s. 4d.	100	66s. 6d.	100	33s. 7d.	100
Upper quartile	34s. 3d.	129	17s. 2d.	129	77s. 9d.	117	39s. 3d.	117

B. 1938 and 1960

	1938				1960			
Lower quartile	58s. 0d.	83	29s. 6d.	85·5	234s. 2d.	83	128s. 2d.	84·5
Median	70s. 0d.	100	34s. 6d.	100	283s. 4d.	100	151s. 7d.	100
Upper quartile	82s. 0d.	117	39s. 6d.	114	344s. 9d.	122	178s. 7d.	118

Notes: A.   1906: those who worked full-time;
                  1938: those who worked 44–8 hours.
              B.   1938: those who worked 44 hours or more;
                  1960: those who worked full-time or more.

[a]Figures include manufacturing; building, transport (excluding railways in 1938 and 1960 and London Transport in 1960), mining and quarrying (excluding coal), gas, electricity and water, local authority services, government industrial establishments.

Thus far, a narrowing of the range of dispersion appears in 1938 as compared with 1906 for both men and women. Between 1938 and 1960, the range between the lower quartile and median was held more or less intact, but for both men and women there was a widening of the median–upper quartile range. On this reckoning, the egalitarian process observed for men in table 24 must have been the net product of a move to greater equality followed by a less pronounced move away from it, while, in the lower half of the manual earnings range, the process appears to have been completed by 1938 and then maintained (or perhaps returned to) in 1960[1].

[1]The inclusion in 1960 of women regularly working 30 hours a week or less, would, of course, add a considerable number to the lower earnings ranges, since they constituted 15·6 per cent of the women employed in the industries included. Their earnings averaged 74s. 10d. in October 1960, compared with an average for full-time women of 148s. 4d. If it is assumed that all of the part-timers were getting less than £5 per week, their inclusion with the full-timers (this still omits those who work more than 30 hours but still regularly work less than 'the normal hours of their class') would lower the lower quartile to £5·75, the median to £7·2 and the upper quartile to £8·65 (80, 100 and 120 per cent respectively). The inclusion of all women in 1906 (that is, those working short-time, ordinary time or overtime) produces a lower quartile of 10·2s., a median of 12·75s. and an upper quartile of 16·75s. (80, 100 and 131 per cent). The remarkable intractability of the lower quartile–median gap again appears, and a similar reduction in that between the median and upper quartile.

The proportion of both relatively low wages and relatively high wages diminished from 1906 to 1938. Then, for 1938 to 1960, there is no discernible change at the lower end, while at the top end, the range of earnings has widened.

Between 1906 and 1938, women's earnings fell slightly in relation to men's, though so little as to be hardly significant within the margin of error involved in the data. But between 1938 and 1960 there was a perceptible narrowing in the male-female differential. Again, it is surprisingly small when one considers the social and economic changes separating the two years. The data, derived from table 27, are as follows:

Women's earnings as percentage of men's earnings in 1906, 1938 and 1960

	1906[a]	1938[b]
Lower quartile	51·0	48·6
Median	50·2	50·5
Upper quartile	51·6	50·5

	1938[c]	1960[d]
Lower quartile	50·9	54·7
Median	49·3	53·5
Upper quartile	48·2	51·8

[a]Those who worked full-time.
[b]Those who worked 44–8 hours.
[c]Those who worked 44 hours or more.
[d]Those who worked full-time or more.

Table 28. *Dispersion of manual earnings, 1906, 1938 and 1960 (unweighted averages for eight industrial groups)*[a]

Shillings per week or percentage of median

	Lowest decile		Lower quartile		Median		Upper quartile		Highest decile	
	s.	%	s.	%	s.	%	s.	%	s.	%
Men										
1906	20·1	68·3	23·5	79·8	29·45	100	35·7	121·2	43·25	146·9
1938	49·3	71·0	58·05	83·7	69·4	100	81·5	117·4	96·0	138·3
1960	204·1	72·9	235·55	84·2	279·9	100	336·0	120·0	397·25	141·9
Women										
1906	8·35	67·3	10·2	82·3	12·4	100	15·5	125·0	18·7	150·8
1938	24·8	71·2	29·1	83·5	34·85	100	40·1	115·1	47·4	136·0
1960	113·2	75·7	129·7	86·8	149·5	100	176·7	118·2	205·0	137·1

[a]The eight industrial groups are:
1. Bricks, pottery, glass, cement, abrasives, chemicals.
2. Metals, engineering and shipbuilding.
3. Textiles.
4. Clothing.
5. Food, drink and tobacco.
6. Woodworking.
7. Paper, printing, bookbinding.
8. Building and contracting.

For woodworking, building and contracting, data are for men only.

But shifts in the industrial distribution of the labour force have played some part in producing these changes or preserving the apparent rigidities[1].

We can eliminate some of the effect of these by considering individual industries and calculating unweighted averages[2]. The results are shown in table 28.

The direction of change is confirmed (a narrowing of differentials below the median, and first a narrowing, then a widening above it), but the magnitude of the changes is a little different: they are rather more moderate between 1906 and 1938.

Relatively to the highest decile, the lowest decile rose quite substantially between 1906 and 1938, after which it hardly changed:

Lowest decile as percentage of highest decile

	1906	1938	1960
Men	40·6	51·9	50·3
Women	44·65	52·3	55·2

(e) *The ratio between men's and women's earnings*

Relative to men's, women's earnings rose substantially between 1906 and 1938. For the six industries included in table 28 for which we have data for both men and women, the relationship was as follows:

Women's earnings as percentages of men's at the median

	1906	1938	1960
Paper and printing	36·1	45·75	49·2
Bricks, chemicals, etc.	41·4	46·1	50·3
Metals, engineering, etc.	37·9	46·0	48·9
Textiles	56·75	57·9	58·0
Clothing	44·8	55·5	56·4
Food, drink and tobacco	43·0	54·3	55·3
Average	42·9	50·5	52·7

Again, remarkable rigidities appear: in textiles, the relationship was almost the same in 1960 as it had been in 1906; in the other industries there has been very little change since 1938.

(f) *Manual earnings and all earnings*

A comparison of the data of table 24 and table 28 reveals some of the mechanism by which the change in differentials has been accomplished. Men in manufacturing and building have moved up the income scale. Their lowest and highest deciles, lower and upper quartiles and median bore the following

---

[1]The decline of the number and proportion of women engaged in textiles, where the gap between men's and women's rates is at its narrowest, has contributed greatly to the preservation, in the all-industry average, of the male-female differential.

[2]The inquiries for 1906 and 1960 give an industrial break-down by what are now called Minimum List Headings; that for 1938 is by Industry Order or, in some cases, the combination of several Orders. Thus, the unweighted averages do not eliminate the effect of changes in the size of the constituent parts of the industries or groups of industries.

relationship to the deciles of the male all-employee distribution in 1911/12 and 1958/9:

*Relationship of deciles for men in manufacturing
and building to those for all male employees*

	1911/12	1958/9
Lowest decile	3·25	3·8
Lower quartile	4·25	5·6
Median	6·1	7·3
Upper quartile	7·3	8·5
Highest decile	8·5	9·6

In 1911, males in manufacturing and building represented 41 per cent of all occupied males; in 1951, 47 per cent. This in itself would have had some effect in narrowing dispersion, for the highest decile was 215 per cent of the lowest decile for men in manufacturing and building in 1911/12, compared with 432 per cent for all male employees.

In addition, the dispersion in manual earnings in manufacturing and building has itself narrowed, so that in 1960, the highest decile was 195 per cent of the lowest. Finally, the manual earnings have spilt over into the highest 10 per cent range which formerly was the preserve of managers, administrators and professional workers.

But the lowest 10 per cent in 1911/12 consisted mainly of boys. By 1958/9, not only was the number of boys in employment much reduced, but their pay had risen proportionately more than that of men: thus pay for all male employees at the lowest decile in 1958/9 was 1,142 per cent of that of 1911/12, whilst the lowest decile for men in manufacturing and building in 1958/9 was 1,021 per cent of the level of 1911/12.

For women, the rise in pay of those in manufacturing quite outstripped the general rise, so that, whilst the lowest decile for all females and for women in manufacturing had been identical in 1911, in 1958/9 the lowest decile for manufacturing was higher than the median for all females. Thus, factory workers spread into the upper tenth, leaving behind them a long tail of other workers in the bottom half of the distribution. For women in factories there was a narrowing, for all females a widening of differentials.

We now turn to an analysis of these changes by occupation and thence, by occupational class.

2. PAY OF OCCUPATIONS AND OCCUPATIONAL CLASSES

(a) *Problems of measurement*

Some occupations are normally paid by the year, some by the month, some by the week and some by the hour[1]. Some are paid for time lost owing to

---

[1]Weekly or hourly paid workers are in fact often paid by the minute, with *pro rata* deductions for lateness or absence.

illness or misadventure. Most, nowadays, have an annual paid holiday, though its length may vary from a week to six months. There is also great variation in the length of the working week, which, again, may be prolonged by paid or unpaid overtime. Finally, the effort, intensity and disagreeableness of different occupations vary through an enormous range, from the depressive boredom of the art gallery attendant to the maniac fervour of the pop singer.

Not only does the expenditure of effort vary greatly between jobs; it has, in many cases, varied greatly in the same job as at different times. In particular, most manual jobs involve much less exertion now than they did thirty or forty years ago.

There is no way of standardizing for these variations. We cannot quantify the expenditure of effort involved in doing a job and it is not easy even to rank different jobs in this respect, for those requiring little muscular effort often involve great nervous strain[1]. Instead, we skirt the problem by saying that what we shall set out to measure is the price of engaging a worker in a particular occupation for one year or 52 weeks. From the worker's point of view, it is the earnings that can be extracted (before tax and other statutory deductions) for a year's work, including payments for overtime and deductions for short-time[2]. We leave until later a consideration of the effects of changes in taxation, unemployment benefit and other forms of social insurance, hours of work and unemployment.

In chapter I we plotted the occupational structure in four years that were determined by the incidence of the population census; logically, it might seem that we should choose the same years for plotting pay structure, but here we are subject to two restraints: one relating to the limitations of the available information, the other to the instability of the pay structure over much of our period of study. The years 1921 and 1951 were both periods of violent economic change, one the aftermath of the first world war, the other in the middle of the Korean war; and 1931 was a year of falling prices, rising unemployment and deepening depression.

But there were periods of comparative stability from 1906 to 1914, 1923 to 1928 and 1934 to 1938 and it is at some point in each of these periods that we shall build our pay structure. For more recent years, we choose 1955/6, because this is the period for which the Royal Commission on Doctors' and Dentists' Remuneration collected its information about professional income, and 1959/60 because this marks the end of our study and was a year following some major readjustments in pay.

[1]Thus the standardized mortality ratio, 1949-53, of the owners of retail shops, aged 20-64, was well above the average; that for shop-assistants well below. By far the highest rate was scored by company directors (so returned). See *The Registrar General's Decennial Supplement, England and Wales, 1951: Occupational Mortality*, part II, vol. 2 (H.M. Stationery Office, 1958), p. 14.

[2]Earnings censuses for manual workers have generally been confined to a particular week in a year, in which case we have multiplied the week's earnings by 52. This, and other usages, are explained in the sections relating to each occupational class.

We proceed, then, to build up the class averages by assessing pay for the constituent occupations in each of the five periods. Having done that, we shall consider the intervening years in an endeavour to identify the periods of significant change and the phenomena that were associated with the changes.

(b) Occupational class 1A (Higher professions)

Men

For the years 1913/14, 1922/3 and 1955/6, professional earnings are well documented[1], and, for these years, we are able to produce measures of dispersion. These are shown in table 29.

Table 29. *Professional earnings, 1913/14, 1922/3 and 1955/6*

	1913/14 £	1922/3 £	1922/3 % of 1913/14	1955/6 £	1955/6 % of 1922/3	1955/6 % of 1913/14
Barristers						
Highest decile	1,820	3,450	189	5,003	145	275
Upper quartile	680	1,533	225	2,619	171	385
Median	210	580	276	1,251	216	596
Lower quartile	155	235	152	579	246	373
Solicitors						
Highest decile	1,410	2,413	171	3,983	165	282
Upper quartile	790	1,453	184	2,630	181	333
Median	390	811	208	1,688	208	434
Lower quartile	185	434	234	1,041	240	562
Doctors						
Highest decile	1,200	1,757	146	3,544	202	295
Upper quartile	700	1,142	163	2,865	251	409
Median	370	723	195	2,300	318	622
Lower quartile	195	439	225	1,794	409	920
Dentists						
Highest decile	1,140	1,681	147	3,746	223	328
Upper quartile	600	950	158	2,806	295	468
Median	310	514	166	2,090	407	674
Lower quartile	155	294	190	1,437	489	928

Over the whole span, the changes display some similarity: income at the median has multiplied six or seven times, at the lower quartile about nine times (except in the case of the solicitors), at the upper quartile about four times and at the highest decile about three times.

Within this pattern, there have been considerable fluctuations in relativities.

[1]For the first two years, information is drawn from the Inland Revenue reports to the Committee appointed to inquire into the standard of remuneration and other conditions of employment of state servants (see *Report of Committee on Pay, etc. of State Servants* (Anderson Committee), H.M. Stationery Office, 1923); for 1955/6, from the *Report of the Royal Commission on Doctors' and Dentists' Remuneration, 1957-1960*, Cmnd 939 (H.M. Stationery Office, 1960). The nature of the material and the methods used are described in Appendix G.

The averages for the medians and quartiles for each profession and their relation to the averages for the four professions were as follows:

	1913/14		1922/3		1955/6	
	£	% of average	£	% of average	£	% of average
Barristers	348	90	783	103	1,483	77
Solicitors	455	118	899	118	1,786	93
Doctors	422	109	768	101	2,320	121
Dentists	322	83	586	77	2,111	110
Average	387	100	759	100	1,925	100

There have been interesting fluctuations over the years: a gain by barristers in 1922 and a more than proportionate fall in 1955. To some extent, this may be explained by changes in the age-structure: the first world war destroyed a high proportion of young men from the professions and, at the Bar, the earnings spread is extraordinarily wide. The road to success is long and hard but the prize (as measured by the highest decile) is considerable. At that level, barristers' earnings are much in excess of those in other professions.

Within each profession, there has been a general narrowing of differentials though, in the case of barristers, the lower quartile was no nearer the upper quartile in 1955 than in 1913.

	Lower quartile as per cent of upper quartile			Median as per cent of highest decile		
	1913/14	1922/3	1955/6	1913/14	1922/3	1955/6
Barristers	23	15	22	11	17	25
Solicitors	23	30	40	28	34	42
Doctors	28	38	63	31	41	65
Dentists	26	31	51	27	30	56

The career pattern of barristers was much the same in 1956 as it had been in 1914, but for the others there has been a great compression of the range of earnings, evident both in 1922 and 1955.

We are able to include data for the medical practitioners for 1935/7 by virtue of the investigation by Sir Austin Bradford Hill[1]. Their earnings in 1935/7 and 1955/6 were as follows:

	1935/7	1955/6	
	£	£	% of 1935/7
Highest decile	1,750	3,148	180
Upper quartile	1,380	2,640	191
Median	1,010	2,058	204
Lower quartile	740	1,528	206

[1]See tables and notes extracted from the report made to the British Medical Association by Professor (now Sir) Austin Bradford Hill: Appendix II, p. 17, *Report of the Inter-Departmental Committee on Remuneration of General Practitioners*, Cmd 6810 (H.M. Stationery Office, 1946). Specialists and assistants were excluded from the inquiry. Returns were received from 3,008 respondents in 1946, relating to accounts accepted by the Inspector of Taxes for the years 1935, 1936 and 1937. This lapse between the event and the inquiry results in some distortion of age-distribution and this has been corrected by weighting the age-ranges in accordance with age-distribution shown in the 1931 census.

There has been little change in the lower quartile/median ratio but the lower quartile shows a modest rise with reference to the upper quartile: from 54 per cent in 1935/7 to 58 per cent in 1955/6. The median was 58 per cent of the highest decile in the earlier period and 65 per cent in the later.

For a comparison between 1922/3 and 1935/7, the earnings for the later year must be raised to allow for the inclusion of consultants and assistants. In 1955/6, this inclusion raises the highest decile by 12·5 per cent, the upper quartile by 8·5 per cent, the median by 11·7 per cent and the lower quartile by 17·4 per cent. The best we can do is to raise the figures for 1935/7 in like proportion. The comparison is then as follows:

	1922/3 £	1935/7 £	% of 1922/3
Highest decile	1,757	1,969	112
Upper quartile	1,142	1,497	131
Median	723	1,128	156
Lower quartile	439	869	198

There appears to have been both a substantial rise in incomes and a substantial narrowing of differentials. The lower quartile was 38 per cent of the upper quartile in 1922/3 and 58 per cent in 1935/7. Thus the major narrowing between 1913 and 1955 took place at some time between 1922/3 and 1935/7.

Table 30. *Average professional earnings (occupational class 1A), 1913/14, 1922/4, 1935/7, 1955/6 and 1960*

	1913/14 £	1922/4 £	% of 1913/14	1935/7 £	% of 1922/4	1955/6 £	% of 1935/7	1960 £	% of 1955/6	% of 1913/14
Barristers	478	1,124	235	(1,090)	(97)	2,032	(186)	..	..	..
Solicitors	568	1,096	193	(1,238)	(113)	2,086	(168)	..	..	..
Dentists	368	601	163	676	112	2,273	336	2,500	110	679
General practitioners	395	756	191	1,094	145	2,102	192	2,552	121	646
Clergy	206	332	161	370	111	(582)ᵃ	157	(582)ᵃ	..	(283)
Army officers	170	390	229	205	53	695	339	1,091	157	642
Engineers	292	468	160	..	..	1,497	..	1,973	132	676
Chemists	314	556	177	512	92	1,373	268	1,717	125	547
Averages: Unweighted	349	665	190	741	103ᵇ	1,580	246ᵇ	1,736	129ᵇ	579ᵇ
Current weights	328	582	177	703	109ᵇ	1,428	243ᵇ	1,755	132ᵇ	606ᵇ
Weighted increases on 1913/14 average	328	582	177	634	109	1,541	243	2,034	132	620

Note: For sources and methods of estimation, see Appendix G.
ᵃ1957.
ᵇAverage increases for those shown in column above.

In table 30, we estimate the averages for the four professions so far considered and, with some other professions added and doctors and dentists brought up to 1960, calculate weighted and unweighted averages for the class[1].

Over the whole period, the increases for dentists, general practitioners, army officers, and engineers have been of similar magnitude. We do not know how barristers and solicitors fared between 1955/6 and 1960. If we grant them the 32 per cent which was the weighted average for the others, their earnings in 1960 would be 531 and 459 per cent respectively of 1913/14. The solicitors have done badly; chemists and barristers have had about four-fifths of the average increase of the others.

While dispersion within each profession was reduced between 1913/14 and 1922/4, that between the professions increased. The mean deviation was 32 per cent of the average in the pre-war year, 47 per cent in the post-war. By 1955/6, it was down to 37 per cent.

The cost of living index stood at about 425 in 1960, with 1913/14=100, so that, on average, higher professional real incomes before tax had increased by nearly 40 per cent; for the parochial clergy, however, real income had fallen by about 30 per cent. Their position was fairly satisfactory until 1935, but after that, they fell substantially in real and relative terms. Relatively, the bishops of the Church of England did even worse: their income, net of expenses, fell from an average of £3,400 in 1913/14 to £2,700 in 1924. In 1957, at £3,200, it was still below the money level of 1913/14 and thus less than a quarter of the real level of that year.

High Court judges, like other high-ranking people paid out of public funds, were also left to suffer from the fall in the value of money. Their 1913 salary of £5,000 was not changed until after the second world war, and in 1960, at £8,000, they were getting only 60 per cent more than their 1913 level. County court judges had had an increase of 193 per cent to £4,400. In 1913/14, they had received 220 per cent of the barristers' upper quartile; in 1922/3, 111 per cent; in 1955/6, 107 per cent[2].

There is a wealth of information available about pay in the Civil Service. Although at the upper levels the numbers involved are small, they have a wider significance because of the fact that pay rates were determined with reference to outside usage. Table 31 gives scale averages for various Civil Service professional jobs.

---

[1]The main omissions are architects, surveyors, authors, editors and journalists, who constituted 18 per cent of the men in the class in 1951. Requests to the national daily papers for information on editors' pay were unanimously refused—in the interests of personal privacy.

[2]But then they were given an increase of 57 per cent that would have raised their pay to about 135 per cent of the barristers' upper quartile.

Table 31. *Professional pay in the Civil Service, 1913/14, 1922/4, 1935/7, 1955/6 and 1960*

		1913/14 £	1922/4 £	% of 1913/14	1935/7 £	% of 1922/4	1955/6 £	% of 1935/7	1960 £	% of 1955/6	% of 1913/14
Accountant: Post Office, Customs and Excise	a	665	854	128	804	94	990	123	1,128	114	170
Legal Adviser: Ministry of Agriculture	b	950	1,644	173	1,593	97	3,100	195	5,000	161	526
Asst. Solicitors: Customs and Excise	b	905	1,220	135	1,375	113	2,245	163	3,180	142	351
Principal Medical Officer	b	1,150	1,383	120	1,395	101	2,450	176	3,700	151	322
Senior Medical Officer	b	560	864	154	1,023	118	2,300	225	3,400	148	607
Engineer-in-Chief: P.O.	b	1,150	1,700	148	2,000	117	3,500	175	5,800	166	504
Asst. Engineer-in-Chief: P.O.	b	810	1,271	157	1,259	99	2,450	195	3,300	135	407
Executive Engineer	c	420	668	159	666	100	837	126	995	119	237
Principal Architect and Surveyor: Ministry of Works		1,200	1,419	118	1,650	116	2,700	164	3,650	135	304
Architect and Surveyor: Ministry of Works	b	712	1,037	145	983	95	1,623	165	2,054	127	288
Asst. Architect and Surveyor, 1st Class: Ministry of Works	b	411	564	137	687	122	1,271	185	1,565	123	381
Government Chemist	b	1,350	1,569	116	1,510	96	2,700	179	4,100	152	304
Deputy Government Chemist	c	787	1,208	153	1,342	111	2,312	172	3,469	150	441
Analysts, 1st Class	a	507	763	150	663	87	1,080	163	1,575	146	311
Analysts, 2nd Class	a	285	505	177	449	89	882	196	1,249	142	438

[a]15 point scale average.
[b]10 point scale average.
[c]20 point scale average.

Increases were more modest than for professionals outside the Civil Service, so that most of the ranks lost ground. Then between 1955/6 and 1960 some of this leeway was made up as a result of the recommendations of the Priestley Commission[1] and the investigations of the Civil Service Pay Research Unit.

[1]Royal Commission on the Civil Service, 1953-55, *Report*, Cmd 9613 (H.M. Stationery Office, 1955).

	1922/4 as % of 1913/14		1955/6 as % of 1922/4	
	Civil Servants	Non-Civil Servants	Civil Servants	Non-Civil Servants
Legal Adviser (C.S.) and barrister	173	235	189	180
Senior Medical Officer (C.S.) and general practitioner	154	191	266	278
Executive Engineer (P.O.) and engineers	..	..	126	320
Analysts, 1st Class (C.S.) and chemists	..	..	141	247
Asst. Solicitors (C.S.) and solicitors	135	193	184	190

As shown later (page 70) the 'non-professional' administrator at a similar salary range did no better than the technical professions.

Women

For the years before 1955/6, we have not sufficient data to estimate average income for women in the higher professions. Women for most occupations in the Civil Service received three-quarters or four-fifths of the men's rate. The Bradford Hill inquiry into the income of general medical practitioners[1] showed an average for 1936/8 of £1,060 for men and £548 for women. But until the last war, their numbers in this occupational class were too small to make much difference to the women's average for all classes.

For 1955/6, the Pilkington Commission[2] gives us the following averages for women professionals:

	£	% of men's average
General medical practitioners	1,591	74
Assistant general medical practitioners	945	93
Medical consultants	2,773	82
Senior hospital medical officers	1,611	79
Average	1,722	78
General dental practitioners	1,630	71

The Institute of Chemistry had 245 women in its inquiry for 1956. In the age group 26-30, their median pay was 79 per cent of the men's median; at 36-40, it was 73 per cent; at 46-50, 67 per cent.

Though professional fees for those working on their own account are generally the same and though equal pay has been applied in the public service for some time to the professionally qualified, age-distribution, time worked and prejudice combine to lower women's earnings, so that we may guess that, for all women professionals, the average would be about 75 per cent of that for men, that is, £1,080 for 1955/6 and £1,425 for 1960.

[1] *Report of the Inter-Departmental Committee on Remuneration of General Practitioners, loc. cit.*
[2] Royal Commission on Doctors' and Dentists' Remuneration. 1957-60, *loc. cit.*

(c)   Occupational class 1B (Lower professions)

The Civil Service again provides a well-defined framework of pay levels and relationships though, until the last war, the relevant grades were filled almost entirely by men. Scale averages at various levels in four occupations are given in table 32.

Table 32. *Lower-professional salaries for men in the Civil Service, 1913, 1924, 1936, 1955 and 1960*

	1913	1924		1936		1955		1960		
	£	£	% of 1913	£	% of 1924	£	% of 1936	£	% of 1955	% of 1913
Chief Veterinary Officer: Board (later Ministry) of Agriculture	900	1,383	153	1,280	92	2,700	211	4,100	152	456
Assistant Veterinary Officer ᵃ	625	962	154	1,107	115	2,300	208	3,350	146	536
Veterinary inspectors ᵇ	381	506	133	548	108	1,016	185	1,248	123	328
Librarian: Patent Office ᶜ	575	754	131	735	97	1,532	208	2,190	143	380
Assistant Librarian: Patent Office ᵃ	430	589	137	545	92	1,285	236	1,775	138	413
Library assistants, 1st Class: Patent Office ᵃ	313	463	148	428	92	1,051	246	1,377	131	430
Draughtsmen, 1st Class: P.O. Eng. ᶜ	191·5	375	196	343	91	795	232	1,099	138	574
Draughtsmen, 2nd Class: P.O. Eng. ᵃ	137	273	199	249	91	621	249	859	138	627
Laboratory assistants: Govt. Chemist ᵈ	..	163	..	145	89	420	290	536	128	..
Laboratory assistants: Board of Agriculture ᵈ	132	201	152	186	92	420	226	536	128	406

Note: Grade names, 1955 and 1960: Chief Veterinary Officer, Deputy Veterinary Officer, Veterinary Officer Grades I and II; Librarians Grades I, II and III; Leading Draughtsmen, Draughtsmen; Assistants (Scientific).
ᵃ15 point scale average.
ᵇ20 point scale average.
ᶜ10 point scale average.
ᵈAverage pay of those in posts 1955 and 1960: 15-year average.

Each period has characteristics of its own: in the first, the cost of living bonus raises the lower paid relatively more than the higher paid; in the second, it goes into reverse so that laboratory assistants with the Government Chemist lose 11 per cent of their £163 while those at the Board of Agriculture lose only 8 per cent of their £201[1]. Draughtsmen and veterinary officers scored a big

[1] Cost of living bonuses were granted in May 1917 to Civil Servants whose pay did not exceed £250 a year and were revised and extended from time to time. From 1 March 1920, a formula was adopted tying bonus to the cost of living index. Up to £91. 5s. 0d. per year, pay was to be compensated in full for the rise in the cost of living since July 1914; on the next slice of pay, up to £200, there was to be 46 per cent compensation; above that level

Table 33. *Pay in the lower professions (constituents of class 1B), 1913, 1924, 1936, 1955 and 1960*

	1913 £	1924 £	1924 % of 1913	1936 £	1936 % of 1924	1955 £	1955 % of 1936	1960 £	1960 % of 1955	% of 1913
Men										
Qualified teachers[a]	154	353	229	348	99	613	176	907	148	589
Draughtsmen[b]	126	250	199	253	101	679	268	905	133	718
Veterinary inspectors[c]	381	506	133	548	108	1,016	185	1,248	123	328
Laboratory assistants[c]	132	201	152	186	92	420	226	536	128	406
Weighted average:										
current weights	155	320	206	308	96	610	198	847	139	546
1911 weights	155	334	215	332	100	634	191	929	147	599
Women										
Qualified teachers[a]	104·5	272	260	265	97	524	198	813	155	778
Nurses[d]	55	106	193	133	125	362	272	424	117	771
Weighted average:										
current weights	89	214	240	211	99	438	208	606	138	680
1911 weights	89	222	249	223	100	473	212	689	146	774

[a]Annual reports of the Ministry of Education and (1913–36) *Statistical Abstract for the United Kingdom*, Board of Trade (H.M. Stationery Office, annual).

[b]1924–60, from annual census of Draughtsmen's and Allied Technicians' Association; 1913, 1924 deflated as for Post Office Engineering Draughtsmen, 2nd Class.

[c]Civil Service.

[d]Includes value of board, lodging, uniform and other allowances. 1913: 1902 average for 13 hospitals, raised in proportion to the increase in scale averages for female clerks in the Civil Service and manipulative workers (women) in the Post Office. 1902 figures from B. Abel-Smith, *A History of the Nursing Profession* (London, Heinemann, 1960), p. 280. 1936 and after: average of minimum and maximum of ward sisters and staff nurses and rate for 2nd year probationers plus estimate for board, etc. averaged by 1937 weights.

advance in the first period and veterinary officers an additional one in the second.

Between 1936 and 1955, increases were in general more substantial than those shown for the higher professional grades; in the last period, usually less substantial.

The tendency up to 1955 was for a narrowing of differentials; after 1955, for a widening. The net results were as follows:

	1913	1960
Assistant Veterinary Officer as per cent of Chief Veterinary Officer	69	82
Assistant Librarian as per cent of Librarian	75	81
Draughtsman, 2nd Class as per cent of Draughtsman, 1st Class	72	78

Outside the Civil Service, there has been no discernible narrowing of differentials within occupations. Between 1913 and 1960, women have generally done much better than men: the 1960 average for qualified teachers was 589 per cent of 1913 for men and 778 for women, while for the public service the movement towards equal pay for men and women was consummated at the

there was to be 35 per cent compensation. In 1921, bonus raising total pay above £2,000 was abolished. See *Appendix to Part I of Minutes of Evidence: Introductory Memoranda relating to the Civil Service* submitted by the Treasury to the Royal Commission on the Civil Service (1929) (H.M. Stationery Office, 1930), pp. 54-6.

F

beginning of 1961. But headmasters averaged 36 per cent more than certificated assistants in 1913; the same in 1924; and 41 per cent more in 1960. In 1924, section leaders had a lead of 12 per cent over draughtsmen aged over thirty; in 1936, 14 per cent; in 1955, 11 per cent; but in 1960, 16 per cent. In the nursing profession, differentials narrowed until 1955:

			Percentages	
	1924	1936	1955	1960
Ward sister	100	100	100	100
Staff nurse	43	45	85	72
2nd year probationer	27	28	50	42

Table 33 shows averages for the dominant occupations in the class. The occupations shown made up about half the men in 1911 and rather more than sixty per cent of them in 1951. The teachers and nurses constituted 83 per cent of the women in 1911 and 78 per cent in 1951.

(d)   *Occupational class 2B (Administrators and managers)*

Administrators in the public service are greatly outnumbered by business managers: in 1951, they formed 107,000 out of 1,246,000. Yet they are an important sub-species, whose pay represents a public bid for the type of labour with which we are concerned. Table 34 shows pay at seven levels in the Civil Service.

Table 34.   *Salaries of administrators and managers in the Civil Service (men) (occupational class 2B), 1913, 1924, 1936, 1955 and 1960 (London rates)*

	1913	1924		1936		1955		1960		
			% of		% of		% of		% of	% of
	£	£	1913	£	1924	£	1936	£	1955	1913
Chancellor of the Exchequer	5,000	5,000	*100*	5,000	*100*	5,000	*100*	5,000	*100*	*100*
Permanent Secretary of the Treasury	a 2,250	3,500	*135*	3,500	*100*	5,000	*143*	8,000	*160*	*356*
Deputy Secretary	b 1,500	2,200	*146*	2,200	*100*	3,250	*148*	5,000	*154*	*333*
Assistant Secretary	c 1,150	1,382	*120*	1,345	*97*	2,117	*157*	3,115	*149*	*274*
Principal	d 855	1,073	*125*	1,017	*95*	1,794	*176*	2,181	*122*	*255*
Assistant Principal	e 380	563	*148*	509	*90*	743	*146*	1,064	*143*	*280*
. Executive Officer	f 195	383	*196*	379	*99*	721	*190*	936	*130*	*480*

a10 point scale average.
b10 point scale average.   1913, Assistant Secretary; 1955, Second Secretary.
c10 point scale average.   1913, Principal Clerks.
d20 point scale average.   1913, 1st Class Clerks.
e20 point scale average.   1913, 2nd Class Clerks.
f30 point scale average.   1913, Lower Division and Lower Division Higher Grade.

The Chancellor, like bishops and judges, is among those whose extraordinary wealth of 1913, society, with equanimity, has seen brought down. The Chancellor and the High Court judges in 1913 had an after-tax income which, in 1960 prices, would have been worth about £20,000. It was three or four times more than the highest decile of the professional men shown in table 29. By 1924, it had been reduced to a little over twice the professional highest decile.

But by 1955, the public administrators were in general a rather depressed class. Principals were getting 210 per cent of the scale average of 1913, compared with 300 per cent for Chief Veterinary Officers, 333 per cent for solicitors and 409 per cent for doctors at the upper quartile, and 293 per cent for the Deputy Government Chemist, the income of all of whom was of a similar order in 1913.

Executive Officers did better, but still much worse than teachers, draughtsmen or librarians.

But another significant thing is the very high increases which were given between 1955 and 1960 after the reassessment of the position of Civil Servants *vis-à-vis* their peers in outside employment. Deputy Secretaries, for example, received an increase in pay nearly equal to the annual income of two Executive Officers. But even with these increases, only Executive Officers in 1960 had a real income higher than that of their equivalent in 1913. That of Principals had been almost halved.

Business managers: 1913 to 1924

The task of assessing the pay levels and movements for business managers is much more difficult. We are faced with an immense range of duties and responsibilities that defy standardization; and, even where standards have been established, by a wide dispersion, between different firms, in the pay for similar jobs[1]. None the less, we shall try to establish two things: changes in business salaries at the very highest level and at or about the mode.

A comparison between 1913/14 and 1924/5 can be made in some detail by virtue of the Inland Revenue report mentioned above in connexion with pay in the higher professions[2]. This showed the rank order of individuals in ten industrial groups who, in 1913/14, were at annual salaries of £2,000, £1,000, £500 and £200 and the salaries of individuals of the same rank order in 1924/5. In addition, it showed the number getting more than £2,000 in 1913/14, and their average in that year, and the average for the same number, counting from the top of the salary range, in 1924/5. These were as follows:

1913/14	1924/5	
£	£	% of 1913/14
4,321[a]	8,292[a]	192
2,000	4,034	202
1,000	1,933	193
500	1,045	209
200	483	241

[a]There were 212 getting more than £2,000 in 1913/14 and their average salary was £4,321. In 1924/5, the top 212 averaged £8,292.

[1]An investigation into company salaries by the National Institute of Economic and Social Research showed a wide dispersion of rates for similar occupations, for example, in the case of chief accountants, there was an average deviation from the average of 18 per cent. For production managers, it was 22 per cent (see p. 76 below).
[2]The calculations are explained in Appendix H.

Thus the increase of the £2,000 man was greater than that of the £1,000 man and only slightly less than that of the £500 man. The increase in the average for the top 212 was almost identical to that of the man at £1,000. It is only at the £200 level that a substantially higher increase occurs. Thus the egalitarian forces, active between £200 and £500, at higher levels seem to have played themselves out, and there is an extraordinary similarity in the increases of those at £500 and above.

The top one per cent

The highest-paid company employees maintained their relative position despite the economic crises of war and slump. How they fared in the inter-war years we cannot say, but after World War II, the Inland Revenue again published tables showing tax-payers by ranges of income, which they had ceased to do early in World War I. With these, we may take up the story again.

We know that in the Inland Revenue sample the 212 highest-paid employees averaged £8,290 in 1924/5 and we are also told that the sample included roughly 5 per cent of company employees assessed to tax. If it was a representative sample, then about $212 \times 20 = 4,240$ at the top were getting an average of £8,290.

The numbers in occupational class 2 increased by 110 per cent between 1921 and 1951, and, assuming the rate of increase constant from top to bottom, we might then conclude that the equivalent of the top 4,240 in 1924/5 would be the top 9,000 of 1957/8.

There were 17·2 thousand employees in the United Kingdom in 1957/8 whose salary was £5,000 or more[1]. Further, there were 26,059 surtax payers with earned incomes of £5,000 or more and for these we are told the numbers in various income ranges up to £20,000 and the number with earned income over £20,000, with the total earned income for each range. Out of 26·1 thousand, 17·2 thousand were employees. On this proportion (0·66) of employees to self-employed, there would be 10,380 in the range £6,000 and over—a number near enough to 9,000 for the rough justice of the method used here—and their average pay was £9,190. For 1958/9, the average for the same number (counting from the top) was £9,582. Projected to 1959/60, this would become £9,990, an increase of 14 per cent over 1955/6.

As a further guide, we investigated the salaries of the directors of the hundred largest companies in the United Kingdom[2]. In 1957, these numbered 1,134 and their salaries and emoluments averaged £8,799. An elimination of double (or treble) counting raises this average to £9,088[3]. But there is a great difference

[1] *102nd Report of the Commissioners of H.M. Inland Revenue*, Cmnd 922 (H.M. Stationery Office, 1960), table 59.
[2] In terms of the Companies Act of 1948, a public company must publish the aggregate emoluments paid to its directors. From *The Directory of Directors* and *The Stock Exchange Official Year Book*, directors and the companies that they direct can be identified.
[3] Thirty-two of the directors each directed two of the 100 largest companies and two more directed three.

between the pay of a full-time and a part-time director and the ratio of one to the other partly explains the very great range in average pay between companies (from £36,270 for Turner and Newall to £3,073 for Charrington and Co. and £894 for Union International). For Woolworths, where one-company directorships seem to be the rule, the average was £19,319.

We can only guess at the effect of eliminating part-time directors from the calculation. *The Financial Times* stated, '. . . although these men probably receive in most cases more than the part-time directors of nationalised Boards, it is unlikely that many of them earn more than £2,000 a year for their advisory services'[1]. If we assume that no one directing more than ten companies can be a full-time director and that part-time directors receive £2,000 each, we arrive at 651 full-time directors of the 100 largest companies, with an average salary of £14,000. It is unlikely that the hundred giant companies have less than six full-time directors each; however, their part-time directors may be paid on average a good deal less than £2,000. If the average were £1,000 instead of £2,000, the full-time directors' average would be raised by £630.

Differentials in gross income are very great at this level, for they must compensate for the fact that a married man with three children at £10,000 a year gets, after tax, only £1,664 more than a man with similar family at £5,000 a year[2]. Thus the average for the highest 10,000 managers might well be £5,000 less than that of the 651, and an average of £10,000 for the former in 1960 seems fairly plausible[3].

Pay at the median

How did the average or typical manager fare in these years—the administrator between the foreman and clerk, on the one side, and the chairman of the board on the other? We calculated that there were 574,000 of these in 1911[4]. In the Inland Revenue 5 per cent sample of 1913/14, there were 14,237 employees getting more than £200 per year: multiplied by twenty to represent the universe of managers, the £200 man would then be 284,740th from the top, very near the 287,000th position that would represent the median of the range. By 1924/5, as we have seen, this had become £483.

We may get some measure of the inter-war changes by comparing the average

---

[1] 19 November 1958.
[2] See *103rd Report of the Inland Revenue*, Cmnd 1258 (1961), table 23.
[3] The question of how the highest-paid salary-earners have fared, outside the public sector, is part of a wider controversy. See J. A. Brittain, 'Some Neglected Features of Britain's Income Leveling', *American Economic Review*, vol. 50, no. 2, May 1960, p. 593; H. F. Lydall, 'The Long-Term Trend in the Size Distribution of Income', *Journal of the Royal Statistical Society, Series A*, vol. 122, part 1, 1959, p. 1; Richard Titmuss, *Income Distribution and Social Change* (London, Allen and Unwin, 1962).
[4] Excluding those in the public service and brokers and agents working on their own account. See table 8.

for employees getting more than £250 in 1922/3[1] and 1938/9[2]. The averages, weighted by the total number of managers in the relevant industries in 1921 and 1931 respectively, were £534 in 1922/3 and £490 in 1938/9: a reduction of 8 per cent. This accords with the downward drift in the inter-war years for a number of the occupations that we have already priced. It would have reduced the £483 of 1924/5 to £444 in 1938/9.

For the generality of managers, we have no bridge to carry us over the second world war and can produce only an impression of where the median would occur. But before we do so, it will be useful to look at the data for bankers and shop managers whom we are able to treat with greater precision.

For data as at 1 January 1956 and 1961, we are greatly obliged to the Committee of London Clearing Bankers who conducted a special inquiry in order to give us the dispersion of their (white-collar) employees by salary range[3]. We were able to produce a comparable dispersion for 1924 by combining the Inland Revenue data with that produced by Bowley from his inquiry of that year[4]. The data do not distinguish between bank managers or assistant managers and those in non-managerial positions, but the highest decile, near the threshold of managerial status, gives an indication of how salaries moved in the upper levels. The number of women in managerial positions is small enough to have little statistical significance. For the men, the highest deciles were as follows:

| | 1924/5 | 1 Jan. 1956 | | 1 Jan. 1961[a] | |
	£	£	% of 1924/5	£	% of 1956
Highest decile	702	1,360	194	1,840	135
Upper quartile	507	990	195	1,325	134

[a]Excluding payments for overtime, which added 0·9 per cent to remuneration in the year ended 1 January 1956 and 4·4 per cent in the year ended 1 January 1961. Overtime would not normally be paid to managers.

For 1924 and 1925, the pay of shop managers can be estimated from the trade board inquiries into the grocery, drapery, outfitting, fancy goods and

[1]From the Inland Revenue figures. The presentation for 1924/5 does not enable the calculations to be made for that year.
[2]From the Marley-Campion inquiry. See J. G. Marley and H. Campion, 'Changes in Salaries in Great Britain, 1924–39', *Journal of the Royal Statistical Society*, vol. 103, part 4, 1940, p. 524. Miss Marley (now Mrs Cox) made available to us the cards on which the data were abstracted.
[3]Further data from this inquiry is given on p. 79 below.
[4]Bowley and Stamp (1924) show for various industries the numbers of men and women getting above and below the tax exemption limit and a dispersion by income ranges for those below: see A. L. Bowley and Sir Josiah Stamp, *The National Income, 1924* (Oxford, Clarendon Press, 1927), reprinted in Bowley and Stamp, *Three Studies on the National Income* (London School of Economics and Political Science, 1938). From Inland Revenue, we have a dispersion by income ranges for those above.

meat trades[1]. The numbers of managers and assistants are given, but in the pay ranges their distribution is not distinguished, so that we must assume that managers come at the top of the respective pay distributions. For managers, then, the averages are £230 for men and £157 for women. But there are in addition a number of managers not employed in shops but working on the administrative side of the businesses. For them, we have no information for 1924/5, but in the 1938 data[2] their inclusion with the shop managers raises the average by 11·4 per cent for men and 2·7 per cent for women. The averages for 1924/5 similarly adjusted become:

| Men | £256 |
| Women | £161 |

Now the £160 average for women shop managers approximates to the average shown in Bowley's investigation in 1924 for women in the distributive trade in the pay range £125 and over. This amounted to £155 in 1924 and, in 1938 (Marley and Campion) to £162. This is an increase of about five per cent, that would raise the 1924 level to about £168 in 1938.

In 1960 minimum provincial 'A' rates for grocery branch managers for weekly sales of £2,400 were £972 for the co-operative societies and £954 for the multiple grocery trade in England and Wales, 380 per cent to 372 per cent of 1924. But these minima understate the level of earnings. A large provision chain store quoted to us a range of £1,025 to £2,400 for branch managers, effective from the latter part of 1959. Another large chain store quoted a range for 1960 of £1,150 to £2,240. In this case, the firm was able to give comparable data for 1939, when the range was £260 to £520, so that 1960 levels would have been 442 to 431 per cent of 1939.

For other managers, it is not possible to produce statistics that are consistent with the pre-war material. However, a number of investigations have been made in recent years into pay levels of various sorts of managers and from these it is possible to get an idea of the managerial pay structure.

In 1960, we invited twelve large companies to rate five jobs for which detailed descriptions were supplied. Specifically, they were asked to put each job through the company's process of job evaluation so as to determine the pay and conditions that would attach to it if it were to be performed in their own company.

After the replies had been analysed, the participants met to discuss the results. In general, it was felt that the replies were comparable and gave a realistic view of salary levels and terms of employment in the organizations concerned.

Quoted levels for each job showed a wide dispersion, but this is a general characteristic of salaries for jobs at this level. For the chief accountant the

---

[1] Published in three reports: Ministry of Labour, *Report on an Inquiry into the Rates of Wages, Hours and Degree of Industrial Organisation in the Wholesale and Retail Grocery and Provisions Trade*, etc. (H.M. Stationery Office, 1926).

[2] Marley and Campion, *op. cit.*

Table 35. *Salaries of five managerial occupations, July 1960, with changes between 1956 and 1960*

	Range of scale, July 1960	Normal working hours	Annual holiday	Company pension contri- butions	Salary for incumbent aged 45 in post 5 years Year ended	
					1.4.56	1.4.60
	£	Hours	Weeks	%	£	£
Chief accountant	2,245—3,276	37·9	2·6	7·2	2,054	2,663
Production manager	2,170—3,331	40·0	3·0	7·2	2,066	2,713
Shift superintendent	1,304—1,942	39·6	2·9	6·8	1,296	1,653
Divisional sales manager	2,087—3,129	37·9	2·8	7·4	2,148	2,673
Area sales manager	1,322—2,023	37·7	2·7	7·3	1,314	1,652

deviation from the average scale minimum itself averaged £412 and from the maximum £441 (sign ignored), 18 per cent in the one case and 13 per cent in the other. Similar dispersions characterized the other jobs.

The question relating to the incumbent aged 45 was partly aimed at assessing the way in which salaries had increased in the four years to April 1960 and partly as a further move towards standardization. But here again, dispersion was wide. For the chief accountant, with an average increase over the four years of 29·6 per cent, the average deviation was 13 per cent. This, again, typified the increases for the other occupations.

The National Institute of Economic and Social Research held an inquiry on a larger scale in May 1962[1]. This time, eighty-eight companies participated and twelve jobs were rated instead of only five. Again, there was a wide dispersion. For the chief accountant, the average deviation from the average was 18 per cent at the scale minimum and 20 per cent at the scale maximum.

Another indication of pay levels and increases is given by the results of the inquiries of the Institution of Works Managers, conducted in the early parts of 1954 and 1960[2]. From those surveys, the category 'general and works managers (excluding directors)' was taken for each year and equal weight given to the distribution of those controlling 1 to 250, 251 to 500, 501 to 1,000 and over 1,000. Pay levels at various points were as follows:

	1954 £	1960 £	1960 as % of 1954
Highest decile	2,450	3,360	*137*
Upper quartile	1,937	2,430	*125*
Median	1,515	1,844	*122*
Lower quartile	1,094	1,375	*126*
Lowest decile	844	1,078	*128*

[1]The Institute published a report of this inquiry (*Company Salary Structure in the U.K. as at 1st May 1962*, report of a Conference on Company Salary Structure and Policy held by the Institute of Personnel Management and the N.I.E.S.R.). Scientists and engineers were included as well as managers.

[2]Institution of Works Managers, *The Works Manager and his Responsibilities: Report of a Membership Survey* (London, 1954) and 'Remuneration Survey', *Works Management*, N.S. vol. 13, no. 3, March 1960, p. 21.

Pay levels for the works managers in 1954 were almost identical to those for graduates aged 35 to 39 in the investigation conducted by the Royal Commission on Doctors' and Dentists' Remuneration[1].

In a survey by George Copeman relating to 700 managers in 1959[2], 38 per cent were getting less than £1,500; 40 per cent between £1,500 and £2,499; 18 per cent between £2,500 and £4,999 and 4 per cent £5,000 and over. This suggests a median somewhere in the range £1,800 to £1,900. Copeman's averages for production managers and personnel managers accord closely with those subsequently published by the Institution of Works Managers (1960) and the Institute of Personnel Management (February/March 1961)[3].

For production management, with the age-range averages weighted together according to the age-distribution shown in the Institution of Works Managers *Remuneration Survey*, Copeman's average is £2,014, while the average of the highest and lowest deciles, quartiles and median from the Institution of Works Managers survey is £2,043. For personnel managers, the two sets of averages compare as follows:

Age	Copeman[a]	I.P.M.
	£	£
25–34	1,315	1,239
35–44	1,715	1,711
45 and over	1,984	2,016

[a]Simple average of age ranges 25–9 and 30–4, etc.

The evidence shows a wide range of pay and function, but what evidence we have suggests that median pay for men in 1960 was about £1,800 to £1,900, with average pay in the neighbourhood of £2,000, and an increase between 1955/6 and 1960 averaging between 20 and 30 per cent.

For women, the average shown by the inquiry on graduates in industry quoted above, was about 50 per cent of that for men. In the Institute of Personnel Management inquiry, 1961, the women's average was 70 per cent of the men's in the case of personnel officers and personnel assistants. But because there were proportionately fewer women in the higher categories, the women's average was only 60 per cent of the men's. The Institute of Personnel Management report for 1956 gives only medians and quartiles, whose sum was 58 per cent of the men's. As a generalization, it seems safe to say that, for managers, women's pay averaged between 50 and 60 per cent of men's between 1955 and 1960. Thus, in table 36 we show women's pay at 55 per cent of men's for 1955/6 and 1960. But in 1924/5, there were comparatively few women managers except in retail trade and catering, so that their average would

[1]The information related to 7,466 graduates in twenty large industrial and commercial undertakings. See the Commission's *Report* (Cmnd 939), *loc. cit.*, presented in February 1960, p. 299.

[2]'Where are the Top Salaries?', *Business*, vol. 89, no. 12, December 1959, p. 68.

[3]Institute of Personnel Management, *Personnel Management Salaries* (London, 1961).

not have varied much from the £161 shown above for the retail trade. This was 63 per cent of the men's average for managers in distribution but only 34 per cent of the estimated median for all men managers.

The median for men, shown in table 36, shows a much greater rise in the first and third periods than we observed for the professions and for administrators in the Civil Service, but in the second and fourth periods they all move more or less in step. The net result, over the whole term, is a substantial relative rise for the managers.

Table 36.   *Managers' pay, 1913/14, 1924/5, 1938, 1955/6 and 1960*

	1913/14 £	1924/5 £	% of 1913/14	1938 £	% of 1924/5	1955/6 £	% of 1938	1960 £	% of 1955/6	% of 1913/14
Men	200	480	*240*	440	*92*	1,480	*336*	1,850	*125*	*925*
Women	..	160	..	..	..	800	..	1,000	*125*	..

(e)   *Occupational class 3 (Clerks)*

Continuing our journey down the scale, we come to occupational class 3, Clerical workers. We can in part trace their pay history by the use of the results of several inquiries that have been held during the period of our study. The Cannan Committee[1] collected information about the pay of clerks in various industries for the years 1909 or 1910.

For 1929/30, we have a dispersion for 2,799 males and 1,915 females living within the London area, from the house sample inquiry of the New London Survey[2].

Since 1942, the Office Mangement Association (now the Institute of Office Management) has taken a census of clerks' pay every two years, so that since that year, we have been well served[3]. We have averages for railway clerks from the British Transport Commission *Annual Census of Staff* and the distribution of bank employees by range of income as at 1 January 1956 and 1 January 1961[4].

Table 37 gives details of the movements of clerks' pay in various sectors.

[1]"The Amount of Distribution of Income (other than wages) below the Income-Tax Exemption Limit in the United Kingdom: Report of the Committee, consisting of Professors E. Cannan (Chairman), A. L. Bowley (Secretary), F. Y. Edgeworth, and H. B. Lees Smith and Dr W. R. Scott', *Report of the 80th Meeting of the British Association for the Advancement of Science, Sheffield, 1910*, p. 170. For 'commercial and industrial clerks' (those not in banking, insurance, railways or the public service), their information related to 16,000 males and 2,600 females in 102 firms 'carrying on a great variety of businesses scattered throughout the kingdom, and of very different sizes'.
[2]*New Survey of London Life and Labour* (London, King, 1934), vol. VIII, *London Industries III*, p. 298 et seq.
[3]*Clerical Salaries Analysis.*
[4]We are much obliged to the Committee of London Clearing Bankers for having collected and tabulated this information for us.

Table 37. *Clerks' pay (occupational class 3), 1911/13, 1924, 1935, 1955 and 1960*

Men	1911/13 £	1924 £	% of 1911/13	1935 £	% of 1924	1955 £	% of 1935	1960 £	% of 1955	% of 1911/13
C.S. clerical officers	116	284	245	260	92	503	193	661	131	570
In business[h]										
Upper quartile	148[a]	213[b]	144	..	..	570[c]	268[d]	762	134	515
Median	96[a]	159[b]	165	..	..	500[c]	314[d]	663	133	691
Lower quartile	60[a]	87[b]	145	..	..	447[c]	514[d]	582	130	970
Railway clerks	76	221	291	224	101	559	250	751	134	988
In banks[i]										
Median	142	280	197	368[g]	131	850	231	1,040	122	732
Lower quartile	83	149	180	227[g]	152	650	286	802	123	966
Lowest decile	46	92	200	103[g]	112	380	339	396	104	861
Weighted average	99	182	184	192[f]	105	523	272	682	130	689
Women										
C.S. clerical officers	..	206	..	190	92	396	208	586	140	..
C.S. clerical assistants	..	143	..	130	91	327	252	481	147	..
	87	177	203	163	92	369	226	544	147	626
C.S. shorthand typists	79	179	226	162	90	367[e]	227	491[e]	134	622
C.S. typists	65	147	226	125	85	315	252	432[e]	137	665
Civil Service	81	171	211	155	91	360	232	520	144	642
In business[h]										
Upper quartile	55[a]	120[b]	218	..	..	344[c]	287[d]	471	137	856
Median	40[a]	84[b]	210	..	..	304[c]	362[d]	409	135	1,022
Lower quartile	..	58[b]	..	..	..	267[c]	460[d]	356	133	..
In banks[i]										
Upper quartile	..	..	..	204[g]	..	460	225	560	122	..
Median	..	178	..	143[g]	80	360	252	412	114	..
Lower quartile	..	145	..	104[g]	72	278	267	348	130	..
Weighted average	45	106	235	99[f]	93	317	320	427	135	949

Note: In calculating the averages, where quartiles, medians or deciles are shown, each is given a weight equal to one-third of the number of clerks in the relevant sector. Where one of these points is missing, only the median is used with weight equal to total number of clerks in the sector.

[a] 1909/10.
[b] 1929.
[c] Average of March 1954 and 1956.
[d] Per cent of 1929.
[e] Grade I.
[f] Assuming business clerks as in previous columns.
[g] 1938.

[h] For clerks in business, 1924, the figures of the *New Survey of London Life and Labour* relating to 1929 have been corrected in the way suggested in the report to compensate for the exclusion from the survey of clerks in some middle-class families (*loc. cit.*, vol. VIII, *London Industries III*, p. 300). A further adjustment has been made to exclude clerks in the public service, transport, banking and insurance and this lowers the male average by about £15 per year and the female by £4·6 per year. For the weighted averages, the 1929 London Survey figures have been used both for 1924 and 1935.

[i] For those entitled to it, it added 0·9 per cent to pay in 1955 and 4·4 per cent in 1960. Upper quartiles were not available for men in 1911/13 or 1935. For 1924, 1955 and 1960 they were, respectively, £507, £990 and £1,325.

In the first period, male clerks in business appear to have done much less well than those in the other sectors. As has been mentioned, the figures in the second column relate to 1929 and are based on the London Survey, corrected for the exclusion of clerks from middle-class families. Klingender suggests that there must have been a substantial cut in the salaries paid in this sector between 1924 and 1929, which, at the lower quartile, would have amounted to about 60 per cent[1]. However, this hardly credible suggestion is based on a comparison of his figures, extracted from the London Survey records, and Bowley and Stamp's survey of 1924. Klingender seems to think that their figures for salaries relate exclusively to clerical workers[2], but in fact they included all salaried employees so that the income shown would necessarily be above that for clerks alone[3].

It is possible, of course, that the authors of the *New Survey of London Life and Labour* may have underestimated the depressing effect of excluding middle-class families[4]. But no fresh evidence has been found to help to decide the issue.

Up to 1955 there seems to have been a general tendency for the lower-paid to rise faster than the higher-paid; after 1955, in the case of clerks in business, this tendency is gently reversed.

For women, the movement for clerks in business between 1909/10 and 1924 is very similar to that for clerks in the Civil Service: there is some confirmation of this given by the Cadbury records[5]. Women clerks in that company averaged £57 in 1912 (£2 above the business upper quartile shown in table 37) and £127 in 1924; 1924 pay was 222·7 per cent of 1912, close to the upper quartile's 218 per cent.

Between 1935 and 1955, the inverse correlation between degree of increase and salary level shows even more clearly for the women than it did for the men. This may partly be for the very reason that women's pay was in any case much below that for men. For business and banks, where we have measures of dispersion, there was a surprisingly constant relationship between the quartiles or first decile and median (as the case may be) pre- and post-World War I, followed by a substantial narrowing pre- and post-World War II. For male business clerks, Q_1 as percentage of Q_3 was as follows:

	Per cent
1911	41
1929	41
1955	78
1960	76

[1] See F. D. Klingender, *The Condition of Clerical Labour in Britain* (London, Lawrence, 1925), p. 77.
[2] *Op. cit.*, p. 67.
[3] A. L. Bowley and Sir Josiah Stamp, *The National Income, 1924, op. cit.*, p. 20.
[4] A family would have been excluded if the head of the family were a clerk.
[5] From material kindly provided by Cadbury Bros. of Bournville.

For females, the median was 73 per cent of the upper quartile in 1911 and 70 per cent in 1929, while the Q_1/Q_3 percentage was as follows:

	Per cent
1929	48
1955	78
1960	76

For bank clerks, the 1st deciles (or, for women, lower quartiles) as percentages of the medians (or upper quartiles) were as follows:

	Men Per cent	Women Per cent
1913/14	32	
1922/3	33	
1938	28	51
1955	45	60
1960	38	62

But, as in the case of men, the egalitarian principle again reverses itself between 1955 and 1960, both in the Civil Service and in business.

Between men and women, differentials have narrowed between each pair of years except 1924 and 1935. Thus, in 1909/10, the women's average was 45 per cent of the men's, and in 1960, 63 per cent. In the Civil Service, however, equal pay was achieved in January 1961.

(f) *Occupational class 4 (Foremen, supervisors, inspectors)*

Men

The earnings reports of 1906[1] distinguish foremen from other occupational categories so that there is no difficulty in establishing their pay level for that year. There is also sufficient information available for the period post-World War II to get an approximation of their present position. Between the wars however, our knowledge is limited to a small number of cases.

Foremen are as a rule manual workers promoted from the ranks and their pay is generally fixed in relation to the pay of those they supervise. The major determinant is the level of the highest-paid occupation in the foreman's charge, in addition to which he will receive a plus-rate for supervision. Thus, if we can establish what was thought to be the appropriate plus-rate in any period we may add this to the rate for the relevant group of manual workers

---

[1]Published by the Board of Trade. They are described briefly in Appendix D.

to give the foreman's rate. In 1906, the relation of foremen's pay to the average for men in their charge was as follows:

Foremen's average earnings

	£	Per cent of men's average
Textiles	100	*140*
Clothing	105	*146*
Metals and engineering	134	*161*
Paper and printing	127	*139*
Pottery, chemicals, etc.	111	*149*
Food and drink	104	*140*
Other manufacturing industries	105	*144*
Building, woodworking	118	*146*
Public utilities and railways	86	*132*
Weighted average	113	*145·5*

Most of the averages lay between 140 and 150 per cent of men's earnings in the industries concerned. In metals and engineering, the differential was higher: more than 160 per cent in the major branches of the industry. It was also high in gas and electricity supply, but rather lower for local authority services and transport.

For the post-1945 period, we have the study of the National Institute of Industrial Psychology[1]. For 446 'level B' foremen[2] averages (converted to annual rates) were:

	£	Per cent of men's average
Metals, engineering, etc.	520	*131*
Chemicals	517	*138*
Textiles	484	*134*
Clothing	476	*131*
Food, drink, tobacco	481	*140*
Weighted average	511	*132·5*
Other	476	··

In food, drink and tobacco the 40 per cent differential is the same as that for food and drink in 1906 (tobacco was not divided occupationally in the report for that year). All the other sectors show a reduction:

	1906	1949	Quotient
Metals and engineering	161	131	·81
Chemicals	151	138	·91
Textiles	140	134	·95
Clothing	146	131	·89

[1]Made between 1948 and 1950: see *The Foreman: a Study of Supervision in British Industry* (London, Staples Press, 1951).

[2]Level B foremen are described in the report as 'the men and women who are probably most generally in mind when the terms "Foreman" or "forewoman" are used . . .'

In 1958, the Institute of Personnel Management collected information about foremen's pay[1]. For five large engineering concerns, the mid-point of the range of pay was £908. The annual rate of earnings for men in engineering, shipbuilding and electrical goods (mean of October 1957 and April 1958) was £692. The foremen's differential would thus have been 31 per cent· the same as that shown for 1949.

Between July 1958 and October 1958, the Civil Service Pay Research Unit submitted eight reports on the pay outside the Civil Service of occupations related to the 'linked departmental classes of the technical works, engineering and allied classes'. The Civil Service Arbitration Tribunal finally fixed their pay in June 1960, with effect from May 1958[2].

These classes are drawn from apprenticed craftsmen who are not less than 26 years old, have had three years' experience as a tradesman and have an Ordinary National Certificate or an equivalent technical education in the appropriate subject[3]. The two lowest grades are roughly comparable to foreman and, since comparison is largely with general engineering, electronics and aircraft, the Tribunal's award may be held to reflect the pay of foremen in those industries at that time. If the scales for Grades II and III are averaged over ten annual points and weighted together according to the totals in each grade, an average is obtained of £940. Average men's earnings in engineering, shipbuilding and electrical goods, vehicles and metal goods not elsewhere specified in April and October 1958 (at an annual rate), were £706. Grades II and III, on the basis of the calculation described, had a lead of 33 per cent on this.

We must now look for evidence of the situation between the wars and see how it differed from that before and after them. There are some cases in which comparisons can be made. In 1906, railway foremen earned 136 per cent of the average for railway manual workers and gangers 120 per cent of permanent way labourers (including, in 1906, lengthmen and relayers). In other years, the relationship was as follows:

		1935	1960
Foremen			
Operating	£	263	938
	% of manual average	160	132
Maintenance and	£	303	1,035
construction	% of manual average	170	135
Gangers	£	146	815
	% of lengthmen and relayers	117	113

[1]*Status and Pay of Supervisory Staff* (London, Institute of Personnel Management, 1958).
[2]*Civil Service Arbitration Tribunal Award 388* (H.M. Stationery Office, 1960).
[3]See Royal Commission on the Civil Service (1953), *Introductory Factual Memorandum on the Civil Service* (H.M. Stationery Office, 1954), pp. 75-6.

Thus, while the gangers' lead was reduced between 1906 and 1935 by three percentage points and between 1935 and 1960 by four percentage points, that of foremen increased quite substantially between 1906 and 1935 and then, between 1935 and 1960, fell to somewhat below the 1906 level.

In electricity supply, the pay and lead of shift-charge engineers moved as follows:

	1924	1935	1959
Amount (£)	476	453	1,039
Per cent of manual average	*281*	*267*	*156*

Foremen in electricity supply in 1906 had a lead of 57 per cent over the men's average, so, again, there appears to have been a reversion in more recent years to the position of 1906.

Further evidence of the rise and fall of differentials in our period of study comes from the Anderson Report of 1923[1]. In 1914, the average pay of the Civil Service inspectorate was £229, compared with an average of £81 per head for Civil Service industrial staff; in 1923, it was £443 for the inspectorate and £142·5 for the industrials. The lead had increased from 183 to 211 per cent.

In the Post Office Engineering Department in 1938, inspectors' pay was 188 per cent of that of skilled workmen Class II; in 1952, it was 159 per cent[2]. The fall in the differential over the second world war was almost identical in proportion to the rise in the inspectorate–industrial staff differential over the first world war.

In general terms, foremen seem to have had a modal lead in 1906 of between 40 and 50 per cent of the men's manual average for the industry concerned with the average at 45 per cent; between the wars, this had risen to between 60 and 65 per cent; post-1945, it returned to somewhere below the pre-1914 level, with a much-reduced inter-industry dispersion and an average lead lying between 30 and 35 per cent. Applying these estimates to the men's average from the earnings censuses[3], we get:

		1906	1924	1935	1955	1960
Men's average	(£)	78	165	168	592	766
Foremen's average	(£)	113	268	273	784	1,015

[1] *Report of Committee on Pay, etc. of State Servants, loc. cit.*, pp. 27 and 32.
[2] The pay scales have been averaged over 20 incremental years.
[3] The industries included are:
Pottery, bricks, glass, chemicals;
Metal manufacture, engineering and shipbuilding;
Textiles;
Clothing, laundries, dry cleaning;
Food, drink, tobacco;
Sawmilling and wood products;
Paper and printing;
Building and contracting;
Gas, electricity and water.

Women

There is little information available about the pay of this occupational class and, at any rate until 1939, their numbers were too small for a mode to have emerged[1]. The 1906 reports distinguish only the following:

	£	Per cent of women's average
Hosiery	45·5	*126*
Dress, millinery, etc. (factory)	67	*174*
Shirts, blouses, underclothing	56	*168*
Tailoring (ready-made)	49	*151*
Corsets (factory)	42	*135*
Dyeing and cleaning	58	*161*
Laundries	55	*175*
Bookbinding	48	*145*
Stationery manufacture	49	*161*
Cardboard, canvas box manufacture	46	*151*
Cocoa, chocalate and sugar confectionery manufacture	47	*146*
Weighted average	52	*160*

We have no evidence of what happened to the forewomen's lead between the wars, but the National Institute of Industrial Psychology study[2] shows an average in 1949 for level B forewomen of £7. 1s. 0d. per week and for level C (supervisors responsible to a level B supervisor) of £5. 14s. 0d. The B and C average was £6. 6s. 0d. Women's earnings in the Ministry of Labour inquiry in October averaged £3. 18s. 9d., so that forewomen's earnings, at £6. 6s. 0d., would have been back at the 1906 level of 160 per cent of the women's average.

In the Post Office, there is some evidence for the rise and fall of differentials that we saw in the case of men. In 1938, telephone supervisors had a London scale averaging £280 over fifteen points; in 1953, the average was £499·5. For telephonists, the scale average (fifteen points from age 18) was £142 in 1938 and £309 in 1953. The supervisors' lead had fallen from 97 to 62 per cent. The fall (just over a fifth) was similar in scale to that experienced by men.

For the earlier period, the change in differentials at Cadbury's Bournville factory gives corroboration. In 1912, forewomen's average earnings were 186 per cent of day-wage operatives and 170 per cent of piece-wage operatives. In 1924, the rank of forewoman had been divided into two: forewomen and deputy forewomen. Their earnings as a percentage of those of operatives, were as follows:

	Day-wage operatives	Piece-wage operatives
Forewomen	360	251
Deputy forewomen	253	176

[1]Table 1 shows 10,000 in 1911, 18,000 in 1921, 28,000 in 1931 and 79,000 in 1951.
[2]*The Foreman, op. cit.*, 1951.

G

We cannot say what the average rise in differential was, for we do not know the numbers in the occupations concerned, but the rise ranged between 93·5 per cent for forewomen compared with day-wage operatives to 3·5 per cent for deputy forewomen compared with piece-wage operatives.

We should probably not be far wrong if we guessed that the forewomen's differential moved similarly to that of foremen and that their 1906 lead of about 60 per cent rose to rather over 90 per cent between the wars and then returned to about 60 per cent.

(g)   Occupational class 5 (Skilled workers)

Men

Again, we may draw on a wide range of occupations for the calculation of the 1906 average:

	'000s	Average earnings £
Coalface workers	586	112
Manufacturing industry		
Pottery turners	14 {	87 } 90
Pottery throwers		93 }
Glass gatherers, blowers, makers	13	113
Engineering and boilermaking		
Patternmakers	18	97·5
Moulders	99	95
Smiths	55	96
Turners, fitters, erectors, millwrights:		
time	231 {	90 } 95
piece		104 }
Platers, riveters, caulkers: time	60 {	96 } 106
piece		120 }
Ship- and boatbuilding and repairing		
Platers, riveters, caulkers: time	13 {	90 } 128
piece		140 }
Shipwrights: time	21 {	91 } 92
piece		119 }
Railway coachmakers	4	93
Buffers and polishers (coal, etc.)	3	86
Engravers	5	93
Mounters (jewellery)	3	97
Cotton spinners	114 {	107 } 103
Wool-worsted spinners		74 }
Cotton weavers	115 {	65 } 65
Wool-worsted weavers		65 }
Textile printers	16	119
Tailoring cutters (ready-made)	19	81
Boot and shoe clickers: time	19 {	71 } 71
piece		69 }
Grain millers	8	62
Bakers	7 {	76 } 77
Confectioners and pastry-cooks		81 }
Cabinet-makers	47	85
French polishers (cabinet-, etc., making)	17	83

	'000s	Average earnings £	
Carriage-makers and body-builders	73	86	
Wheelwrights	18	76	
Compositors, general	54 {	90 }	98
Compositors, daily news		141 }	
Building			
Bricklayers	100	94	
Masons	56	90	
Carpenters and joiners	223	93	
Plumbers	63	94	
Painters and decorators	183	89	
Electrical wiremen (electricity supply)	8[a]	93	
Railways			
Engine drivers	33	119	
Guards	24	80	
Signalmen	30	71·5	
Mechanics	27[b]	82	
Weighted averages			
Coal	586	112	
Manufacturing and maintenance	1,116	90·7	
Building and electricians	633	91·8	
Railways	114	89·5	
All	2,449	96·0	

[a]Electricians and electrical fitters.
[b]No. shown in earnings report.

Table 38 gives a selection of representative occupations by which the 1906 average may be projected to the relevant years. The weights used are the numbers of skilled workers of whom the occupation cited is typical; for example, engineering fitters are taken to represent all skilled metal-workers, carpenters all skilled woodworkers, bakers all skilled food-workers.

Table 38 gives the following indexes:

	Weighted	Unweighted
1906	100	100
1924	188	205
1935	203	209
1955	648	659
1960	829	863

The major divergence between the two series comes between 1906 and 1924, when the weighted index is pulled down by the relatively small rise in the pay of coalface workers who, in 1924, constituted 605,000 out of the total of 2,892,000 employees of whose pay the index is representative. Engineering fitters, too, were a large class whose rise in pay was below the mode. Between 1924 and 1960, by contrast, there is less divergence and it is then the weighted index that shows the greater rise: from 100 to 441 as compared with 421 in the unweighted index.

Table 38.   *Earnings of skilled men (occupational class 5), 1906, 1924, 1935, 1955 and 1960*

	1906[a] £	1924 £	% of 1906	1935 £	% of 1924	1955 £	% of 1935	1960 £	% of 1955	% of 1906
Coalface workers[b]	112	180	*161*	149	*83*	834	*560*	922	*111*	*831*
Pottery turners[c]	90	153	*170*	166	*109*	..	..	758	..	*842*
Pottery throwers[c]	110	198	*180*	203	*103*	..	..	678	..	*617*
Engineering fitters[d]:										
time	90	157	*174*	212	*135*	649	*306*	828	*128*	*916*
piece	103	191	*185*	243	*127*	686	*282*	876	*128*	*848*
Boot and shoe clickers[e]:										
time	71⎱	165	*232*	159	*96*	464⎱ *324*		620	*134*⎱ *731*	
piece	69⎰					555⎰		751	*135*⎰	
Bakers[f]	75	159	*212*	156	*98*	508	*326*	691	*136*	*921*
Carpenters[g]	98	191	*195*	176	*92*	507	*288*	674	*133*	*688*
Bricklayers[g]	94	191	*203*	176	*92*	507	*288*	674	*133*	*717*
Railway engine drivers[h]	119	276	*232*	258	*94*	622	*241*	863	*139*	*725*
Railway guards[h]	80	196	*245*	192	*98*	540	*281*	745	*138*	*931*
Compositors[i]	91	209	*230*	218	*104*	561	*257*	723	*129*	*795*
Weighted average[j]	97	182	*188*	197	*108*	629	*319*	804	*129*	*829*
Unweighted average	92	189	*205*	192·5	*102*	585	*315*	754	*131*	*820*

[a]Except coal, from earnings inquiry.

[b]From Finlay A. Gibson, *A Compilation of Statistics (technological, commercial and general) of the Coal Mining Industry of the United Kingdom* (Cardiff, The Western Mail, 1922). Coal earnings figures relating to June 1914 have been reduced in proportion to average earnings per shift for all coalminers and average number of shifts worked per week to approximate to earnings in 1906. *Other years:* Coalface workers annual averages include payments in kind.

[c]Employers' federation inquiries. 1960: 1959 raised by increase in earnings shown in Ministry of Labour inquiries.

[d]Employers' federation inquiries.

[e]1924 and 1935 average earnings for all men aged 21 and over. 1955 and 1960: Employers' federation inquiries.

[f]1906 earnings raised proportionately with rates for 1924 and 1935. 1955 and 1960: average quotations for 1958 from thirty-six firms notifying vacancies to employment exchanges in Edinburgh, Manchester, Birmingham and London lowered and raised respectively, proportionately to earnings in Ministry of Labour reports. Amounts include addition for overtime.

[g]1924 and 1935, average rates 39 towns. 1955 and 1960 rates Grade A districts. Amounts include addition for overtime.

[h]Total cash earnings from Ministry of Transport or British Transport Commission reports.

[i]Jobbing book and weekly newspapers. For 1924 and 1935, raised proportionately with rates in 26 large towns. 1955 and 1960: same methods as for bakers. Amounts include addition for overtime.

[j]Weights: number in occupation at nearest population census, except for the following: fitters—all skilled engineering workers; bakers—all skilled food-workers; carpenters—all skilled woodworkers; bricklayers—all skilled building workers except carpenters; compositors—all skilled printing workers. 1960: numbers from Census 1951 adjusted in proportion to change in industrial totals for employees end-May 1951 to October 1960.

Applying the indexes to the average of £96 for 1906 we get:

	Weighted	Unweighted
1906	96	96
1924	180	197
1935	195	201
1955	622	633
1960	796	828

Women

Averages for the skilled occupations about which information was available were as follows for 1906:

	'000s	£
Pottery transferers	14	32
Wire weavers	1	21
Polishers (jewellery)	1	36
Chain makers (goldsmiths)	1	36
Ring spinners (cotton)	15	39
Reelers, winders, beamers, warpers (cotton)	69	39
Weavers (cotton)	163	50
Winders, reelers, warpers (wool)	10	37
Weavers (wool and worsted)	49	39
Hosiery frame tenters and knitters	47	36
Boot and shoe closers: time	34	36 ⎫ 36
piece	10	38 ⎭
Women's clothing cutters (factory)	13	49 ⎫ 41
Shirt cutters		38 ⎭
Dress, corset and light clothing makers	183	37
Milliners, hat and cap makers	53	37
Upholsterers	9	32
Food and tobacco workers	24	34
Paper makers	43	30
Case makers, sewers and stitchers (bookbinding)	22	32
French polishers, signwriters[a]	7	26
Total	768	39 (average)

[a] E. Cadbury, M. C. Matheson and G. Shann, *Women's Work and Wages* (London, Fisher Unwin, 1906).

The average of £39 compares with the range of £30 to £34 for the semi-skilled women in the clothing, engineering and laundry trades, but is well below the £50 of cotton frame tenters, shop-assistants and domestic servants (including an estimate of the value of board and lodging).

In table 39 we attempt to gauge the movement of skilled women's earnings between 1906 and 1960. For pottery transferers and boot and shoe closers the information is based on returns collected by employers' associations and is satisfactory; for clothing cutters and upholsterers the figures relate directly to those occupations and probably give a fair reflection of the reality. For cotton weavers, we rely on average women's earnings for the weaving section of the cotton textile industry: since about two-thirds of the female manual working force of this section consisted of weavers, the approximation is not too wide.

But to be comparable with later years, the 1906 average for weavers (£50) must be diluted to allow for admixture of winders, warpers, sizers and drawers in, whose average was £38·5 in 1906. There were 9·4 thousand of these last in 1951, to 51·1 thousand weavers in the cotton weaving industry, and the use of these proportions brings the average for 1906 down to £48. For wool and worsted, hosiery and dressmakers, again dominated by workers of class 5, the best we can do is to follow average earnings for all women in those industries, with the assumption that they approximate to the relative movements of the earnings of skilled women.

Table 39. *Earnings of skilled women manual workers (occupational class 5), 1906, 1924, 1935, 1955 and 1960*

	1906[a] £	1924 £	1924 % of 1906	1935 £	1935 % of 1924	1955 £	1955 % of 1935	1960 £	1960 % of 1955	% of 1906
Pottery transferers[b]	32	65	203	76	117	305	401	366	120	1,144
Cotton weaving[c]	48	93	194	80	86	327	409	404	124	842
Wool and worsted[c]	35	94	269	80	85	303	379	378	125	1,080
Hosiery[c]	36	75	208	93	124	329	354	394	120	1,094
Boot and shoe closers[d]:										
time	32	94	294	86	91	260	302	344	132	1,075
piece	37	..	..	..	..	330	..	441	134	1,192
Clothing cutters[e]	41	100	244	103	103	322	313	410	127	1,000
Dressmakers[c]	37	76	205	93	122	294	316	367	125	992
Upholsterers[e]	32	102	319	114	112	405	355	518	128	1,619
Average (weighted)[f]	40	87	217·5	86	99	317	369	395	125	987
(unweighted)	37	87	235	91	105	319	354	402	126	1,086

[a]Earnings and hours inquiry, *loc. cit.*
[b]Employers' federation census; 1960 and 1955, Oct. 1959 figures adjusted proportionately with Ministry of Labour earnings averages.
[c]For sources, see text, p. 89–90.
[d]1924 and 1935, standard rates; 1955 and 1960, employers' federation census.
[e]1929 (*New Survey of London Life and Labour, op. cit.*, vol II (1)) adjusted by change in women's earnings in the clothing and furniture industries 1924 and 1925.
[f]Weights: from table 12, with cotton weaving, wool and worsted and hosiery combined in proportion to all females in those industries in 1911, 1921, 1931, 1955 and 1960.

Table 39 gives indexes based on 1906 as follows:

	Weighted	Unweighted
1906	100	100
1924	217·5	235
1935	215	247
1955	795	873
1960	993	1,101

Applying these indexes to the skilled women's average of £39 for 1906, we get:

	Weighted £	Unweighted £
1906	39	39
1924	85	92
1935	84	96
1955	310	340
1960	387	429

The weighted average is dominated by skilled textile workers who accounted for nearly half the total of skilled women workers in 1911 and 35 per cent in 1951. Dressmakers formed 24 per cent of the toal in 1911 and 6·7 per cent in 1951.

Cotton weavers remained above the average in 1960, but never fully recovered from their relative decline of 1906-24 and 1924-35 despite their rally between 1935 and 1955. It is this in particular that has depressed the weighted in relation to the unweighted average.

(h) *Occupational class 6 (Semi-skilled workers)*

Men

The following average earnings for 1906 are taken from the earnings reports[1], with the addition of some manipulative grades of Post Office workers[2], shop-assistants and army privates.

	£
Agricultural labourers	48
Manufacturing industry	
Cotton textiles, mixers, scutchers, grinders and card-room jobbers	70
Wool teazers, fettlers, scribblers, combers, dressers and finishers	58
Textile bleachers, crofters and dyers	59
Ready-made tailoring machinists and pressers	72
Wooden box makers	75
Shipbuilding platers' helpers	60
Shipbuilding drillers and hole cutters	88
Engineering machinemen: time	73
piece	84
Lettterpress assistants	74
Packers, The Potteries	88
Transport	
Carters and carmen (sawmilling)	58
Carters and carmen (borough and urban district councils)	65
Tram drivers	80
Bus drivers	93
Bus conductors	70
Railway platelayers	55
Railway engine firemen	71
Railway ticket collectors	64
Railway carmen and draymen	65
Post Office	
Postmen (London)	81
Sorters (London)	109
Telephonists (London)	77
Electricity and gas supply	
Boiler attendants (gas)	85
Firemen (electricity)	81
Jointers' mates (electricity)	71
Shop-assistants	83
Army privates[a]	40
Unweighted average	72

[1]Board of Trade, *loc. cit.*

[2]So called because they manipulate telephones, telegraphs or (as postmen or sorters) letters.

Sectional averages

Weights		£
1118	Agriculture	48
550	Manufacturing industry	72
665	Transport	65
97	Post Office	94
30	Electricity and gas	81
546	Shop-assistants	83
196	Army[a]	40
	Weighted average	63

Note: Manufacturing industry, transport, and electricity and gas sectional averages obtained using weights in accordance with numbers shown in the earnings reports, loc. cit. For overall average, weights according to 1911 Population Census.
[a]Includes pay and living-out allowance for married men.

Table 40.   Earnings or rates for semi-skilled men (occupational class 6), 1906, 1924, 1935, 1955 and 1960

	1906	1924		1935		1955		1960	
	£	£	% of 1906	£	% of 1924	£	% of 1935	£	% of 1955	% of 1906
Packers, The Potteries[a]	88	153	174	159	104	..	..	653	..	742
Other semi-skilled pottery workers[a]	77	171	222	173	101	..	..	585	..	760
Engineering machinemen:[b] time	73	(151)	195	168	(111)	547	369	672	123	921
piece	84	..	..	..	..	634	..	808	127	962
Railway platelayers[c]	55	147	267	128	87	549	429	720	131	1,309
Railway engine firemen[c]	71	199	280	203	102	507	250	712	140	1,000
Railway ticket collectors[c]	64	166	259	164	99	510	311	680	133	1,062
Railway horse carters[c]	65	151	232	147	97	458	312	634	138	975
One-horse carters average rates[d]	66	139	211	135	97	372	276	492	132	745
Bus and tram conductors (London) rates[e]	72	147	204	157	107	399	254	485	122	674
Bus and tram drivers (London) rates[e]	107	190	178	218	115	476	218	546	115	510
Postmen (London) rates[f]	81	160	199	149	93	430·5	289	527	122	651
Weighted average[i]	73	158	216	168	106	532	317	662	124	908
Shop-assistants[g]	83	120	145	113	94	390	345	487	125	587
Weighted average[i]	75	153	204	159	104	520	327	647	124	863
Agricultural labourers[h]	48	82	171	89	109	423	475	512	121	1,067
Weighted average[i]	68	136	200	144	106	506	351	627	124	923
Unweighted average	74	152	205	154	101	474·5	308	607·5	128	821

[a]Potteries, 1924 onwards: British Pottery Manufacturers' Federation censuses.
[b]1935 onwards: Engineering and Allied Employers' National Federation censuses. 1926: semi-skilled earnings assumed in same position relative to skilled and unskilled as in 1934.
[c]Average earnings for a week in March 1924 and 1935, Railways (Staff) Return (H.M. Stationery Office, annual); 1955 and 1960: Annual Census of Staff (London, British Transport Commision).
[d]1914, 1924 and 1936, average of recognized rates in twelve large towns (Ministry of

Notes to table 40 continued on next page.

Labour, *Abstract of Labour Statistics*). 1955 and 1960: average of standard rate for brewing in nine districts and corn trade in four districts.
e*Abstract of Labour Statistics*.
f1924, scale averaged over 25 years. Other years, averaged over 20 years. 1955: scale operative from 1 November 1955 to 31 March 1956. 1960: scale operative from 1 December 1958. In all cases, beginning at 18 years of age.
g1909: estimate from inquiry by National Union of Shop Assistants. See *The Case for Minimum Wages in Distributive Trades* (National Amalgamated Union of Shop Assistants, 1913). 1924-5: reports of Trade Board inquiries. 1938: Marley and Campion inquiry, *op. cit. (Journal of the Royal Statistical Society*, vol. 103, part 4, 1940, p.524). 1955 and 1960: average quotations for 1958 from 155 firms notifying vacancies to employment exchanges in Edinburgh, Manchester, Birmingham and London, reduced by 17 per cent for 1955 and raised by 3·5 per cent for 1960, these being the approximate percentage changes for retail co-operative, retail multiple grocery and Retail Food Wages Council wage rates.
hIncludes allowance for payments in kind. 1924: A. L. Bowley's estimate, *Wages and Income in the United Kingdom since 1860* (Cambridge, University Press, 1937). 1935: J. R. Bellerby's estimate for 1936-8, *Agriculture and Industry: Relative Income* (London, Macmillan, 1956).
iWeights: numbers in the occupation in Population Census 1911 for 1906; in immediately preceding census for subsequent years. Engineering machinemen are weighted according to the number of all semi-skilled engineers, postmen (London), *all* postmen, etc., and those other than shop-assistants and agricultural labourers are given a group weight equal to numbers of all semi-skilled men other than shop-assistants and agricultural labourers.

Of course, the class average is pulled down by the average for the agricultural labourer which was below that of any of the unskilled averages cited below[1]. If agriculture is excluded, the average becomes £71, well above that of £56 for unskilled men.

We may now gauge the movement of semi-skilled earnings from table 40, limited to occupations for which data are available for all or most of the five required years.

Our calculations showed a semi-skilled male average for 1906 of about £63 including agricultural labourers and £71 without them. We may now calculate average pay series for semi-skilled men by applying to these estimates the ratios of inter-year change from table 40. The results are shown in table 41.

Table 41. *Average pay for semi-skilled men (occupational class 6), 1906, 1924, 1935, 1955 and 1960*

| | Including agriculture | | Without agriculture | |
	£	Index	£	Index
1906	63	100	71	100
1924	126	200	145	204
1935	134	212	151	212
1955	469	744	493	694
1960	581	923	611	860

In the event, the index including agriculture (100:923) is almost identical in its ratio 1906-60 with that given for semi-skilled factory and construction workers in table 46 (100:923·5). But when agricultural labourers and shop-

[1]See p. 96-7.

assistants are excluded the 1960 average is reduced to 908 per cent of 1906 (table 40).

There have been important differences between the performance of the different groups in the various periods: between 1906 and 1924, agricultural labourers and shop-assistants were well below the average in percentage increase and bus and tram drivers did not get on much better. In the next period, bus drivers and agricultural labourers had increases much larger than the average, but shop-assistants were again near the bottom.

In the period 1935-55, agricultural workers were well in the lead and shop-assistants staged a partial recovery. In the last period, railway workers led the field, engineering machinemen and shop-assistants were very near the average and agricultural workers near the bottom.

In the beginning and end years, the occupations were ranked as follows:

1906	£	1960	£
Bus and tram drivers	107	Engineering machinemen (piece)	808
Pottery packers	88	Railway platelayers	720
Engineering machinemen (piece)	84	Railway engine firemen	712
Shop-assistants	83	Ticket collectors	680
Postmen (London)	81	Engineering machinemen (time)	672
Semi-skilled potters	77	Pottery packers	653
Engineering machinemen (time)	73	Carters (railways)	634
Bus and tram conductors	72	Semi-skilled potters	585
Railway engine firemen	71	Bus drivers	546
One-horse carters	66	Postmen (London)	527
Carters (railways)	65	Agricultural workers	512
Ticket collectors	64	One-horse carters	492
Railway platelayers	55	Shop-assistants	487
Agricultural workers	48	Bus conductors	485
Unweighted average	74		607·5
Average deviation	11		87·5

The average deviation from the unweighted average (sign ignored) amounted to 14·8 per cent of the average in 1906 and 14·4 per cent in 1960, so that the degree of dispersion was almost unchanged; but bus and tram drivers in 1960 were 90 per cent of the average compared with 145 per cent in 1906, shop-assistants had fallen to 80 from 112 per cent and agricultural labourers had risen to 84 from 65 per cent.

Women

Table 42 shows movements in the average earnings of representative occupations in occupational class 6.

For the whole period, the occupations listed divide themselves into two: textile workers, shop-assistants and domestic servants whose 1960 averages as a percentage of 1906 were 734, 630 and 633, and clothing machinists, engineering machine operators and laundry workers, for whom the comparable figures were 1,276, 1,269 and 1,033. In table 46 we estimate semi-skilled

Table 42. *Earnings of semi-skilled women (occupational class 6), 1906, 1924, 1935, 1955 and 1960*

	1906	1924		1935		1955		1960		
	£	£	% of 1906	£	% of 1924	£	% of 1935	£	% of 1955	% of 1906
Cotton frame tenters[a]	50	94	*188*	80	*88*	310	*388*	367	*118*	*734*
Clothing machinists[b]	34	78	*230*	73	*94*	294	*403*	434	*148*	*1,276*
Shop-assistants[c]	50	69	*138*	80	*116*	255	*319*	315	*124*	*630*
Waitresses[d]	..	113	..	(113)[e]	..	280	*(248)*	323	*115*	..
Domestic servants[f]	49	115	*235*	(115)[e]	..	255	*(222)*	310	*122*	*633*
Engineering machine operators[g]	32	79	*247*	85	*108*	328	*386*	406	*124*	*1,269*
Laundries and dry cleaning[h]	30	68	*227*	73	*107*	246	*337*	310	*126*	*1,033*
Weighted average	46	97·6	*212*	99·6	*102*	269·2	*270*	339·1	*126*	*737*
Index	100	212		216		584		736		

[a]1906 average earnings; 1924, 81 per cent over 1914. See *18th Abstract of Labour Statistics of the United Kingdom*, Cmd 2740 (H.M. Stationery Office, 1926), p.117, but excluding effect of increase in hourly rates to compensate for reduction in length of working week. Allows for 2·8 per cent increase, Sept. 1906 to July 1914; see J. Jewkes and E. M. Gray, *Wages and Labour in the Lancashire Cotton Spinning Industry* (Manchester, University Press, 1935). 1936, 59·2 per cent over 1914. 1955 and 1960: quotations from 10 firms in north-west region, May 1958, adjusted by changes in minimum rates, 1955 and 1960.

[b]Bowley gives 130 per cent increase for females making 'other clothing', 1914-24. See *Wages and Income in the United Kingdom since 1860, op. cit.*, p. 17. 1935: 1924 adjusted *pari passu* with women's earnings in the clothing industry. 1955 and 1960: 107 employment exchange quotations for 1958 adjusted according to changes in earnings.

[c]1909: inquiry by National Amalgamated Union of Shop Assistants, Warehousemen and Clerks, *loc. cit.;* 1924/5 Trade Board inquiries; 1938: Marley/Campion inquiry, *op. cit.;* 1955 and 1960: 143 employment exchange quotations for 1958 adjusted according to per cent changes for retail co-operative societies, retail multiple grocery and wages councils for retail food and drapery, outfitting and footwear.

[d]1929: from Trade Board reports. Averages of quartiles and median by licensed hotels with more than 10 bedrooms, non-licensed hotels, etc., and light refreshment and dining-rooms, without tips but including value of meals and accommodation. 1955 and 1960: average quotations for 1958 from 179 firms notifying vacancies to employment exchanges in Edinburgh, Manchester, Birmingham and London, adjusted forward and backward according to per cent changes in waitress rates, licensed residential establishments and licensed restaurants, plus £47 for value of meals.

[e]Assumes no change 1924 and 1935.

[f]W. T. Layton, 'Changes in the Wages of Domestic Servants during Fifty Years', *Journal of the Royal Statistical Society*, vol. 71, part 3, September 1908, p. 515. 1929: housewives' returns to the *New Survey of London Life and Labour* and *Survey of Merseyside*, ed. D. Caradog Jones (Liverpool, University Press, 1934). 1958/9: 90 employment exchange quotations, adjusted according to per cent changes in rates for chambermaids, licensed residential establishments, Area B.

[g]Time- and piece-workers. Federation average 1935: 1924—all women plus 12·3 per cent, to equal relationship of 1935. 1955 and 1960, Federation average.

[h]Laundries, etc.: earnings for all females.

women's earnings in textiles in 1960 to have been 760 per cent of those for 1906 and in clothing manufacture 1,072·5 per cent[1].

[1]Of course, these are the estimated changes in the medians for all semi-skilled women in all branches of the two industries.

The 1906 averages in the first group were all in the vicinity of £50, compared with £30 to £34 for the second. The decline, in the case of shop-assistants, comes between 1906 and 1924, after which their increases are above or near the average. In cotton, the relative fall is between both 1906 and 1924, and 1924 and 1935; then comes a recovery between 1935 and 1955, followed by a further decline. In domestic servants, by contrast, the decline was between 1935 and 1955.

By 1960, the income relationship between the service occupations and two of the three manufacturing occupations had been reversed: the averages for shop-assistants, waitresses, domestic servants, laundresses and dry cleaners were all within the range £310 to £323; engineering and clothing were in the region of £400 with cotton midway between.

(i)   Occupational class 7 (Unskilled workers)

Men

The earnings reports of 1906 give the following average earnings for general labourers, aged 20 and over, in the United Kingdom[1]:

		No.	Average earnings £ per year
Cotton		1,944	52·65
Wool and worsted		535	51·35
Textile bleaching, printing, dyeing and finishing		3,337	52·4
Building			
Bricklayers' labourers		10,814	60·9
Masons' labourers		4,393	58·9
Plasterers' labourers		2,185	62·6
Painters' labourers		1,631	68·5
Excavators		3,920	57·6
Builders' labourers		7,706	62·8
Civil engineering			
Excavators and labourers:	time	5,952	54·8
	piece	246	85·4
Sawmilling, machine joiners, etc.:	time	5,147	53·9
	piece	199	94·5
Cabinet-making, etc.		902	57·0
Road, sanitary, etc. services (borough and urban district councils):			
General roadmen		5,096	58·3
Paviours' labourers		2,612	60·5
Sweepers and scavengers (able-bodied)		20,228	58·9
Yardmen and general labourers		10,361	59·4
(county and rural district councils):			
Road labourers		13,208	41·8
Gas supply		9,090	62·2
Electricity supply		2,413	63·5
Water supply		3,211	59·6
Tramway and omnibus services		3,428	65·6

[1]Board of Trade, *loc. cit.* The weekly average has been multiplied by 52 to give an annual rate to facilitate comparison with classes 1, 2 and 3. Note that at this stage no allowance is made for unemployment or unpaid holidays.

		No.	Average earnings £ per year
Pig iron manufacture		2,020	55·9
Iron and steel		3,824	59·8
Engineering and boilermaking:	time	4,262	52·2
	piece	4,629	62·6
Ship- and boatbuilding and repairing		12,534	54·4
Railway carriage and wagon building:	time	4,262	52·2
	piece	4,629	62·6
Railways (1907):			
Porters (loading and traffic)		23,906	50·1
Porters (goods)		18,506	56·8
Engine cleaners		9,930	52·4
Carriage cleaners		4,478	52·6
Locomotive, etc. labourers		8,518	56·5
Permanent way labourers		27,197	56·3
Paper manufacture		1,305	55·7
Printing		469	66·1
Pottery		459	56·8
Bricks, etc.		1,779	51·8
Chemical manufacture		4,921	55·7
Grain milling		2,010	50·3
Brewery		1,033	59·1
Cocoa, chocolate and sugar confectionery		319	63·9
Total		306,487	56·45 (average)

While the average for the above is £56 per year, the median for the groups (disregarding the numbers in each group) is between £57 and £58 and the unweighted average is £59. We may say that the 'representative rate' for unskilled men in 1906 lay between £55 and £60 per year, or between 94·5 and 103 per cent of the manual workers' average as shown in the Board of Trade earnings reports.

In 1924, we are much less well served with information. For many of the industries listed above we have no information about labourers' earnings. There are some for whom earnings information is available, however, and others for whom we shall have to depend on changes in standard rates. Thus we have:

Table 43. *Earnings or rates for unskilled men (occupational class 7), 1906 and 1924*

	Weights	1906	1924	1924 as % of 1906
		£ per year		
Building labourers' standard rate[a]	250	65	144	*221·5*
Railway permanent way labourers[b]	25	56	133	*237·5*
Railway workshop labourers[b]	14	57	147	*258*
Railway platform porters[b]	94	50	133	*261*
Engineering labourers[c]: time	170	57	116[d]	*203·5*
piece	30	69	138[d]	*200*
Brewery labourers (London)[e]	15	72	149	*207*
Local authority labourers[f]	30	58	138	*238*
Weighted average[g]	628	60	134	*223*
Unweighted average	8	60·5	137	*226*

Footnotes on next page.

[a]Average weekly rates in 39 large towns.
[b]Average weekly earnings from *Railways* (*Staff*) *Return* (annual, *loc. cit.*).
[c]October 1926, Employers' Federation census.
[d]1926.
[e]1924, Meux's Brewery.
[f]Average of rates in 28 large towns.
[g]Weights: approximate numbers in 1921 in thousands.

The range of increases is from 100 per cent for engineering piece-workers to 161 per cent for platform porters. Applying the average increase of 123 per cent to the range of £55 to £60 for 1906, we get a range of £123 to £134 as likely to have included the mode in 1924.

Table 44 illustrates the relative positions in 1924, 1935, 1955 and 1960.

Table 44. *Earnings or rates for unskilled men* (*occupational class 7*), *1924, 1935, 1955 and 1960*

	1924	1935	% of 1924	1955	% of 1935	1960	% of 1955
	£	£		£		£	
Building[a]	144	131	*91*	419	*320*	496	*118*
Railways[b]:							
Civil eng. labourers and length-men	133	135	*101·5*	478	*355*	720	*150*
Shedmen	147	146	*99*	452	*309*	616	*136*
Signal and telegraph (1955 and 1960: handymen)	158	145	*92*	509	*351*	707	*139*
Marine and dock (1955 and 1960: porters)	123	124	*101*	476	*383*	637	*134*
Platform porters	133	114	*86*	441	*387*	614	*139*
London Transport stationmen/porters	140	148	*106*	..	..	524	..
Engineering[c]: time	116	144	*124*	499	*347*	620	*124*
piece	138	158	*114*	543	*344*	684	*126*
Brewery labourers, London[d]	149	162	*109*	447	*276*	583	*130*
Local authorites[e]	138	135	*98*	342	*253*	460	*135*
Weighted averages	134	136	*101*	458	*337*	565	*123*

[a]1924 and 1935: average weekly rates in 39 large towns.   1955: Grade A districts, 45½ hours.   1960: from April, Grade A districts, 44 hours.

[b]Earnings from *Railways* (*Staff*) *Return* or British Transport Commission *Annual Census of Staff*.

[c]From Employers' Federation censuses.   1935: 1938 average reduced by 8·1 per cent, i.e. difference in average shown in Ministry of Labour inquiries.

[d]1924, Meux.   Later years, Guinness.

[e]1924 and 1935: average of rates in 28 large towns.   1955 and 1960: Group I, weekly rates Zone A.

The calculations shown above indicate a pay level for unskilled men in 1960 9·3 times that of 1906 and we may now check this by drawing on other evidence.

Labourers' earnings in the Potteries increased 9·6 times; the basic rate for labourers in gas supply 8·0 times and in electricity supply (London) 8·6 times.

Labourers other than those listed in table 44 averaged £55 in 1906 and may be compared with a group of 589 employment exchange quotations for Camden Town, Birmingham and Manchester for 1957-60, which, if adjusted to take account of increases to the latter year, give an average of £469.

We may say, then, that the modal rate for unskilled men in 1960 is somewhere about nine times that for 1906.

Tables 43 and 44 give the ratios by which the unskilled average for 1906 must be raised to yield averages for the subsequent years:

1906	1924	1935	1955	1960
£57·5	£128	£129	£435	£535

Women

In *Women's Work and Wages*[1], the authors wrote: 'In the inquiry as to wages one of the outstanding facts elicited was, that whenever women had replaced men the former always received a much lower wage, and that this wage was not proportionate to the skill or intelligence required by the work but approximated to a certain fixed level—about 10s. to 12s. per week. The wage that the man previously received gave no criterion as to what the woman would get, though as a general statement approximately correct, we may say that a woman would get from one-third to one-half the wages of a man'.

The tendency to fix women's pay without particular regard to the skill or intelligence required makes it difficult to distinguish between the pay of occupational classes 5, 6 and 7 in 1906 and a greater variation appears between rates of pay of different women for the same job than between the averages for different jobs. The following are some examples of average earnings in unskilled work in 1906 (converted into annual rates)[2]:

		£
Rag sorters (paper manufacture):	time	26
	piece	28
Rag cutters (paper manufacture):	time	25
	piece	26
Folders (printing):	time	31
	piece	42
Gummers (stationery manufacture):	time	32
	piece	28
Soap and candle manufacture		32
Cleaners (borough and urban district councils)		31

But in other industries, the 1906 reports do not distinguish unskilled occupations and sometimes give no occupational classification for women. The average for all women aged 18 and over was £36 (annual rate) and for girls

---

[1] E. Cadbury, M. C. Matheson and G. Shann, *op. cit.*, p. 119.
[2] From the earnings and hours reports, *loc. cit.*

under 18, £20, so that the unskilled averages for the two age-groups must have been somewhere below these. Cadbury and others[1] cite an average of 10s. per week for door-attendants aged 18 and over; 7s. 9d. for charwomen, with a minimum of 1s. 6d. and a maximum of 2s. per day. The average earnings of firewood choppers were 9s. 10d., tin pressers 8s. 6d., mineral water bottlers 9s., laundry general workers 7s. 4d.

In August 1910, the Trade Board for the chain industry established a minimum rate of 2½d. per hour. The average normal week was 46·8 hours in 1906, for which the minimum pay in 1910 would then have been 9·7s.

In 1911, a Trade Board minimum of 2¾d. per hour was established for machine-made lace and net or 12·4s. for a 54-hour week. In 1912, 3d. per hour was laid down as a minimum for cardboard-box making. It would probably be safe to say, then, that the mode for unskilled women in 1906 would have been at an annual rate of about £26.

By the mid-1920's, the Trade Board minima had been raised to 6½d. or 7d. per hour: between 26s. and 28s. for a 48-hour week and the number of industries covered had been increased to 41. At an annual rate, this would represent between £67 and £73 per year. This matches the rate of £70 paid to charwomen in the Civil Service. The median remuneration of kitchen and scullery maids was shown in the Trade Board investigation of 1929 as somewhat higher: 35·5s. per week or £92 per year[2].

The earnings inquiry of 1924 did not distinguish women from girls and showed an average for females of £71. Applying the same women : females ratio as in 1935, one gets an amount of £81 as the approximate average for all grades of women's manual work. This would be higher than the average or mode for unskilled women, which would have been nearer to the Trade Board minimum of £67 and probably within the range £70 to £75: about 2·8 times the level of 1906. From about 45 per cent of the manual average in 1906, they had risen to about 58 per cent of it in 1925.

Between the mid-1920's and the mid-1930's, there were some reductions in Trade Board minima and some increases, but in the main they were unchanged. The earnings inquiry of 1935, too, showed an average for females almost identical to that for 1924.

On 1 April 1955, the average of 105 minima laid down in wage regulation orders[3] was at an annual rate of £223. At 1 April 1956, it was £238, so that, by interpolation, the mid-1955 figure would have been £227.

The equivalent figure for mid-1960 was £283. This figure is almost identical to that yielded by the application of the occupational class proportions to the

---

[1]*Op. cit.*, p. 329.

[2]This included cash wages, tips, other allowances in cash and the value (estimated at the cost to the employer) of meals and lodging, where provided, and of other allowances in kind.

[3]I.e., by Wages Councils (which supplanted Trade Boards in 1948), the Agricultural Wages Boards and the various Catering Wages Boards.

earnings distribution for manufacturing industry[1]. Women in manufacturing industry in 1951 were divided as follows:

	Per cent
Occupational classes 4 and 5	41
Occupational class 6	44
Occupational class 7	15
	100

On this basis, median earnings would be at the annual rate of £510 for classes 4 and 5 combined, £373 for class 6 and £286 for class 7[2]. The inter-period movements thus suggested are set out in table 45 and compared with those of the manual average and of the women's average.

Table 45. *Average earnings of unskilled women workers compared with average for all women manual workers (selected industries)[a] and the manual average (selected industries)*

	Unskilled women	Women's average[b]	Manual average
1924 as % of 1906	280	225	213
1935 as % of 1924	100	101	101
1955 as % of 1935	310	363	391
1960 as % of 1955	125	126	127
1960 as % of 1906	1,090	1,044	1,075

[a]Those listed in footnote 3, p. 84.
[b]The women's constituent of the manual average.

We see here a suggestion of periods with contrasting characteristics: a first period where women's pay rises more than that of all workers and that of unskilled women more than that of all women; a third period where the reverse holds; and a second and fourth where pay at these three levels moves in step.

3. CLASS AVERAGES FOR MANUAL WORKERS

In §1(d) we compared the distribution of manual workers by level of earnings in 1906 and 1960, but made no adjustment for change in occupational class distribution.

For 1906, we are given for each industry quartile and median earnings by occupation for those who worked full-time, though for women the detail is sufficient for an occupational class analysis in only two industries.

For 1960, for which dispersions by occupation were not given, we insert

---

[1]The proportions shown in Appendix B, applied to the earnings distribution shown in the *Ministry of Labour Gazette*, vol. 69, no. 4, April 1961, at p. 149.
[2]Assuming that the area of overlap between the classes is not so great as to affect unduly the position of the median.

H

the occupational class frontiers in the earnings dispersions by applying the data from Appendix B[1]. The results of this calculation appear in table 46.

Table 46. *Median earnings for occupational classes 4 and 5, 6 and 7 in various industries, 1906 and 1960*

Amounts in £ per year

Men		1906 Occupational class			1960 Occupational class		
		4 and 5	6	7	4 and 5	6	7
Food, drink and tobacco	Amount	77·7	61·6	51·5	845·0	656·2	528·6
	Per cent	*100*	*79·2*	*66·3*	*100*	*77·7*	*62·5*
Metals and engineering	Amount	98·3	74·4	55·9	920·4	673·4	550·2
	Per cent	*100*	*75·7*	*56·9*	*100*	*73·2*	*59·7*
Textiles	Amount	79·8	64·2	51·0	916·5	611·0	483·1
	Per cent	*100*	*80·45*	*63·8*	*100*	*66·7*	*52·7*
Woodworking	Amount	86·8	64·6	55·1	761·3	525·7	497·6
	Per cent	*100*	*74·4*	*63·5*	*100*	*69·1*	*65·4*
Paper and printing	Amount	97·8	74·4	55·6	920·4	669·2	561·6
	Per cent	*100*	*76·1*	*56·9*	*100*	*72·7*	*61·0*
Construction	Amount	97·5	..	64·0	768·0	618·3	557·4
	Per cent	*100*	..	*65·6*	*100*	*80·5*	*72·6*
All above	Amount	89·7	67·9	55·5	855·3	627·1[a]	529·75
(Unweighted average)	Per cent	*100*	*75·7*	*61·9*	*100*	*73·3*[a]	*61·9*
Women							
Textiles	Amount	46·0	42·6	..	448·5	323·7	258·7
	Per cent	*100*	*92·6*	..	*100*	*72·1*	*57·7*
Clothing	Amount	36·4	32·0	..	494·0	343·2	219·7
	Per cent	*100*	*87·9*	..	*100*	*69·5*	*44·5*

[a]Excluding construction.

For men as between classes 4 and 5 (taken together) and 7 there has, on this evidence, been a general narrowing of differentials for four out of the six industrial groups.   But the narrowing in these groups is cancelled by the widening in the others, so that the percentage relationship of the averages is the same in the two years.

Between the semi-skilled and classes 4 and 5, the data shows an actual widening of differentials between the two years, substantial in textiles and, in other groups, small but general.

For women, the widening of the difference between the top groups and the semi-skilled has been considerable in the two industries shown in the table.

We may now check these calculations against those previously made for occupational classes 4 to 7[2].   For males in classes 4 and 5, we get an average of £97 for 1906 and £857 for 1960; table 46 shows £90 and £855.   The major

[1]Occupational classes by industry, England and Wales 1951.   The degree of validity of this calculation depends on how far the occupational composition of the industries has changed since 1951 (insofar as their manual work force is concerned) and to what extent the location of class medians has been disturbed by overlaps of the range of earnings for the different classes.

[2]In §§ 2(f) to (i) above.

omissions from table 46 are coalface workers and railwaymen. If these are included we get an unweighted average of £94·4 for 1906 and £850·0 for 1960. The difference is one of 2·7 per cent in 1906 and 0·8 per cent in 1960. For semi-skilled men, we get the following alignment:

	1906	1960	
	£	£	% of 1906
Table 46[a]	68	627	922
Table 40[b]	68	627	922

[a]Unweighted average, manufacturing industry.
[b]Weighted average, manufacturing, transport and communication, agriculture and retail trade.

The identity is fortuitous, for when the average from table 46 is adjusted to include agriculture and retail distribution, the averages become £67 and £591. None the less, it is of interest that the ratio of the average for 1960 to 1906 should be the same despite the contrasting methods of calculation.

For unskilled workers, table 46 shows £55·5 for 1906 and £529·75 for 1960, so that 1960 is 955 per cent of 1906, while the calculations in §2(i) suggested a ninefold increase, with 1960 between 850 and 960 per cent of 1906.

The indications are that the method used in table 46 for standardizing occupational class changes does not understate the rise of labourers' pay. The earnings gap between skilled and unskilled has not narrowed to any marked extent in the industries represented, and in some has actually widened; that between skilled and semi-skilled has shown a slight but general tendency to widen.

4. COMPARISON OF OCCUPATIONAL CLASS AVERAGES

Now the time has come to assemble the class averages and to assess the performance of the classes relative to one another. In table 47, the 1906 averages for classes 4 to 7 have been raised by 9 per cent to approximate to the level of 1913/14[1].

(a) *Effect of changes in numbers*

In the case of the men, part of the increase in average pay has been due to a shift in numbers from lower to higher-paid classes: this is measured by the difference between the current-weighted and the 1911-weighted averages. The divergence was greatest between 1935/6 and 1955/6 and barely discernible between 1955/6 and 1960. Over the whole period, the move from lower to higher classes has accounted for 8 per cent of the total increase (64 percentage points).

For the women, too, the overall increase resulting from movements to higher-paid classes has accounted for about 8 per cent of the total increase,

---

[1]A rough approximation based on Bowley's estimates, *Wages and Income in the United Kingdom since 1860, op. cit.*, pp. 6 and 7.

but in their case these shifts actually lowered the average slightly between 1913/14 and 1935/6, while in 1960 the current-weighted average was 419 per cent of that of 1935/6, while the fixed-weighted average was only 386 per cent. Of course, movements between the classes have been larger than this would suggest, but in part they have cancelled one another out.

Table 47. *Average earnings, seven occupational classes, 1913/14, 1922/4, 1935/6, 1955/6 and 1960*

	1913/14	1922/4		1935/6		1955/6		1960		
			% of		% of		% of		% of	% of
	£	£	1913/14	£	1922/4	£	1935/6	£	1955/6	1913/14
Men										
1. Professional										
A. Higher	328	582	177	634	109	1,541	243	2,034	132	620
B. Lower	155	320	206	308	96	610	198	847	139	546
2B. Managers, etc.	200	480	240	440	92	1,480	336	1,850	125	925
3. Clerks	99	182	184	192	105	523	272	682	130	689
4. Foremen	113	268	237	273	102	784	287	1,015	129	898
Manual										
5. Skilled	99	180	181	195	108	622	319	796	128	804
6. Semi-skilled	69	126	183	134	106	469	350	581	124	842
7. Unskilled	63	128	203	129	101	435	337	535	123	849
Averages										
Current weights[a]	92	180	194	186	104	634	340	808	127	874
1911 weights	92	177	191	185	104	590	319	746	126	807
Women										
1. Professional										
A. Higher	..	..	..	..	..	(1,080)	..	(1,425)	(138)	..
B. Lower	89	214	240	211	99	438	208	606	138	680
2B. Managers, etc.	(80)[b]	160	..	(168)	105	800	(524)	1,000	125	(1,250)
3. Clerks	45	106	235	99	93	317	320	427	135	949
4. Forewomen	57	154	270	156	101	477	306	602	126	1,056
Manual										
5. Skilled	44	87	198	86	99	317	369	395	125	898
6. Semi-skilled	50	98	196	100	102	269	270	339	126	678
7. Unskilled	28	73	261	73	100	227	280	283	125	1,000
Averages										
Current weights[a]	50	103	204	104	101	319	307	436	137	866
1911 weights	50	103	205	104	101	307	295	402	131	797
Men and women										
weighted average[c]	80	157	196	162	103	531	328	683	129	854

[a]According to number of men or women in relevant class. 1959: 1951 adjusted for changes in industrial distribution.

[b]Included in weighted average. Their exclusion lowers the average fractionally.

[c]According to proportions in occupational classes in nearest census year until 1935/6 and to proportions in total labour force, 1955 and 1960.

(b) *Men's and women's averages*

Over the whole span, women have done better than men in every class except that of semi-skilled manual workers (occupational class 6), whose pay increase was relatively so small and whose numbers are so large that the women's overall increase was reduced to below that of the men[1].

Women's averages as percentages of men's averages

		1913/14	1922/4	1935/6	1955/6	1960
1A.	Higher professional	..	..	..	(75)	(75)
1B.	Lower professional	57	67	69	72	72
2B.	Managers and administrators	(40)	33	38	54	54
3.	Clerks	42	46	46	57	61
4.	Foremen	50	57	57	61	59
5.	Skilled manual	44	48	44	51	50
6.	Semi-skilled manual	72	78	75	57	58
7.	Unskilled manual	44	57	57	52	53
	All (current weights)	54	57	56	50	54
	All (1911 weights)	54	58	56	52	54
	Unweighted average	50	55	55	58	58

The women's average moved up in the first period, the women in each class (excepting the managers and administrators) gaining on the men. Then inter-class movements worked against the women. Their currently weighted average fell until, in 1955/6, it was lower than it had been in 1913. But by 1960 it had regained its former level. On a class-by-class comparison, however, the women improved their position so that the unweighted average rose from 50 to 58 per cent of the men's. The improvements occurred in the two war periods; in between, the women merely held their own.

The relative improvement was greatest amongst the clerks, but all classes showed a gain except the semi-skilled, whose position deteriorated substantially. The proportions (women's of men's averages) themselves changed by the following percentages between 1913/14 and 1960:

1B.	Lower professional	26
2B.	Managers and administrators	35
3.	Clerks	45
4.	Foremen	18
5.	Skilled manual	14
6.	Semi-skilled manual	—20
7.	Unskilled manual	21

In relation to the men, the women clerks have made the greatest gain; only the semi-skilled lost in this comparison, and their loss was considerable.

(c) Inter-class pay structure

In table 48, class averages have been converted into percentages of the average for all classes. Thus we eliminate the confusing effect of measuring in money of inconstant value, and express the movements in the simplified form of 'pay units'. The average for each class is then shown as a percentage of the

---

[1]Class 6 accounted for 53 per cent of the women in 1911 and 43 per cent in 1951 (table 1).

average for men and women of all classes. The all-class average becomes, in effect, the unit of account, in which the earnings for each class are then expressed. The second column for each year (after 1913/14) measures the percentage change in the relative position of each class. Thus, in 1913/14, the average for the higher professional men was just over four times the overall average; in 1922/4 it was 3·7 times the overall average, a fall of 9 per cent.

The bottom line in each sub-table, the mean percentage deviation, gives a measure of the dispersion of the class average. For the men's classes the mean deviation was 67 per cent in 1913/14. Inequality had increased in 1922/4, so that the mean deviation was 73 per cent. By 1955, it had been substantially reduced (48 per cent) and was still at about that level in 1960. For the women, the deviation increased over the war periods and fell between 1955 and 1960.

During the half-century, the only really big changes have been the decline in the differential for professionals, clerks and foremen between 1935 and 1955 and for skilled manual workers between 1913 and 1924. The fall in the relative position of the professionals was substantial and affected both men and women: 1955 found them at between 60 and 70 per cent of their relative position of 1935. Between 1955 and 1960, however, they showed some gain.

The all-women's average has changed very little in relation to the overall average for men and women: it rose between 1913 and 1924, fell between 1935 and 1955 and in 1960 was almost back to what it had been in 1913. But the inter-class pattern shows changes that explain the peculiar inter-decile changes noted in table 24. There, we observed that the lower deciles had fallen relatively to the higher ones between 1911 and 1958. In table 48, we see that the unskilled (the lowest-paid 8 per cent of occupied women) have improved their relative position by 17 per cent, but the semi-skilled, occupying the next income layer, have suffered a relative decline of 19 per cent. Skilled workers have improved their position, and foremen and managers and administrators have done better still, but the lower professionals have done no better than the semi-skilled.

(d)   *Differentials between complementary occupations*

But changes in the class averages are caused partly by changes in the pay of individual occupations, partly by changes in the numbers occupied in occupations at different levels of pay. This last effect can be eliminated by the comparison of occupations in different classes but complementary to one another in the process of production.

In engineering, the time-working fitters' average in 1926 was 174 per cent of that of 1906; the time-working labourers' was 203 per cent; for piece-workers the relevant percentages were 185 and 209. The increase was 15 per cent higher for labourers than for fitters. From 1926 to 1938, fitters' earnings rose one per cent more than labourers'; from 1938 to 1955, labourers' rose 8 per cent more than fitters'; from 1955 to 1960, fitters' earnings rose 28 per cent, labourers' 24 per cent (time-workers) and 26 per cent (piece-workers).

Table 48. *Occupational class averages as percentages of the average for all occupational classes, men and women, 1913/14, 1922/4, 1935/6, 1955/6 and 1960*

	1913/14	1922/4		1935/6		1955/6		1960		
	% of av.	% of av.	% of 1913/14	% of av.	% of 1922/4	% of av.	% of 1935/6	% of av.	% of 1955/6	% of 1913/14
Men										
1. Professional										
A. Higher	410	372	91	392	105	290	74	298	103	73
B. Lower	194	204	105	190	93	115	60	124	108	64
2B. Managers, etc.	250	307	123	272	89	279	103	271	97	108
3. Clerks	124	116	94	119	103	98	82	100	102	81
4. Foremen	141	171	121	169	99	148	88	149	101	106
Manual										
5. Skilled	124	115	93	121	105	117	97	117	100	94
6. Semi-skilled	86	80	93	83	104	88	97	85	97	99
7. Unskilled	79	82	104	80	98	82	102	79	96	100
Men's average (current weights)	115	114	99	115	100	119	103	118	99	103
Mean deviation (per cent)	67	73		70		48		49		
Women										
1. Professional										
A. Higher	..	..	..	..	..	(203)	..	(209)	(102)	..
B. Lower	111	137	123	130	95	82	63	89	109	80
2B. Managers, etc.	(100)	102	(102)	104	102	151	145	146	97	(146)
3. Clerks	56	68	121	61	90	60	98	62	103	111
4. Forewomen	71	98	138	96	98	90	94	88	98	124
Manual										
5. Skilled	55	56	102	53	94	60	113	58	97	105
6. Semi-skilled	62	63	102	62	98	51	82	50	98	81
7. Unskilled	35	47	134	45	96	43	96	41	95	117
Women's average (current weights)[a]	63	66	105	64	97	58	91	64	110	102
Mean deviation (per cent)[a]	31	37		38		43		39		
Average men and women %	100	100		100		100		100		
£	80	157		162		531		683		

[a]Excluding class 1A.

The pattern repeats itself on the railways: unskilled earnings rose more than the skilled in the first period, fell more in the second and rose substantially more in the third. In the last period, porters' and engine drivers' earnings each rose 39 per cent.

In building, the labourers' standard rate rose 121·5 per cent between 1906 and 1924; the bricklayers' rate 103 per cent. Then the unskilled rate fell to 90 per cent, one percentage point more than the skilled. In the period 1935 to 1955, the labourers' rate rose 220 per cent and the skilled rate 188 per cent; in the final period the unskilled rate rose 18 per cent and the skilled 33 per cent.

The semi-skilled (outside agriculture and the distributive trade) also fit into this pattern: in period 1 they did better than the skilled but not so well as the unskilled; in period 2, they did less well than the skilled but better than the unskilled and so on. There are some exceptions, however. Engine firemen have in each of the four periods done better than engine drivers, and their 1935-55 gain was smaller than that of 1907-24.

But more important, agriculture and retail distribution have followed a rhythm of their own:

	1924 as % of 1913	1935 as % of 1924	1955 as % of 1935	1960 as % of 1955
Agricultural labourers	171	109	475	121
Shop-assistants	145	94	345	125
Other semi-skilled	216	106	317	124
Unskilled	223	101	337	123
Skilled	188	108	319	129

Agricultural labourers were the lowest paid male occupation in 1913: despite this, their relative position by 1924 had still further deteriorated. Their atypical pattern continued to 1935, when they registered an increase even larger than that of the skilled class, and in the next period, too, their rise was extraordinarily large.

The women's groups did not conform to the patterns set by the men. In period 1 the unskilled women did much better than the others; in the second period the three manual groups moved almost in unison; in the third period, the skilled did much better than the other two; in the fourth they moved again in virtual unison.

What were the forces generating the changes we have observed? And what were the forces preventing changes from taking place?

The next stage will be to track the course of change between the years to which attention has so far been directed in order to uncover the routes by which pay rates reached their positions of temporary rest. We shall also note associated economic and social changes and subsequently try to assess the relationship between them.

CHAPTER III

THE TIME AND CIRCUMSTANCES OF PAY CHANGES

We have now reconstructed the national pay and occupational structure for various years between 1906 and 1960, but this tells us nothing about the relationship between the numbers in any occupation and its relative pay. A rise or fall in relative pay may go equally well with a rise or fall in employment. But in economic terms, this may be because both the demand and supply schedules have changed, thus changing the shape or position of the curves that give expression to them. We have a snapshot for each class and its principal occupations showing pay and employment in various years; to interpret the changes (or lack of change) we need a moving picture of the years between in which we can glimpse the conflicting forces that have been operative.

Two aspects of the economy seem to be of peculiar relevance: the level of unemployment in any occupation and the rate and direction of price changes. The first is the best indicator we have of the strength of demand and supply, though for recent years we can reinforce unemployment data with information about unfilled vacancies; the second is important because price changes throw on to the institutions of the labour market (firms, groups of workers, employers' associations, local or national government) the task of adjusting money contracts to give expression to the real relationships that underlie them. The speed at which these institutions work may itself cause changes in the pay structure.

As a starting-point, we set out in table 49 percentage unemployment and indices showing average wage rates and the cost of living between 1906 and 1960. We have many contrasts against which to examine the behaviour of the relative pay rates of occupational classes and occupations and may be able to deduce something about causal relationships.

1. 1906 TO 1924

A period of gently rising prices and wage rates is followed by one of mobilization for war. A post-war boom is followed by a sharp decline with heavy unemployment and, after 1923, partial recovery. The final outcome, as we saw in tables 47 and 48, was a radical improvement in the relative pay of the unskilled, though there was no general tendency for lower-paid classes to do better than the higher-paid. Skilled and semi-skilled men on average did no better than clerks and higher professionals and considerably worse than foremen, managers and lower professionals. The pattern amongst the women was similar, except that female clerks did particularly well.

Table 49.   *Indices of wage rates and the cost of living and percentage unemployment (trade unions, 1906-23; insured workers, 1924-60), United Kingdom*

	Wage rates	Cost of living	Unemployment %
	Average for 1906-10=100		
1906	97	98	*3·6*
7	103	102	*3·7*
8	100	98	*7·8*
9	99	99	*7·7*
1910	100	102	*4·7*
1	101	103	*3·0*
2	104	106	*3·2*
3	106	108	*2·1*
4	106	106	*3·3*
5	111-117	131	*1·1*
6	122-127	155	*0·4*
7	143-148	187	*0·7*
8	185-191	216	*0·8*
9	223-228	230	*2·4*
1920	$\left\{\begin{array}{c}276\\\overline{314}\end{array}\right.$	266	*2·4*
1	307	241	*16·6*
2	226	194	*14·1*
3	208	184	*11·6*
4	211	185	$\left\{\begin{array}{c}8·1\\\overline{10·2}\end{array}\right.$
5	212	186	*11·0*
6	211	182	*12·3*
7	210	177	*9·6*
8	207	175	*10·7*
9	206	173	*10·3*
1930	205	167	*15·8*
1	203	156	*21·1*
2	198	152	*21·9*
3	196	148	*19·8*
4	196	149	*16·6*
5	199	153	*15·3*
6	203	156	*11·9*
7	210	164	*10·6*
8	218	166	*11·1*
9	218	170	*8·2*
1940	245	198	*4·4*
1	264	216	*1·3*
2	288	231	*0·6*
3	300	237	*0·4*
4	313	242	*0·4*
5	327	245	*0·8*
6	353	249	*2·5*
7	365	266	*1·7*
8	387	287	*1·4*
9	398	295	*1·5*
1950	401	305	*1·5*
1	434	333	*1·2*
2	471	362	*2·0*

	Wage rates *Average for 1906-10=100*	Cost of living	Unemployment %
1953	493	373	*1·6*
4	518	381	*1·3*
5	555	397	*1·1*
6	599	417	*1·2*
7	633	432	*1·4*
8	645	445	*2·1*
9	666	449	*2·2*
1960	684	454	*1·6*

Sources: Unemployment: *Abstract of Labour Statistics of the United Kingdom* (H.M. Stationery Office, 1926 and 1937); *Ministry of Labour Gazette.* Wage rates and cost of living, 1906-14: A. L. Bowley, *Wages and Income in the United Kingdom since 1860, op. cit.,* p. 6, col. 1; 1914-20: Bowley, *Prices and Wages in the United Kingdom, 1914-1920,* Economic and Social History of the World War, British Series (Oxford, Clarendon Press, 1921), p. 106 (July each year); 1920-60: Ministry of Labour index of weekly wage rates (annual averages) and index of retail prices, *London and Cambridge Economic Bulletin.*

Prices rose with great rapidity on the outbreak of war and continued their rise until November 1920, so that considerable revisions in pay were required. By 8 August 1914, four days after the declaration of war, the cost of living index had risen 15 per cent and, though there was an immediate fall from this level, by 1 January 1915 the rise was 18 per cent. Year-to-year increases were then as follows:

	Per cent
Year ended 1 January 1916	23
1917	29
1918	10
1919	11
1920	3
10 months ended 1 November 1920	23

Pay movements

Bowley has given a detailed account of wage movements between 1914 and 1920[1]. Earlier in 1914, a wage-offensive was being mounted by the trade unions; on the outbreak of war, their programmes were postponed and outstanding disputes settled. In the next six months or so, wages in many industries remained unchanged; in others, increases seldom exceeded 10 per cent. But a general move for higher rates became evident about the middle of 1915. 'The patriotic efforts of men to work their best, irrespective of wage questions and without much notice of the rise of prices . . . showed signs of diminution. The demand for labour was acute and there was no difficulty in obtaining moderate increases.'[2]

[1]*Prices and Wages in the United Kingdom, 1914-1920, op. cit.*
[2]*Ibid.,* p. 98.

In the next phase, standard rates rose rapidly, the form of the rise varying from case to case[1]. The net effect was generally a narrowing of differentials between kindred manual occupations. Thus in 1920, the bricklayer's rate was 235 per cent of that of 1914, his labourer's 300 per cent. The engineering craftsman's rate was 231 per cent of 1914, the engineering labourer's 309 per cent.

Standard rates lagged behind prices until 1920, but earnings probably caught up sooner. Thus in July 1920, when Bowley estimated standard time- or piece-rates at 260 per cent of July 1914, returns furnished to the Ministry of Labour showed that earnings averaged 275 per cent of 1914.

How did salaries behave in this period of high demand for labour and rapidly rising prices? After 1913/14, the Commissioners of Inland Revenue no longer gave a frequency distribution for tax-paying employees in different income ranges.

Changes in total salaries liable to tax (between years with the same lower limit) are due either to an expansion of employment, a rise in pay for employees who had previously been below the limit and are now over it, or to increases in pay for those already paying tax. It is the extent of the latter that we must try to measure.

The Inland Revenue reports tell us how many Schedule E tax-payers there were in each year except 1915/16, 1916/17 and 1917/18[2]. We can fill in these years by a calculation based on total abatements[3]. Despite the downward extension of the lower limit, no increase in total salaries was registered between 1914/15 and 1915/16 for corporation and public company officials, owing, no doubt, to the large number of enlistments. Between then and 1920/1, the total salary bill for this group (for employees at more than £130) rose 263 per cent. For all Schedule E income, the rise was 230 per cent.

This, of course, is much more than the increase per head, given by dividing total income by total numbers, that amounted to only 35 per cent. But the 35 per cent understates the rise for any member of the group because, when incomes are rising, there is an annual influx of those who, the year before, were below the exemption level. We may place an upper limit on the percentage increase per head by assuming that all the additional tax-payers each year were

[1]When increases were given as cost of living bonuses, they sometimes took the form of equal percentage additions at all levels of pay, on the grounds that loss from rising prices was proportional to income, or they gave more to the poorer than to the richer, on the grounds that the latter could better afford the sacrifice involved. In engineering and building, artisans and labourers generally received the same money increase. In woollen textiles, flat rates were abandoned in June 1917 and replaced by percentage increases.

[2]Government, corporation and public company officials were taxed under Schedule D, all other employees under Schedule E.

[3]£120 was allowed on incomes exceeding £130 but not exceeding £400; £100 on those exceeding £400 but not exceeding £600; and £70 on those exceeding £600 but not exceeding £700. By deducting the estimated numbers in each of these ranges from the total, we get estimates of those exceeding £700. Totals in this group have been extrapolated for the three missing years to retain their proportion to the numbers in the range £600–£700.

receiving only £131 and calculating what the average salary of the remainder would then be. The results of this calculation are shown in table 50.

Table 50. *Estimated increase in the average salary of Schedule E tax-payers with new arrivals excluded each year, 1915/16 to 1920/1*

	Last year's average	This year's average	Per cent increase	Cumulative per cent increase
1916/17	209	226	*8·1*	*8·1*
1917/18	204	218	*6·8*	*15·4*
1918/19	208	246	*18·3*	*36·6*
1919/20	227	259	*14·1*	*55·8*
1920/1	242	312	*28·9*	*100·8*

Of course, the new entrants to the tax range would average more than £131 in their first tax-paying year, and the calculation in table 50 overstates the increase for the remainder accordingly.   None the less, we may maintain with confidence that annual increases would not be more than the percentage shown. The cumulative increase of 101 per cent between 1915/16 and 1920/1 compares with one of 154 per cent for railwaymen; 126 per cent for coalminers; 186 per cent for cotton textile workers; 113 per cent for postmen; 67 per cent for Civil Service administrators; 93 per cent for Civil Service lower division clerks.

By the end of 1920, average salaries were probably little more than double what they had been in 1914, while average weekly wage rates had risen 2·7 or 2·8 times for a working week that, in 1919, had been reduced to between 44 and 48 hours from its former range of 48 to 60 hours[1].

The year 1919 is curious for having produced this great reduction of hours concurrently with a general rise in weekly wage rates and a sudden increase in unemployment to levels that had not been experienced since before the war. In November 1918, less than one per cent of insured workers were unemployed; by March 1919, their numbers had risen to nearly 9 per cent: 753,000 civilians and 306,000 ex-servicemen.   From May, conditions improved and unemployment was down to 5·4 per cent by November.   By March 1920, it was down to 2·8 per cent but, towards the end of the year, began rising again.

The Ministry of Labour recorded negotiated increases for 7,867,000 wage-earners in 1920, at an average of 12s. per worker per week.

By January 1919, standard wage rates had just about caught up with the cost of living, measured from July 1914; during 1919, standard rates[2] rose 9 per cent and the cost of living index just under one per cent, while hours of work were greatly reduced; from December 1919 to December 1920, standard rates rose 20·4 per cent and the cost of living 19·5 per cent.

---

[1]See *Ministry of Labour Gazette*, vol. 29, no. 2, February 1921, p. 64. According to the Ministry's records, in 1919, 6·3 million workers had their hours reduced by an average of 6·4 per week. 'If the number of agricultural labourers, shop assistants and police whose hours have been reduced could be included, the total number would be substantially increased'. See *Ministry of Labour Gazette*, vol. 28, no. 1, January 1920.
[2]Bowley's index.

Then followed the collapse of wages that we have noted above. From December 1920 to December 1921, Bowley records a fall in standard rates of 8 per cent; for the next twelve months, of 22 per cent, and there rates rested with very little change until 1931. The average decrease recorded by the Ministry in 1921 was 17s. 6d. per week for 7·2 million workers and in 1922 a further 11s. for 7·6 million. The reductions were most severe for coalminers: an average of more than £2 per week for 1·3 million in 1921, and a further 10s. in 1922[1]. Excluding coalminers, the average reduction for 1921 was 11·7s., but for 1922 was slightly above 11s.

Wage rates, prices and unemployment moved as follows in this period:

	Weekly wage rates[a]	Cost of living	Wholesale prices All articles	of which iron and steel	Per cent unemployment of insured workers
1920					
Oct.	..	100	100	100	..
Nov.	..	107	95	95	5·4[b]
Dec.	..	103	87	90	6·6[b]
1921					
Jan.	100	101	81	85	11·0
Feb.	98	92	74	76	12·9
March	98	86	70	67	15·0
April	97	81	68	61	19·9
May	95	78	67	59	23·0
June	94	73	65	57	21·9
July	89	73	64	54	17·4
Aug.	87	74	63	52	15·1
Sept.	85	73	62	49	13·9
Oct.	83	67	60	46	14·3
Nov.	78	63	57	43	16·9
Dec.	77	60	56	41	17·7
1922					
Jan.	75	56	54	39	17·5
Feb.	74	54	54	38	16·9
March	72	52	53	37	15·8
April	70	50	53	37	15·6
May	68	49	53	37	14·4
June	67	49	53	37	13·5
July	66	51	53	37	12·9
Aug.	64	49	52	36	12·6
Sept.	64	48	51	35	12·5
Oct.	63	48	51	35	12·4
Nov.	62	49	52	35	12·8
Dec.	62	49	52	35	12·6

[a]Ministry of Labour index.
[b]United Kingdom.

The wholesale price of cotton textiles showed an even more calamitous fall: the average for 1922 was only 30 per cent of the high point reached in April 1920.

[1]Using the Ministry's figures, this would have left weekly rates about 10s. above the level of 1914, and represented a severe reduction in real rates.

The advances in pay and conditions in 1919 had been gained with the loss in strikes of 36 million man-days; the reductions of 1921 were accompanied by the loss of 82 million man-days and those of 1922 by 20 million. But most of these man-days were lost in two great disputes: coal in 1921 (85 per cent) and engineering in 1922 (88 per cent).

Of the aggregate reductions in rates, 55 per cent in 1921 (measured in pounds per week) and 38 per cent in 1922 were under sliding scale agreements related to the cost of living, and just as these had very often benefited the lower-paid relatively more than the higher-paid, so reducing differentials, they now reduced the pay of the lower-paid relatively more, thus widening them again.

In 1921, despite the reduction in money rates, there was a rise in real rates, for, while money rates fell 23 per cent, retail prices fell just over 40 per cent, But in the next twelve months, the fall of rates was 19 per cent, almost the same as that in prices.   Of course, family incomes must have suffered more than these figures suggest by the increase in unemployment, short-time working and loss of job opportunities.

Table 51 shows the magnitude of the changes in standard rates between 1920 and 1924[1].

Table 51.   *Number of workpeople*[a] *reported as affected by changes in weekly full-time rates of wages and aggregate amount of such changes in the years 1920-4*

	Number of separate individuals reported as affected by			Amount of change in weekly rates		
	Net increase	Net decrease	Total[b]	Increase	Decrease	Net increase (+) Net decrease (−)
1920	7,867,000	500	7,868,300	4,793,200	180	+4,793,020
1921	78,000	7,244,000	7,432,000	13,600	6,074,600	−6,061,000
1922	73,000	7,633,000	7,706,700	11,450	4,221,500	−4,210,050
1923	1,202,000	3,079,000	4,685,000	169,000	486,000	−317,000
1924	3,019,000	481,500	3,873,000	616,000	62,100	+553,900

[a]The statistics exclude changes affecting agricultural labourers, domestic servants, shop-assistants and clerks.   In many cases the changes arranged by individual employers and affecting unorganized workers were not reported to the department.
[b]Workpeople whose wages were changed during any year and at the end of that year stood at the same level as at the beginning, are included in the above Total column, though not in either of the preceding columns.

The years 1922 and 1923 were a time of almost universal reductions in wage rates; in 1923, the increase registered was largely accounted for by a modest rise in miners' rates and there was a further general reduction though on a much more moderate scale.   It was not until 1924 that there was a general move in the opposite direction.   So, from the level of 1920, two and a half to three times that of 1914, standard rates were reduced to about twice the 1914 level.

[1]These calculations, published monthly in the *Ministry of Labour Gazette*, are not based on reductions or increases in actual wage bills but are calculations of what would happen if changes in negotiated (standard) rates were literally implemented by employers.

The Anderson Committee produced a table showing the increase in pay per head of various sections of the Civil Service between 1914 and 1923[1]. This, together with data for women Civil Servants[2], was as follows:

	Pay per head, 1914 £	1923 as per cent of 1914
Administrative	662·1	*139*
Professional, scientific and technical	234·2	*179*
Inspectorate	229·0	*193*
Executive and clerical	138·0	*170*
Writing assistants and typing	65·4	*197*
Manipulative	67·4	*220*
Messengers, charwomen, etc.	49·9	*203*
Industrial[a]	80·9	*176*
Women only		
Clerks, writing assistants, etc.	79·5	*186*
Manipulative (mainly P.O.)	61·3	*229*

[a]Civil Service industrial workers are skilled, semi-skilled and unskilled workers employed on repair and production in government factories, dockyards, etc. Their rates are fixed in relation to those of similar workers outside the Civil Service.

The path by which various classes reached these temporary resting points was largely the same as that noted for manual workers: a substantial rise to 1920 (1921 in the Civil Service) and a substantial fall to 1923[3].

	1914	1915	1916	1917	1918	1919	1920	1921	1922	1923	1924
Administrative class	100	100	100	101	106	129	167	180	144	134	134
Executive class	100	100	102	106	126	151	264	290	238	197	197
Women clerks	100	105	108	111	129	155	221	247	220	196	196
Postmen and sorters (men)	100	106	109	119	148	177	221	224	193	173	173
P.O. engineers (professional)	100	101	102	106	140	178	237	261	216	197	197
P.O. engineers (manual)	100	108	110	121	151	209	259	291	227	200	200

We have already noticed that salaries in general must have risen much less than wages between 1914 and 1920. But by 1923, they bore a relationship to their 1914 level similar to that of wages. Table 29 (*Professional earnings*) records a narrowing of differentials within each profession, but at the median, barristers' income had risen 2·76 times, solicitors' 2·08, doctors' 1·95 and dentists' 1·66.

Certificated teachers, whose pay rose nearly two and a half times between 1914 and 1924, followed a different pattern. By 1921, the men's average had risen 2·24 times, the women's 2·47. By 1923, the ratios to 1914 had become 2·35 and 2·64 and only in 1924 did they suffer a modest decline[4].

[1]Committee on Pay, etc. of State Servants, 1923, *loc. cit.*, p. 22.
[2]*Ibid.*, p. 34.
[3]Guy Routh, 'Civil Service Pay, 1875 to 1950', *Economica*, N.S. vol. 21, no. 83, August 1954, p. 201.
[4]See *Statistical Abstract for the United Kingdom, 1913 and 1923 to 1936*, Cmd 5627 (H.M. Stationery Office, 1938), p. 54.

We have noted that salary-earners taxed in terms of Schedule E also fell behind wage-earners to 1920.   Did they participate in the general reductions that followed?   Table 52 sets out some of the data provided for the Anderson Committee by the Department of Inland Revenue.

Table 52.   *Salaries in public companies in various industries, 1920/1 to 1924/5*

A.   Average salaries, 1920/1 to 1922/3

	1920/1 £	1921/2 £	1922/3 £
Coal, metal and engineering	364	368	359
Textiles	411	389	383
Chemicals	420	449	467
Food, drink and tobacco	378	398	408
Paper	410	417	419
Shipping	482	450	440
Banking	424	406	407
Insurance	478	476	456
Wholesale and retail distribution	355	327	320
All the above	408	401	400
Railways	302	282	275

B.   Average of highest salaries and amount of salaries at various rank points, 1920/1 to 1924/5

	1920/1 £	1921/2 £	1922/3 £	1924/5 £
All the above industries except railways:				
Average of 204 highest	8,720	7,200	8,100	8,416
205th	4,350	4,020	4,372	4,211
697th	2,010	1,970	1,955	1,949
2,462nd	1,025	1,128	1,114	1,079
13,571st	429	466	526	534
Railways:				
Average of 8 highest	3,850	3,600	4,698	5,125
9th	3,000	2,860	3,333	3,750
28th	1,733	1,615	1,583	1,545
122nd	840	824	812	832
744th	453	422	415	419

Salaries in the industries listed had a remarkable stability when compared with manual wage rates or earnings in the years 1920 to 1924.   There are significant differences in the performance of different industries, but the average falls only 2 per cent between 1920/1 and 1922/3.

Again, for the values of salaries of different rank order or for the highest-paid, there is not much fluctuation.   For all the industries listed (except railways), the top 204 fell by 17·5 per cent between 1920/1 and 1921/2, but by 1924 had returned to within 3·5 per cent of the 1920/1 level.   In 1924/5, the 205th was within 3·2 per cent of the 1920/1 level; the 697th within 3 per cent, the 2,462nd had actually risen 5·2 per cent and the 13,571st 24·5 per cent.   Fortunes in different industries varied, some in particular suffering substantial cuts in 1922

I

or 1923.   But, like the teachers, they neither climbed so high nor fell so far as manual workers.

A high degree of stability is manifest for the professions, too, whose averages for 1921/2 and 1922/3 are shown in table 53[1].

Table 53. *Professional incomes in 1921/2 and 1922/3*

	Average income of those liable to tax	
	1921/2	1922/3
	£	£
Barristers	1,088	1,309
Solicitors	1,040	1,173
Doctors	909	943
Dentists	745	759
Scholastic professions[a]	538	586

[a]Heads of universities and colleges, university and college teachers, headmasters and housemasters.

Unemployment

Unemployment data derived from National Insurance returns is classified by industry and not by occupation and until 1948 was limited, with some exceptions, to manual wage-earners.   Percentages represent the number registered for employment at employment exchanges as a proportion of all insured workers in the industry in which they are normally employed or, if they are not attached to a particular industry, in the industry in which they last worked.

The series relating to those insured under the National Insurance Act of 1911 dates from September 1912, when some two million workers were included. Until 1926, the Ministry of Labour also published a series showing percentage unemployment amongst members of certain trade unions that paid unemployment benefit and made regular returns to the Ministry.   Since the latter refers almost exclusively to craftsmen and the former to all workers, a comparison of the two rates gives a rough indication of the variation of unemployment at different levels of manual skill.

In engineering, shipbuilding and metal, the trade union rate was 2·2 per cent in 1913, while for all insured males in shipbuilding and engineering it was 2·6 per cent.   Since skilled workers formed 78 per cent of all workers in the metal-making and -using trades, unemployment must have averaged about 4·0 per cent for the semi-skilled and unskilled.   In 1921 and 1922 the related figures would have been:

	Percentages	
	1921	1922
Trade union	22·1	27·0
All	27·1	28·9
Semi-skilled and unskilled	45·0	35·6

[1]For those assessed under Schedule D, an adjustment was made by the Inland Revenue to accord the income shown with the assessment for the year concerned instead of with the average for the previous three years.

We cannot get any other near industrial comparison before 1914, but for 1921 and 1922 may compare the following:

	Percentages	
	1921	1922
Trade unions		
Printing and bookbinding	7·3	6·6
Furnishing trades	10·3	6·2
Boots and shoes	7·1	4·5
Carpenters, joiners, plumbers	4·8	7·6
All trade unions, including above	14·8	15·2
National Insurance[a]		
Printing, publishing and bookbinding	7·2	7·2
Furniture and upholstery	12·9	10·0
Boots and shoes	12·3	10·3
Building	15·2	16·8
All insured males	17·0	16·3

[a]Average of rate at end of each quarter.

In November 1923 and 1924, the Ministry of Labour investigated the personal circumstances of a representative sample of claimants of unemployment benefit[1]. Here again, the high proportion of unskilled men is demonstrated, though for the women the semi-skilled percentage was rather near their proportion of the manual work force.

Level of skill	Males		Females	
	1923	1924	1923	1924
Apprenticed	2,135	2,093	270	228
Trained	2,082	2,180	868	1,094
Neither	4,016	4,557	626	731

2. 1924 TO 1934

The downward rush of the early 1920's now gives way to a gentle decline. Unemployment again reaches the depths of 1921 but now the agony is prolonged over years instead of months:

	Weekly wage rates	Cost of living	Wholesale prices		Per cent unemployment of insured workers
			All articles	of which iron and steel	
1924	100	100	100	100	*10·2*
5	102	101	96	88	*11·0*
6	101	98	89	86	*12·3*
7	101	96	85	84	*9·6*
8	99	95	84	79	*10·7*
9	99	94	82	80	*10·3*
1930	98	90	72	79	*15·8*
1	96	84	63	73	*21·1*
2	95	82	61	72	*21·9*
3	94	80	61	74	*19·8*
4	94	81	63	78	*16·6*

[1]10,000 in 1923 and nearly 11,000 in 1924. See *18th Abstract of Labour Statistics of the United Kingdom*, Cmd 2740 (H.M. Stationery Office, 1926), pp. 74 and 76.

Pay movements

The dimensions of unemployment and the fall in prices are again on a grand scale, but instead of a 38 per cent fall in wage rates, there is one of 6 per cent. There is a further contrast with 1921/2, in that the fall was by no means general. Of the net fall in the weekly aggregate of £772,000 recorded by the Ministry for the years 1930 to 1933 (inclusive) nearly half was accounted for by textiles and building. Engineering rates, raised in 1927, were not reduced at all, nor were compositors' rates. Of the decreases in rates between 1924 and 1933, 59 per cent came about in terms of sliding scales tied to the cost of living index or to product prices[1].

This stability was not merely one of appearance, for industrial earnings showed even less fluctuation than did standard rates, despite the increase in short-time working in 1931[2].

Earnings in 1928 and 1931 as percentages of those in 1924 were as follows:

	1928 Oct.	1931 Oct.
Pottery, bricks, glass, chemicals	102·5	96·8
Metal manufacture, engineering and shipbuilding	104·0	95·6
Textiles	102·2	94·4
Clothing, including laundries	97·1	96·1
Food, drink and tobacco	95·8	94·4
Wood products	102·9	93·4
Paper and printing	112·3	107·8
Building and contracting	103·0	100·2
Gas, electricity and water	103·0	102·3
Weighted average	102·4	96·8

Bowley estimated that full-time earnings in 1931 were, for males, 97·3 per cent and for females 98·5 per cent of their 1924 level.

Non-manual salaries or earnings showed even greater stability except those within the control of the government. Their course in various sectors, for the years 1924 to 1934, is shown in table 54.

Unemployment

For the first time the unemployed were distinguished from the employed by occupation in the Census of 1931. The unemployed represented 15·7 per cent of all operatives (employees, excluding managers and directors).

---

[1]Product price sliding scales operated in coal and steel.
[2]The Ministry of Labour took earnings censuses in 1924, 1928, 1931 and 1935 (reported in *Ministry of Labour Gazette* vols. 34 and 35, 1926-7; vol. 37, 1929; vol. 41, 1933; and vol. 45, 1937).

Table 54. *Indices of pay movements (for non-manual workers), 1924-34*

	1924	1925	1926	1927	1928	1929	1930	1931	1932	1933	1934
Railway earnings											
Station and yard-masters and supervisory staff	100	99	99	98	97	95	96	98	94	94	94
Clerical staff	100	99	99	97	100	98	99	102	98	99	100
Civil Servants Administrative class[a]	100	100	100	100	98	98	98	93	92	92	93
Post Office engineering Professional and supervisory	100	100	102	102	97	97	97	91	89	89	101
Certified full-time teachers[b] Public elementary schools (England and Wales) average salaries:											
Men	100	99	..	99	99	99	99	99	88	88	88
Women	100	100	..	96	95	95	95	95	86	86	86
Manufacturing industry (December)[c]	100	100	100	100	100	100	99½	95½	95	95	97
Distribution (December)[c]	100	100	100	100	100	100	100	99	99	99	99
Finance (December)[c]	100	100	100	100	100	100	98	95	95	95	95
Local authorities (December)[c]	100	100	99	99	98	98	98	96	95	97	97½
Draughtsmen (all men over 30)[d]	100	99	99	99	98	102	101	100	100	96	97

[a]From Guy Routh, 'Civil Service Pay, 1875 to 1950', *op. cit.*

[b]*Statistical Abstract for the United Kingdom, 1913 and 1924 to 1937*, Cmd 5903 (H.M. Stationery Office, 1939), pp. 54 and 58.

[c]Marley and Campion, 'Changes in Salaries in Great Britain, 1924-39', *op. cit.*

[d]From the Association of Engineering and Shipbuilding Draughtsmen (later the Draughtsmen's and Allied Technicians' Association).

Unemployment amongst professionals and clerks was much lower than the general average:

Percentage unemployment, 1931

	Males	Females
All occupied	13·3	8·9
Higher professionals	1·8	1·9
Lower professionals	4·1	4·2
Clerical workers	5·7	4·4

For men in religion, law, teaching and medicine, unemployment was almost non-existent in 1931. In occupational class 1A, chemists and metallurgists returned the highest figure, with 5·7 per cent. In the lower professions, 4·0 per cent of laboratory attendants were unemployed, 5·2 per cent of medical auxiliaries and 6·8 per cent of draughtsmen. For women, 4·4 per cent of nurses and midwives were unemployed, 1·6 per cent of teachers and 3·8 per cent of social welfare workers. Actors and musicians formed exceptions, with unemployment high above the overall average.

For twelve industrial groups, unemployment amongst employers and managers averaged 1·9 per cent[1]; for ten industrial groups, it averaged 5·2 per cent for foremen. But for skilled manual workers it was much higher:

		Per cent
Coal hewers and getters		21·6
Pottery kiln and ovenmen		13·6
Chemical grinders and mixers		10·2
Blacksmiths		20·8
Fitters, mechanics		16·1
Tool setters, setter-operators		14·3
Electricians		11·3
Spinners, piecers	M	25·2
	F	27·3
Weavers	M	24·9
	F	25·5
Bakers and pastry-cooks	M	11·7
	F	8·0
Carpenters		17·3
Bricklayers		13·4
Compositors		7·3
Engine drivers		3·2

But there did not seem to be any clear-cut difference between the rate of unemployment for skilled workers and their associated semi-skilled assistants. The two rates were generally close, with the skilled sometimes above the semi-skilled, sometimes below. The dominant factor was the industry rather than the level of skill. The position of the major groups was as follows:

		Per cent
Agricultural labourers		8·5
Motor drivers: goods		10·7
passenger		6·2
Shop-assistants	M	8·4
	F	8·4
Indoor domestic servants	M	12·1
	F	7·3
Waiters	M	18·9
	F	14·7

But it was the unskilled who were most adversely affected:

		Per cent
Building labourers		19·3
Dock labourers		21·2
Other labourers	M	32·0
	F	22·9

The group 'other labourers' included 481,000 unemployed men and 57,000 unemployed women: 24 per cent of all the unemployed in the case of men and 10 per cent in the case of women.

As in the previous period, there is no simple relationships between unemployment and pay. In table 47, we noted a small increase in average pay between

---

[1]An unemployed employer may seem a contradiction in terms but, as already mentioned, employers and managers were not separately coded in 1931.

1924 and 1935—4 per cent for men and 3 per cent for women. Amongst the men, the higher skills did better than the lower: an 8 per cent rise for the higher professionals, a 4 per cent fall for the lower; an 8 per cent rise for skilled manual workers, a one per cent rise for the unskilled. Perhaps the same influences were at work in causing a 5 per cent rise for male clerks and a 7 per cent fall for female clerks. But between 1928 and 1931, the effect of unemployment seems to assert itself in the rather greater general fall in the pay of manual workers as compared with that of non-manual workers.

3. 1935 TO 1955

Between 1931 and 1951 we have noted substantial increases in the numbers of professional workers, managers, clerks and foremen. The number of skilled and semi-skilled workers hardly changed, while unskilled workers fell by 13 per cent. In pay, on the other hand, professionals, higher and lower, suffered a drastic relative reduction. There was also some reduction for male clerks and foremen, and, to a smaller extent, female clerks and forewomen. Skilled men lost a little ground, but managers, semi-skilled and unskilled men improved their positions. In general, white-collar workers (excluding managers) lost considerable ground to manual workers.

By 1935, prices were rising, after having reached their trough in 1933 and 1934; unemployment had fallen to 15 per cent after the 22 per cent of 1932; the fall in wage rates was at last reversed.

Pay movements

From 1935, there was a significant contrast in the behaviour of manual and non-manual pay. We noted a fall in manual earnings between 1928 and 1931. By 1935, the level of 1928 had been more or less regained and between 1935 and 1938 there was a rise of 8 per cent.

Manual earnings

	Percentages of 1928	
	Oct. 1935	Oct. 1938
Pottery, bricks, glass, chemicals	97·5	104·1
Metal manufacture, engineering and shipbuilding	99·1	111·2
Textiles	94·2	98·1
Clothing (including laundries)	101·3	101·3
Food, drink and tobacco	101·3	106·2
Wood products	98·4	99·7
Paper and printing	92·1	95·7
Building and contracting	95·1	102·2
Gas, electricity and water	99·3	105·3
Weighted average	99·2	107·3

Civil Servants, manual and non-manual, had their pre-1931 rates restored in 1935 and 1936, but ended the decade generally a little below the level of 1928, while most salaries in the Marley–Campion series got back in 1936 and 1937 to pre-depression levels and remained there until 1940. By contrast, manual earnings rose by 30 per cent between 1938 and 1940. Year-to-year increases for manual workers were then as follows:

	Per cent
1940 to 1941	10
1941 to 1942	14
1942 to 1943	7
1943 to 1944	5
1944 to 1945	−2

It was only after 1942 that salaries rallied and regained some of their lost differentials. We calculated that the median pay of male clerks in 1929 was 128 per cent of average manual earnings; in 1942, it was 111 per cent For females, the relevant percentages were 68 and 60. By 1946, the clerks had more than recovered their lost ground; but by 1952, the males had slipped back to their 1942 position and the females had again lost some ground[1].

	Percentage of manual average			
	1929	1942	1946	1952
Male clerks	128	111	135	110
Female clerks	68	60	70	66

We can get a year-by-year picture of what was happening in the Civil Service, and this may serve to fill in some of the gaps. With 1938=100, pay indexes moved as follows:

	1940	1941	1942	1943	1944	1945	1946	1947	1948	1949	1950
Administrative class	100	101	101	102	105	108	112	112	116	116	128
Executive class	100	102	104	108	113	116	122	122	132	132	132
Clerical officers	102	108	111	116	120	124	131	140	140	140	154
Women clerks	100	106	109	113	117	120	135	135	138	138	143
Postmen and sorters	114	122	126	133	136	141	171	171	184	194	194
P.O. engineers, professional and supervisory	102	105	106	111	117	119	124	128	128	129	140
P.O. engineers, manual	115	122	128	135	138	144	155	188	196	196	207
Weekly earnings, all in earnings census	130	142	160	176	182	180	182	198½	217	226½	236½

While differentials are narrowing between related classes in the Civil Service, all are declining in relation to manual earnings. The decline reaches a trough about 1944, then reverses itself in 1945 or 1946, then resumes its downward drift. The pattern is repeated in the case of engineering draughtsmen[2]:

	1940	1941	1942	1943	1944	1945	1946	1947	1948	1949	1950
1. Section leaders	109	115	118	126	131	140	148	153	161	163	168
2. All men over 30	109	116	122	129	134	141	151	155	163	166	170
3. 1 as per cent of manual earnings index	82	80	72	72	71	77	79	75	72	71	69
4. 2 as per cent of manual earnings index	83	81	74	74	73	78	79	76	73	72	70

[1]From the Office Management Association (now Institute of Office Management) inquiry, *Clerical Salaries Analysis*, first conducted in 1942.

[2]From the Draughtsmen's and Allied Technicians' Association (formerly the Association of Engineering and Shipbuilding Draughtsmen).

Here again, the decline is reversed in 1945 and 1946 and then resumed. The year 1944 seems to have been the time when non-manual pay reached its lowest point in relation to manual earnings. In the case of Civil Service clerical officers, 66 per cent of the decline had taken place by 1940; for draughts-men aged over 30, 63 per cent of the decline had taken place by that year. Indeed between 1938 and 1940, a major shift in income in favour of manual workers seems to have taken place: compared with their 30 per cent rise, that for all employees, according to the national income estimates, was only 14 per cent[1]. This is certainly true as regards the Civil Service where the pay of manipulative and manual engineering grades rose 15 per cent between 1935 and 1940, while that of the non-manual classes hardly moved at all.

It is also supported by a comparison of draughtsmen's pay with that of the engineering craftsmen. Between July 1938 and July 1940, hourly earnings of the engineering craftsmen rose by 25·5 per cent. Engineering draughtsmen are a group of non-manual workers with close links with engineering craftsmen, yet the average rate for section leaders and draughtsmen over 30 rose only 9 per cent. One would expect the effect of the rise in manual pay to be still further diluted in more remote non-manual groups.

The relation between the national income estimates of changes in wages and salaries per head for those in civil employment and changes in manual weekly earnings indicates that, in subsequent years, there were fluctuations about the 1940 relationship and no further radical changes. From 1944, a series is available relating pay-as-you-earn income and the number of earners concerned. The resulting average actually rose faster than average manual weekly earnings from 1944 to 1947; then fell relatively in 1947, then resumed an upward course.

---

[1]From this we may approximate the change for various sections. The average for coal-miners and for agricultural labourers was about 23 per cent up, which indicates that the overall average must have been pulled down by the sluggish behaviour of non-manual rates and/or those of shop-assistants and domestic servants.

In 1940, non-manual workers earning up to £420 became subject to unemployment insurance, so we do not know exactly how many workers there were whose average earnings would conform to the movement shown in the earnings inquiries. The Ministry of Labour estimated that the 5,550,000 workers about whom details were obtained in the 1938 inquiry represented about 70 per cent of the labour force concerned, so that the labour force would be just under 8 million. For 1940, no such estimate was made, but it was probably not less than a million below the 1938 number. To this, about 1·3 million must be added for coalmining and agriculture.

The total in civil employment in June 1940 was estimated to be 17·8 million. Employers and self-employed may be estimated by interpolation between 1931 and 1951 at 1·5 million, giving an employee population of 16·3 million. Of these, the earnings of 7 million were about 30 per cent above the 1938 level; 1·3 million, 23 per cent above the 1938 level, so that, to reduce the average rise to 14 per cent, the earnings of the other 8 million must have been 1·5 per cent below the 1938 level.

Whether there was an actual reduction in the average of the non-manual industrial employee population or not (and it could have been brought about by the substitution of female for male labour) it does appear that a major income change in favour of manual industrial workers took place between 1938 and 1940.

This is not just a result of fluctuations in industrial hours: the pay-as-you-earn average and hourly earnings show a similar relationship, the former rising relatively to 1946 and 1947, dipping in 1948, then rising again.

We have calculated that average earnings in the higher professions in 1955/6 were 256 per cent of their level of 1935/6[1]. We get a glimpse of their level between these two years from the evidence before the Danckwerts Tribunal[2], which showed that professional income (as indicated by tax returns) was in 1949/50 188 per cent of the level of 1937. In this year, earnings in earnings census industries were 230 per cent of the level of 1938 and 249 per cent of the level of 1935. Interpolation by means of the index of wage rates[3] would show 1949 to be 241 per cent of 1937. We get this picture of the relative progress of manual and professional earnings:

	1937	1949		1955/6
Manual earnings	100	241	100	160
Higher professions	100	188	100	136
Percentage gap		22		15

Thus the erosion of manual/professional differentials must have had a second period of activity after it had spent itself about 1944.

Average earnings for all employees moved in step with those for manual workers between 1944 and 1950 or 1951. Then followed further narrowing:

	Nos. 000's	Average earnings, 1955 as per cent of 1950
1. All employees[a]	19,850	138
2. Manual earnings[b]	10,500	147
3. Coal	700	143
4. Agriculture	660	141
5. Railways	418	147
6. 1 minus 2 to 5	7,572	124

[a]From PAYE tax tables.
[b]Ministry of Labour earnings census (*Ministry of Labour Gazette*).

Those in lines 2 to 5 were, in 1955, getting 353 per cent of their earnings of 1938; the residue 244 per cent. The inclusion of professional individuals and partnerships, as shown in the Schedule D analysis of the tax reports, would widen the gap fractionally.

Unemployment

The drastic reduction in the differential between manual and non-manual workers occurred in a period when unemployment amongst the former remained

[1]See table 47, p. 104.
[2]Arbitration proceedings between the British Medical Association and the Minister of Health, March 1952, reported in Supplement to *The British Medical Journal*, 29 March 1952, p. 129. Between 1949/50 and 1950/1, there was an increase of only 0·8 per cent (1937=100, 1950/1 was 189·5 per cent).
[3]Table 49.

high.   Unemployment was falling between 1932 and 1937, but in 1938, when it was once more on the increase, wage rates continued to rise.

Per cent unemployment, insured males

1935	17·5
1936	14·6
1937	12·0
1938	13·5

It is curious that employers should have found it necessary to increase the pay of their manual workers in these years when, at best, one in eight of the male work force was unemployed; what is still more curious is that rates for the unskilled should generally have risen more than those for skilled workers, for, as in 1931, unemployment was much heavier amongst the former.   An analysis for the Special Areas in 1937 showed that of the unemployed in coal-mining, shipbuilding, engineering and building, 63 per cent were unskilled[1]. In March 1940, when unemployment was still high by modern standards, nearly half the unemployed were labourers: 295,000 out of 631,000[2].

Unemployment remained extraordinarily low after the war, even allowing for the fact that the insured population of which it is expressed as a percentage is no longer limited to manual workers.   In April 1951, only 253,000 work-seekers were registered with employment exchanges, who had been notified of 437,000 vacancies.   The registered unemployed represented 1·9 per cent of all civilian employees.   The Census, however, listing all unemployed and not only those who were registered, shows them to have been 2·3 per cent of all employees. Again, rates for non-manual workers were lower than those for manual workers:

Percentage unemployed, 1951

	Males	Females
All occupied	2·2	2·0
Higher professionals	0·7	1·8
Lower professionals	1·4	2·0
Clerks	1·2	1·2

For skilled and semi-skilled manual workers, unemployment was above average for coal hewers and getters (3·9 per cent), indoor domestic servants (males, 8·6; females 2·5) and waiters (males, 7·2; females 4·5).   Again, it is amongst the unskilled that unemployment is highest:

Percentage unemployed, 1951

Building labourers		5·1
Dock labourers		3·4
Other labourers	M	5·1
	F	2·5

[1]See *Report of the Commissioners for the Special Areas in England and Wales, 1937*, Cmd 5595 (H.M. Stationery Office, 1937), p. 30.   These were areas of high unemployment designated under the Special Areas Acts.

[2]*Ministry of Labour Gazette*, vol. 48, no. 5, May 1940, p. 128.   The analysis relates to males aged 18 and over.

4. 1956 TO 1960

Pay movements

This period was characterized by a widening of differentials. Table 48 showed a pronounced relative decline for semi-skilled and unskilled men and for all women manual workers, while clerks and professionals enjoyed a relative advance. However, the lower professions did better than the higher professions and managers did no better than manual workers (though they did no worse).

In manufacturing industry the narrowing process seems to have been reversed about 1956 or 1957. There, average wages rose in relation to average salaries between 1950 and 1956 and fell thereafter[1]:

Average wages as per cent of average salaries

1950	59·6
1956	68·0
1957	66·3
1958	66·0
1959	65·3
1960	64·8

The Ministry of Labour's indices of average weekly earnings and average salary earnings show a similar relationship[2]:

	Average weekly earnings	Average salary earnings
1955	100·0	100·0
1956	108·0	107·3
1957	113·0	114·8
1958	116·9	118·5
1959	122·2	126·3
1960	130·6	133·4

There are various other traces of this reversal of trend in the pay history of the period. On the railways, station-masters and clerks gained relatively to the manual grades[3]. In various industries, Grade D clerks lost relatively to manual earnings between 1952 and 1954, remained steady between 1954 and 1956 and gained between 1956 and 1958[4].

From 1955 to 1957, the manual earnings of boys, women and girls all improved *vis-à-vis* those of men in manufacturing industry, then lost ground again.

---

[1]See Central Statistical Office, *National Income and Expenditure, 1961* (H.M. Stationery Office, 1961), p. 13.

[2]Weekly earnings are those of manual workers covered by the Ministry's earnings census. Salary earnings are those of administrative and technical grades (including employees with professional qualifications) and clerical and analogous grades. The distributive trade is not included. See *Statistics on Incomes, Prices, Employment and Production*, no. 2, September 1962 (H.M. Stationery Office), p. 7.

[3]This reflects the findings of the Guillebaud Committee on conditions outside the railways (British Transport Commission, etc., *Report of Railway Pay Committee of Inquiry* (London, Special Joint Committee on Machinery of Negotiation for Railway Staff, 1960).

[4]See the *Clerical Salaries Analysis* published biennially by the Institute of Office Management. The 1960 report does not include an industrial analysis.

Between related grades of manual workers, too, differentials reached their narrowest about 1953 or 1954, then fluctuated about that level or widened slightly. Table 55 illustrates this in respect of the engineering industry[1].

Table 55. *Engineering industry: interrelationship of earnings in various occupations, 1950-60*

Rate	1950	1951	1952	1953	1954	1955	1956	1957	1958	1959	1960
Labourers as per cent of fitters	86·0	84·7	86·3	87·0	86·2	85·2	84·5	84·3	84·3	84·3	84·3
Women as per cent of fitters	62·2	63·5	66·0	67·2	67·1	67·2	67·1	67·6	67·6	67·8	67·8
Earnings (time-workers)											
Fitters as per cent of tool-room fitters	..	90·1	89·9	88·9	91·0	90·8	92·3	..	90·4	90·2	90·2
Turners and machinemen, semi-skilled as per cent of fitters	..	82·2	81·8	82·5	80·8	81·2	81·4	..	80·7	80·6	81·8
Labourers as per cent of fitters	..	79·2	78·1	78·4	76·5	76·9	73·9	..	74·8	74·3	74·5
Women as per cent of fitters	..	47·8	48·1	48·5	47·1	46·5	46·8	..	46·8	48·1	..

Unemployment and unfilled vacancies by occupation

From 17 March 1958, the Ministry of Labour has given a quarterly analysis of unemployment and unfilled vacancies for adult men and women on a broad occupational basis[2]. Again, this refers to people registered for employment and vacancies notified to employment exchanges, so is not exhaustive either of unemployment or vacancies. However, it gives a useful indication of the state of demand and supply relating to the occupations cited. The tables that follow average the data for June and December 1958, 1959 and 1960.

On average, there has been an excess demand for all skilled craftsmen except painters and shipwrights. The occupations listed contributed 4·6 per cent to the unemployed and 19·3 per cent to the vacancies. For tool setters, setter-operators, the demand has been particularly acute: nearly four vacancies for each applicant.

For the semi-skilled men, excess supply was the rule, with the exception of bus drivers and conductors, for whom there were, on average, more than eight vacancies for each applicant. But for drivers of goods vehicles, the reverse applies: nearly six applicants for each vacancy. On balance, the semi-skilled supplied a lower proportion of unemployed (11 per cent) than of vacancies (17 per cent).

---

[1]Information about earnings is taken from the inquiries of the Engineering and Allied Employers' National Federation.

[2]See *Ministry of Labour Gazette*, vol. 66, No. 5, May 1958, p. 190, for the first of these analyses.

Table 56. *Unemployment and unfilled vacancies from employment exchange records, average for 1958, 1959 and 1960, June and December each year*

Men	Unemployed	Vacancies
A. Skilled		
Carpenters, joiners (construction)	1,552	3,788
Bricklayers	1,029	2,477
Painters	3,598	2,036
Shipwrights	377	92
Electricians	1,177	1,347
Precision fitters (other than toolroom)	1,743	2,061
Maintenance fitters, erectors	835	1,075
Tool setters, setter-operators	877	3,459
Electronic equipment, installers, testers	528	1,005
Vehicle-body-builders	256	464
All the above	11,972	17,804
Per cent of all occupations	*4·63*	*19·33*
B. Semi-skilled		
Manufacturing process workers	5,958	4,482
Motor drivers (not public passenger)	12,495	2,223
Bus drivers, conductors	458	3,888
Shop-assistants	4,524	2,885
Hotel and catering occupations	4,127	1,932
All the above	27,562	15,410
Per cent of all occupations	*10·7*	*16·7*
C. Unskilled		
Light labourers	52,784	190
Other labourers	93,333	12,908
All the above	146,117	13,098
Per cent of all occupations	*56·5*	*14·2*
All occupations	258,610	92,093
Women		
D. Office workers		
Clerks	8,963	3,363
Book-keepers, cashiers	1,946	1,424
Shorthand typists	1,523	4,104
Typists	1,097	2,151
Office machine operators	650	740
All the above	14,179	11,782
Per cent of all occupations	*14·27*	*15·79*

E. Skilled and semi-skilled process workers

Mechanical and electrical engineering and metal		
goods manufacture	3,034	3,514
Pottery	142	356
Food, drink, tobacco	1,275	2,074
Boot and shoe manufacture	349	367
Textile spinning	539	803
Textile weaving	1,028	846
Wholesale heavy clothing	1,211	3,218
Light clothing	1,439	4,301
All the above	9,017	15,479
Per cent of all occupations	*9·07*	*20·74*

F. Semi-skilled service workers

Motor drivers	291	133
Bus conductors	290	477
Shop-assistants	11,300	7,248
Hotel and catering service:		
Kitchen staff	4,652	4,092
Barmaids, service hands	2,161	2,849
Waitresses	3,365	2,854
All the above	22,059	17,653
Per cent of all occupations	*22·2*	*23·7*

G. Unskilled

Kitchen staff	4,652	4,092
Others	52,183	27,212
All the above	56,835	31,304
Per cent of all occupations	*57·2*	*42·0*

All occupations	99,337	74,604

It is again amongst the labourers that unemployment is most highly concentrated. They supplied 56·5 per cent of the unemployment and had only 14 per cent of the vacancies: eleven applicants for each job.

In the case of women, general clerks were substantially in excess supply, while the reverse applied to shorthand typists and typists. On balance, office workers supplied just about the same percentage of unemployed as there were office vacancies.

There was a considerable excess demand for skilled and semi-skilled process workers (except in textile spinning), while semi-skilled service workers were in excess supply, though they contributed equal proportions to the totals of unemployed and vacancies.

The contrast in the case of unskilled women is not as great as in the case of the men. There are nearly two for every vacancy and they supply about the same proportion of the unemployed (57 per cent for the women, 56·5 per cent for the men), but have 42 per cent of the vacancies (compared with only 14 per cent in the case of the men).

5. PERIODS OF CHANGE

We can distinguish seven major stages in the pay history of our period:

1914 to 1920

There was a general narrowing of differentials. Money earnings of manual workers increased rapidly, while non-manual earnings lagged behind. The narrowing included related occupations at different levels of skill and the range of earnings in particular professions. These movements were associated with a high rate of inflation and a high demand for labour.

1920 to 1923

Wage rates and manual earnings came tumbling down, in the wake of a drastic fall in prices and heavy unemployment. Non-manual earnings were much more stable, so that the two converged at about twice the money level of 1914.

1924 to 1933

There was a downward drift of money earnings, more pronounced amongst manual than non-manual workers, and more pronounced amongst the unskilled than the skilled. Unemployment again approached the extraordinary levels of 1922 and 1923 and retail prices between 1924 and 1933 fell even more than between 1920 and 1923, but the change was now spread out over a much longer period.

1934 to 1944

Manual earnings moved upward at accelerating pace, with maximum rise between 1938 and 1940. Salaries regained their pre-depression level somewhat later (1936 or 1937) and, by 1940, had failed to improve on it. The erosion of differentials came to an end between 1942 and 1944. The change in pay structure was again associated with a substantial rise in prices (nearly 30 per cent between 1935 and 1940; 22 per cent between 1940 and 1944) but, in contrast to the narrowing of 1914 to 1920, with a high level of unemployment. Unemployment was highest amongst those whose relative pay rose most.

1944 to 1950

There was an upward movement of money earnings, with the pay structure generally unchanged; a high level of employment temporarily disturbed in 1946; a somewhat slower rise in retail prices—26 per cent spread over the six years.

1951 to 1955

A further narrowing of differentials accompanied a high level of employment and a somewhat faster rise in prices (30 per cent from 1950 to 1955).

1956 to 1960

A fairly general widening of differentials, with relative declines for semi-skilled and unskilled manual workers. Employment remained high though it fell slightly in the recession of 1958/9. The rise in prices continued but at a much more moderate pace: 15 per cent between 1955 and 1960.

CHAPTER IV

INTERPRETATIONS

At the basis of all economic theorizing and analysis since the time of Sir William Petty has been a belief that price is determined by the interaction of demand and supply and that this mechanism has the power to bring demand and supply into equilibrium[1]. This was the basic assumption of Ricardo and Marx no less than of Jevons and Marshall, Chamberlin and Keynes; it has today almost the same sort of status amongst educated people as the belief that the earth is round.

The marginalists propounded the idea that this mechanism maximized utility in, all things considered, the best of all possible economic worlds; the Marxists that it depressed the real wages of the proletariat to a range of values centred on the subsistence level; the Keynesians that it perpetuated unemployment but might be so manipulated as to eliminate it.

Nearly a century ago, Cairnes, while not questioning its truth, was critical of its significance:

'Nothing is easier than to say that the price of labor . . . like the value of other things, depends upon supply and demand—we may find the formula in any newspaper we take up; but what light does this throw upon the causes which govern the values either of labor or commodities? Simply none at all, or next to none at all. What we want to know is, not whether an increase of supply will cheapen a commodity or will cheapen labor, and an increase of demand raise the price of each—every costermonger will tell you this much—but what it is which governs supply and demand in each case'[2].

1. THE ORIGIN OF PAY STRUCTURE

What was it that determined supply and demand with reference to different occupations and gave the national pay structure its peculiar shape? Cantillon dealt with the subject at some length[3]. A craftsman's labour would be dear in

---

[1]In the sense that, at the end of the term of trading, there do not remain some buyers who would have liked to have bought more nor some sellers who would have liked to sell more at the prevailing price.

[2]J. E. Cairnes, *Some Leading Principles of Political Economy Newly Expounded* (London, Macmillan, 1874), pp. 151-2.

[3]R. Cantillon, *Essai sur la Nature du Commerce en Général*, ed. Henry Higgs, for the Royal Economic Society (London, Macmillan, 1931), p. 19.

proportion to the time lost in learning his trade and the cost and risk incurred in becoming proficient:

> 'The Crafts which require the most Time in training or most Ingenuity and Industry must necessarily be the best paid. A skilful Cabinet-maker must receive a higher price for his work than an ordinary Carpenter, and a good Watchmaker more than a Farrier.

> 'The Arts and Crafts which are accompanied by risks and dangers like those of Founders, Mariners, Silver miners, etc. ought to be paid in proportion to the risks ... When Capacity and trustworthiness are needed the labour is paid still more highly, as in the case of Jewellers, Bookkeepers, Cashiers and others.

> 'By these examples and a hundred others drawn from ordinary experience it is easily seen that the difference of price paid for daily work is based upon natural and obvious reasons'[1].

Cantillon did not describe the mechanism by which differences in pay were regulated, but did suggest an aspect of the subject that was developed later by Cairnes and the modern sociologists:

> 'As the Handicraftsmen earn more than the Labourers they are better able to bring up their children to Crafts; and there will never be a lack of Craftsmen in a State when there is enough work for their constant employment'[2].

Adam Smith, too, devoted considerable thought to the considerations that led to differences in pay. He listed five of the 'principal circumstances' that must be considered when estimating what Marshall subsequently called the *net advantages* of a particular occupation: agreeableness or disagreeableness, easiness and cheapness or difficulty and expense of learning it, regularity of employment in it, degree of trust reposed in those that follow it and the probability of success or failure in it. For someone whose profession had been learnt at the expense of much time and labour, earnings must be high enough to replace the whole expense of his education 'with at least the ordinary profits of an equally valuable capital'[3].

Far less than was generally supposed was accounted for by innate ability:

> 'The difference between the most dissimilar characters, between a philosopher and a common street porter, for example, seems to arise not so much from nature as from habit, custom and education'[4].

Public education for the learned professions would have a radical effect on their level of pay:

> 'It has been considered of so much importance that a proper number

---

[1]R. Cantillon, *op. cit.*, pp. 21-3 [7].
[2]*Ibid.*, p. 27.
[3]*An Inquiry into the Nature and Causes of the Wealth of Nations*, Everyman ed. (London, Dent, 1910), vol. 1, p. 90.
[4]*Ibid.*, vol. 1, p. 14.

of young people should be educated for certain professions, that sometimes the public and sometimes the piety of private founders have established many pensions, scholarships . . . etc., for this purpose, which draw many more people into those trades than could otherwise pretend to follow them'. In the church, despite the length, tedium and expense of the education required, this had resulted in the pay of a curate being less than that of a mason. In other professions, if an equal proportion were educated at public expense, 'the competition would soon be so great, as to sink very much their pecuniary reward. It might then not be worth any man's while to educate his son to either of those professions at his own expense. They would be entirely abandoned to such as had been educated by those public charities, whose numbers and necessities would oblige them in general to content themselves with a very miserable recompense . . . '[1].

Malthus expressed Adam Smith's five determinants unambiguously in terms of demand and supply. They influenced pay not because of any intrinsic value they added to the labour in various professions, but because they 'are causes of a nature to influence the supply of labour in the particular departments in question, and to determine such wages by the demand compared with the supply of the kind of labour required'[2].

In the Marxist system, the value of labour power, like that of other commodities, is determined by the amount of labour power necessary for its production, that is, required to produce the things needed for the subsistence of the labourer and his family:

'In order to modify the human organism, so that it may acquire skill and handiness in a given branch of industry, and become labour-power of a special kind, a special education or training is requisite, and this, on its part costs an equivalent in commodities of a greater or less amount. This amount varies according to the more or less complicated character of the labour-power. The expenses of this education (excessively small in the case of ordinary labour-power), enter *pro tanto* into the total value spent in its production'[3].

Thus, in the same way that a machine passes its congealed labour-time into its products, so the professional man passes something of the labour-time that has gone into his own training into the services that he subsequently renders. Engels followed Adam Smith in maintaining that at such time as this training is given free by society to the individual, so will the profit of this training accrue to society and not to the individual, whose pay will then sink to a level much nearer that of the untrained worker.

[1] Adam Smith, *op. cit.*, vol. 1, pp. 118 and 120.
[2] T. R. Malthus, *Principles of Political Economy*, second ed. (Oxford, Blackwell, 1951), p. 220.
[3] K. Marx, *Capital: a Critical Analysis of Capitalist Production* (Moscow, Foreign Languages Publishing House, 1954-9), vol. 1, p. 172.

We noticed in Cantillon and in Adam Smith the beginnings of a sociological theory of labour supply to different occupations. This was taken a step further by John Stuart Mill, who added a qualification to Adam Smith's determinants:

> 'These inequalities of remuneration, which are supposed to compensate for the disagreeable circumstances of particular employments, would, under certain conditions, be natural consequences of perfectly free competition: and as between employments of about the same grade, and filled by nearly the same description of people, they are, no doubt, for the most part, realized in practice. But it is altogether a false view of the state of facts, to present this as the relation which generally exists between agreeable and disagreeable employments. The really exhausting and the really repulsive labours, instead of being better paid than others, are almost invariably paid the worst of all, because performed by those who have no choice . . . The more revolting the occupation, the more certain it is to receive the minimum of remuneration, because it devolves on the most helpless and degraded, on those who from squalid poverty, or from want of skill and education, are rejected from all other employments'[1].

Mill's pupil, J. E. Cairnes, developed these ideas still further and thus laid the foundation for subsequent investigations into social class stratification and inter-class mobility. Once trained, labour became somewhat immobile as between different occupations, so that changes in demand had to be met largely from the constantly emerging stream of young workers (the equivalent of liquid capital) who could direct themselves into the most profitable occupations. There was, however, an important limitation to this process: each individual could choose his employment only 'within certain tolerably well defined limits', set by the qualifications required for each occupation. Thus the sons of unskilled workers would have all forms of mere unskilled work open to them, but beyond this they were practically shut out from competition. 'The barrier is his social position and circumstances, which render his education defective, while his means are too narrow to allow of his repairing the defect, or of deferring the return upon his industry till he has qualified himself for a skilled occupation'. The sons of artisans suffered from similar limitations of choice, and so on up the occupational scale:

> 'The limits imposed are not such as may not be overcome by extraordinary energy, self-denial, and enterprise; and by virtue of these qualities individuals in all classes are escaping every day from the bounds of their original position, and forcing their way into the ranks of those who stand above them... But such exceptional phenomena do not affect the substantial truth of our position. What we find, in effect, is, not a whole population competing indiscriminately for all occupations, but a series of industrial

---

[1]*Principles of Political Economy*, Book 2, chap. XIV, para. 1.

layers, superposed on one another, within each of which the various candidates for employment possess a real and effective power of selection, while those occupying the several strata are, for all purposes of effective competition, practically isolated from each other...so...that the average workman, from whatever rank he be taken, finds his power of competition limited for practical purposes to a certain range of occupations, so that, however high the rates of remuneration in those which lie beyond may rise, he is excluded from sharing them. We are thus compelled to recognise the existence of non-competing industrial groups as a feature of our social economy; and this is the fact which I desire here to insist upon'[1].

Wicksteed, while applying marginal analysis to the labour market, came to rather similar conclusions. There are many factors that interfere with 'the flow of undifferentiated human talent in the direction which would best minister to the want highest on the collective scale...Thus, those occupations which require an elaborate and expensive preparation will, so long as present conditions remain, always be recruited from a small section of society; and the talent which exists in the great mass of people will be either undetected or left untrained'[2].

He then states the conditions that would be required for the fulfilment of Adam Smith's formula for the determination of pay by job-content. The educational system would have to play the part of a 'great sorting machine for adjusting opportunities to capacities throughout the whole population'[3]. A flow would follow from less pleasant, less highly paid, occupations, to pleasanter and more highly paid ones, so that the marginal productivity of the latter would be lowered and that of the former raised. The Utopian ideal would then be approached 'of a higher payment for the more monotonous services rendered to society by the manual workers, than for the more varied and pleasant ones rendered by the exercise of the artistic and intellectual powers'[4].

Marshall shares these ideas, but adds another, relating to bargaining strength, that may help to explain differences in occupational pay. The unskilled labourer is in the weakest position, because his wages leave him very little margin for saving, and because if he stops work, there are large numbers who are capable of replacing him. It is also more difficult for unskilled workers to form 'strong and lasting combinations' and thus bargain on equal terms with their employers. At the other extreme are the professional classes who 'are richer, have larger reserve funds, more knowledge and resolution, and much greater power of concerted action with regard to the terms on which they sell their services, than the greater number of their clients and customers'[5].

[1]Cairnes, *Some Leading Principles of Political Economy Newly Expounded, op. cit.*, pp. 64-8.
[2]*The Common Sense of Political Economy* (London, Routledge, 1935), p. 334.
[3]*Ibid.*, p. 335.
[4]*Ibid.*, p. 336.
[5]*Principles of Economics*, eighth ed. (London, Macmillan, 1920), p. 568.

In more recent years, sociologists have collected data to measure social stratification and mobility. Lipset and Bendix note that

'before World War II, studies of social mobility were usually limited to investigations of the social origins of different occupational groups, employees of single factories, or inhabitants of single communities. Since World War II there have been at least fifteen different national surveys in eleven countries which have secured from representative samples of the population information that relates the occupations of the respondents to the occupations of their fathers. In addition, there have been a number of studies conducted in different cities of various countries. Taken together, these investigations permit the comparison of current variations in occupational mobility, as well as some estimate of differences during the past half century'[1].

After examing the results of these investigations, Lipset and Zetterberg cautiously concluded:

'In effect, the principal impression which may be derived from the summary of mobility studies around the world is that no known complex society may be correctly described as "closed" or static. Although the paths of mobility and the extent to which the mobile may enter or leave different strata are not the same in all such societies, the number of persons in each who are able to rise above the position of their parents is large enough to refute the statement that "class barriers are insurmountable" '[2].

Lipset and Zetterberg use only three broad classifications to delineate their classes: non-manual occupations, manual occupations and farm occupations. Generally, though, a more detailed system is used. Pitirim A. Sorokin defines social class as a coalescence of occupational and economic bonds associated with a totality of social and legal rights and duties:

'We have seen that economic and occupational bonds taken separately exert a powerful influence on the body and mind, the behavior and way of life of an individual. Their combined influence, re-enforced by similarity of status in the stratified pyramid of the population, is still greater. Persons having essentially similar occupations, economic position, and rights and duties cannot fail to become similar in a great many other ways, physical, mental, moral and behavioral'[3].

The Department of Sociological Research at the London School of Economics investigated the social origins, education, occupation, marriage and fertility of

[1]S. M. Lipset and R. Bendix, *Social Mobility in Industrial Society* (London, Heinemann, 1955), pp. 13-14.
[2]*Ibid.*, chapter II, p. 74.
[3]'What is a Social Class?', *Journal of Legal and Political Sociology*, 1947, p. 21, reprinted in R. Bendix and S. M. Lipset, *Class, Status and Power* (London, Routledge and Kegan Paul, 1954).

a random sample of 10,000 adults. The findings show a high (though changing) degree of social stratification in Britain. This stratification was by no means completely rigid, and there was, in fact, a fair degree of mobility between classes, 'nevertheless the general picture is of a rather stable social structure, and one in which social status has tended to operate within, so to speak, a closed circuit. Social origins have conditioned educational level, and both have conditioned achieved social status. Marriage has also to a considerable extent taken place within the same closed circuit'[1].

The facts seem to lend themselves to interpretations in the way suggested by Cairnes and the others: an occupational distribution and occupational pay structure supported by class stratification, not completely rigid and yet set enough to limit severely competition for higher-paid jobs. We have noted Adam Smith's and Wicksteed's conditions for the break-up of this system: public education for higher occupations, with the educational system as a sorting machine to adjust opportunities to capacities.

Since the war, the education system has been more and more adapted to serve this end and, as we have seen, between 1935 and 1955, higher professional pay fell from 395 to 269 per cent of the all-class average; lower professional pay from 188 to 114 per cent. This was associated with a substantial increase in the proportion of full-time university students and in the number receiving public grants for full-time study.

Teachers give an example of this process. Between 1913 and 1924, they increased their pay lead over the averages for all men and women respectively, but between 1936 and 1955, they suffered a substantial relative reduction. Despite this reduction, it was possible to make up for the wartime fall in the number of teachers and then to increase their numbers, between 1949 and 1956, by over 20 per cent[2]. By 1955, there were more qualified applicants than places in the training colleges. This the government had been able to do by, in effect, paying entrants from the date their specialized training commenced and thus relieving them (or their parents) of the expense of fees, maintenance and wages forgone.

In order to examine more closely the extent of upward mobility between occupational classes, we conducted an inquiry into the social origins of engineering draughtsmen and design technicians. This, it seemed, might be one of the gateways to the professions. If there were a high degree of exclusiveness in the recruitment of draughtsmen, that is, if son followed father in this occupation or if father's occupation was predominantly also in the lower professions, this would indicate a restriction of supply that might well serve to maintain class differentials. On the other hand, if this were in fact a 'gateway occupation',

---

[1] *Social Mobility in Britain*, ed. D. V. Glass (London, Routledge and Kegan Paul, 1954), p. 21.

[2] 35,000 teachers were produced under the Emergency Training Scheme between 1945 and 1951.

it would suggest that there were facilities for adequate supplies of professional labour.

Table 57 summarizes the results of this inquiry in so far as it relates to fathers' occupational class[1]. The first line shows the percentage distribution of respondents classified according to their father's occupational class. The second line of figures shows the occupational class distribution of all occupied men in

Table 57. *Percentage distribution of draughtsmen by fathers' occupational class, 1960, and distribution of occupied men by occupational class, 1931*

	Professional		Managerial	Clerical	Foremen	Manual workers		
	Higher	Lower				Skilled	Semi-skilled	Unskilled
Draughtsmen's fathers	3·8	3·5	14·1	5·6	10·0	40·6	17·4	4·9
Occupied males, 1931	1·5	2·0	12·0	5·5	2·0	30·0	29·0	18·0

Great Britain in 1931. If there had been an equal chance for all to become draughtsmen, then, by the laws of probability, the percentage distribution in both lines would have been similar. But in fact there are great differences. It is only in the case of the sons of clerks that there are neither more nor less than a random distribution would suggest. Proportionately, the sons of foremen are five times more numerous than would have been expected, of higher professionals two and a half times; skilled workers, one and a third times. But sons of semi-skilled workers have only 60 per cent of the places equal opportunity would have given them, and those of unskilled workers only 27 per cent.

This is in keeping with the findings of other inquiries: the great under-representation of the sons of semi-skilled and unskilled manual workers; much talent is going to waste; there is great inequality of opportunity. But at the same time, 70 per cent of the entrants to this profession were the sons of foremen or manual workers; 43 per cent of them had in fact entered draughtsmanship after a craft apprenticeship, that is, had themselves switched from a manual to a non-manual occupation.

There were two other indications that the occupation is associated with high mobility: it is a 'young' occupation, not only because the rate of intake is accelerating, but because it offers a favourable stepping-stone to promotion; secondly, the children of draughtsmen are in a favourable position to enter the professions. So, in 1931, in England and Wales, there were 15,380 draughtsmen in the age-group 25 to 34. But in 1951 in the range 45 to 54,

---

[1]The report, based on 941 satisfactorily completed questionnaires, was published in G. Routh, 'The Social Co-ordinates of Design Technicians', *The Draughtsman*, vol. 44, no. 9, September 1961, p. 7.

there were only 9,086, despite the fact that in the intervening years the total number of draughtsmen had more than doubled. Draughtsmen in the sample had fifty-five sons who were at work and sixty daughters. Their occupational distribution is shown in table 58.

Table 58. *Occupational classes of draughtsmen's children*

	Professional		Managerial	Clerical	Foremen	Manual workers		
	Higher	Lower				Skilled	Semi-skilled	Unskilled
Boys	23	12	5	5	—	9	1	—
Girls	—	25	2	28	—	2	3	—

Even though the sons of semi-skilled and unskilled manual workers are hardly in the running for the higher and get much less than their share of the lower professions, the supply of professional workers may be increased simply by easing the way for the children of the other classes, and not least for those of professional workers themselves. In the sample study of 1949, 38·8 per cent of the sons of fathers who had been professional men and high administrators were employed in the same class; 15·5 per cent of the sons of managers and executives had become professional men or high administrators[1]. There was thus some scope for an increase in recruitment from these classes themselves.

In 1960, class 1A (Higher professions) would have required nearly 20,000 new male entrants to provide for its growth and to make up for deaths and retirements[2]. On the same basis, 3,500 women would have been needed. A calculation based on the age and number of married men in Census Order XIX (the professions) and mean family size for socio-economic group 3 suggests that in 1960, sons and daughters of higher professional fathers must have been coming off the educational assembly line at the rate of seventeen or eighteen thousand a year. Potentially, this class could thus supply a high proportion of men and a superabundance of women.

However, the children of fathers in occupational classes 1B (Lower professions), 3 (Clerks) and 4 (Foremen) and in the lower divisions of class 2 (Managers and proprietors) are in one respect in an even more favourable position: parents' incomes here would not be so high as to disentitle them to

---

[1] The Social Survey investigation reported in *Social Mobility in Britain*, ed. D. V. Glass, *op. cit.*, p. 183.

[2] Our estimate for the growth in the number of men in the class between 1951 and 1960 was 2·1 per cent compound per year, while in 1960 we estimated there were 480,000 men in the class. *The Registrar General's Decennial Supplement, England and Wales, 1951*, showed a death rate of 0·66 per cent per year in the age-group 20–64 for men in socio-economic group 3 (Higher administrative, professional and managerial), while about 1·16 per cent would turn 65 and (in the main) retire (*Occupational Mortality*, part II, vol. 2, *loc. cit.*).

public grants, so that their higher education would not involve their parents in much financial sacrifice. At the same time, their home environment is not unfavourable to social and educational advancement.

The relative shortage of certain professional workers is now due rather to limitations of the educational system than to a shortage of boys and girls with the basic education and financial resources to undertake the required training.

2. THE DRIVING FORCE OF COMPETITION

Theories at the level of abstraction of those outlined above can never be subjected to really satisfactory empirical tests. All we can do is to see whether the broad pattern of changes in pay structure suggests that the supply and demand forces to which the theories have given emphasis seem to be the *major* factors in the changing pattern of incomes. The examples given below strongly suggest that some of the big movements in relative pay do *not* seem to have been due at least to the obvious pattern of the forces of supply and demand; and that there have been big obvious movements in supply and demand which have not in fact been reflected in the expected changes in relative pay. We shall later suggest that other factors, sometimes conflicting with supply and demand forces, are the more important determinants.

We shall not explore the break-down of the supposed supply-demand mechanism that is implied by the existence of involuntary unemployment[1], but shall confine ourselves to a consideration of the circumstances surrounding changes, or failures to change, in the relative pay of various classes or occupations.

The average pay of men in occupational class 7 (Unskilled manual workers) was, in 1924, a little more than double the average for 1914, while that for skilled men had risen by 80 per cent. By 1935, the relative position of these two classes had almost been restored, but between 1935 and 1955, unskilled men again drew ahead. Their average in 1955 was 337 per cent of that for 1935, while for skilled men the 1955 average was only 319 per cent of the 1935 figure.

Over the following five years, 1955 to 1960, the trend was again in favour of skilled workers, whose increase we estimated at 28 per cent, compared with 23 per cent for the unskilled.

The net result was a skilled average in 1960 equal to 800 per cent of that of 1914; an unskilled average equal to 850 per cent of that of 1914.

Can these changes be explained in terms of changing demand and supply schedules? The absolute numbers of skilled workers in each census year show an extraordinary constancy, while the absolute numbers of unskilled workers

---

[1]This, of course, was one of the major themes of Keynes's *The General Theory of Employment, Interest and Money* (London, Macmillan, 1936).

fluctuate, rising between 1911 and 1931, then falling by 13 per cent between 1931 and 1951 (table 2).

We know that in 1916, 1917 and 1918, unemployment was below one per cent of the insured population.   This may conceivably have placed unskilled men in a more favourable bargaining position than skilled men (though this seems unlikely), but both before the war and in the economic collapse that followed the post-war boom, we have estimated that unemployment was considerably higher amongst the semi-skilled and unskilled than amongst the skilled[1].

In particular, the Ministry of Labour investigations of 1923 and 1924 showed a much lower rate of unemployment amongst the apprenticed (approximating to occupational class 5) and the trained (approximating to occupational class 6) than amongst the untrained (occupational class 7).   The apprenticed constituted 21 per cent of the unemployed and (including foremen) 42 per cent of the manual work force, while the unskilled constituted 20 per cent of the manual work force and 40 per cent of the unemployed.   With an overall rate of unemployment of 10 per cent, this would mean that the rate of unemployment was 5 per cent amongst the skilled and 20 per cent amongst the unskilled.   Thus the differential increase for the unskilled is the reverse of what demand-supply relations would suggest.

There is a similar contradiction between demand and supply theory and the relative changes in the period including the second world war.   We estimated that in 1955, the unskilled men's average was 337 per cent of their average in 1935, compared with 319 per cent for the skilled men (table 47). Yet by 1940, when the major narrowing had taken place, there was still substantial unemployment amongst unskilled workers[2].   Even in 1951, when overall unemployment, according to the population census, was down to 2·2 per cent, for unskilled workers it was 5·1 per cent.

Movements in the relative pay of manual and non-manual workers have also contradicted the prognostications of the theory of demand and supply.   Between 1935 and 1955, there were substantial relative reductions for all the non-manual classes except managers (table 48), with the greatest reduction between 1935 and 1940.   This was brought about by a high degree of stability in non-manual pay, juxtaposed with large increases in pay for manual workers, which were paid in the face of heavy unemployment of manual workers[3].

In table 56, we assembled data about the state of demand and supply in respect of various occupations in the years 1958, 1959 and 1960.   This shows great variation between occupations, which demand and supply theory postulates should be equalized by changes in relative pay, yet there was little correlation between excess demand or supply, on the one hand, and pay on the other.

---

[1]See p. 118 *supra*.
[2]See p. 127 *supra*.
[3]See above pp. 126 and 127.

This lack of correlation is illustrated by the following:

Occupation	Unfilled vacancies per	Pay in 1960
Men	unemployed worker, 1958/60	as % of 1955
Bricklayers	2·4	*133*
Engineering fitters	1·2	*128*
Bus drivers ⎫	8·5	⎧ *115*
Bus conductors ⎭		⎩ *122*
Shop-assistants	0·6	*125*
Unskilled workers	0·1	*123*
Women		
Clerks	0·4	*135*
Waitresses	0·8	*115*
Shop-assistants	0·6	*124*

One may cite two occupations in which there was a consistent and exceptionally high degree of excess demand: tool setters, setter-operators, with an average of 877 unemployed for 3,459 vacancies (that is, four vacancies for each applicant) and shorthand typists, with 1,523 unemployed for 4,104 vacancies (2·7 vacancies for each applicant). Far from increases in pay moving the demand for and supply of tool setters towards equilibrium, the state of disequilibrium had become more pronounced by 1960 when (averaging the figures for June and December) there were 463 applicants for 5,679 vacancies (more than twelve vacancies per applicant). We can watch the progress of their pay, relative to that of other engineering workers, from the earnings inquiries of the Engineering and Allied Employers' National Federation. Between September 1954 and June 1960, the earnings of this grade (designated skilled turners and machinemen) rose 46·9 per cent for time-work and 49·4 per cent for payment by results. In the same period, fitters' earnings rose by 43·3 and 45·8 per cent respectively. But even this slight lead fluctuated: fitters made up some lost ground between 1958 and 1959, then lost it again between 1959 and 1960. Thus the very great excess demand for tool setters, setter-operators, compared with the very modest excess demand for fitters, is reflected in an irregularly dispersed increase of a little more than half of a percentage point per year.

The Ministry of Labour's analysis of unemployment and unfilled vacancies has shown an excess supply of women clerks, book-keepers and cashiers (for 1958-60, an average of 12,656 unemployed for 7,678 vacancies) and an excess demand for shorthand typists and typists. But this overall shortage has been concentrated in the London and south-eastern region.

The Institute of Office Management distinguished typists from other clerks in their report for 1960. In Grades C, D and E, in London, median pay for typists was between 8 and 15 per cent more than that for female clerks. In north-western England, the range was between 0 and 10 per cent; in the south-east Lancashire conurbation, minus 6 to 4 per cent[1].

[1]The Civil Service between 1957 and 1960 maintained the relativities between female clerical officers, clerical assistants and shorthand typists Grade I (100 w.p.m. shorthand and 40 w.p.m. typing) and tackled the typist problem by shuttling typing between London and Brighton and providing clerical officers with typewriters.

These are two cases in which there has been acute excess demand. Earnings have risen, but not in such a way as to reduce demand and increase supply so as to bring the two into equilibrium. In general, the labour market does not operate in the way conceived by the theory of demand and supply; the price of labour may rise in face of high unemployment; it may rise at similar pace for occupations showing contrasting demand-supply relationships, or at different rates for occupations showing similar demand-supply relationships.

3. AN EXPLANATORY HYPOTHESIS

The outstanding characteristic of the national pay structure is the rigidity of its relationships. Adam Smith remarked upon this nearly two hundred years ago[1]. He noticed that, though the price of provisions fluctuated, nominal wages did not, so that, if workers could subsist when prices were high, they were well off when they were low. Secondly, he noted the persistence of regional differences. Wages might be 25 per cent higher in a great town than in the surrounding countryside, though the price of necessities in the town was no higher and was frequently lower:

'Such a difference of prices, which it seems is not always sufficient to transport a man from one parish to another, would necessarily occasion so great a transportation of the most bulky commodities, not only from one parish to another, but from one end of the kingdom, almost from one end of the world to the other, as would soon reduce them more nearly to a level. After all that has been said of the levity and inconstancy of human nature, it appears evidently from experience that a man is of all sorts of luggage the most difficult to be transported'.

On the side of occupational distribution, change has been markedly sluggish: the number of skilled and semi-skilled manual workers has hardly changed; the number of unskilled workers has fluctuated, but in 1951 was little different from the number in 1921; the *proportion* of employers and managers has hardly varied, while that of professional workers has moved through only a few percentage points.

In employee income distribution, we noted in table 24.3 that there had been a narrowing in dispersion for males between 1911 and 1958, but that this had been partly offset by a widened dispersion for females, so that the combined change was surprisingly small, except for the region of the highest decile and above.

For manual workers in manufacturing and building, we noted moderate changes in 1960 as compared with 1938 and 1906 (tables 27 and 28). However, when earnings distribution was standardized for changes in occupational class distribution (table 46), we found that, on average, the relative positions

---

[1] *The Wealth of Nations* (Everyman ed.), *op. cit.*, vol. 1, pp. 66-7.

of the class medians for men in manufacturing industry were little different in 1960 from what they had been in 1906.

This is not to say that relationships between class averages and between various occupations do not fluctuate: they do. But they seem to have the capacity to regain previous shapes, sometimes after lapses of many years. Thus class relations were similar in 1935 to those of 1913, and, as between managers, foremen, skilled, semi-skilled and unskilled manual workers, the structure was not much different in 1960 from what it had been in 1913. Coal-miners and agricultural workers suffered relative declines after the first world war, but regained their previous position after the second. The relative pay of railwaymen and Civil Servants was allowed to deteriorate during and after the second world war and was then restored by drastic upward revisions in the middle or late 1950's.

It is not perhaps very surprising that those who share a common occupation should be dedicated to the maintenance of its status relative to other occupations; the misteries of the Middle Ages were so engaged, as are the trade unions and professional bodies of the present day. St Thomas Aquinas justified this phenomenon in the thirteenth century in a system of thought that was further developed by subsequent scholastic thinkers[1]. The test of justice was whether or not income was adequate to maintain the recipient in his due social status:

'The things that can be said without reservation to be necessary to a state of life are those without which a man would be forced to lower his status. He might have to change from living as a nobleman to practising a trade, or to make a notable cut in his domestic staff, in the liberality of his entertainment, or in his sons' education or his provision for them. The goods necessary to a state of life include provision for contingencies such as sickness. All these things also contribute to the decency of a state in life, and can be provided for according to custom, and within the limits of an honourable liberality. And in so far as a man's current status is inferior, he can also count as one of the requirements of decency the ac-quisition of the goods he needs for a moderate rise in status'[2].

Elliott Jaques, using psycho-analytic techniques, identified in workers what he regarded as an intuitive knowledge of what their pay ought to be, having regard to the work that they were doing.

'Payment at the equitable level is intuitively experienced as fair relative to others...Deviations in payment below the equitable level are accompanied by feelings of dissatisfaction which become stronger the greater is the deviation...

'Deviations above the equitable are level... accompanied by feelings of

[1]See 'The Scholastic Theory of the Just Wage', Appendix to Michael Fogarty, *The Just Wage* (London, Chapman, 1961).
[2] A. Lehmkuhl, *Theologia Moralis*, 5th ed. (Freiburg i. Breisgau, Herder, 1888), I.362: quoted by Fogarty, *op. cit.*, p. 269.

being *relatively* well off as compared with others; at the 10 to 15 per cent level of deviation there is a strong sense of receiving preferential treatment, which may harden into bravado, with underlying feelings of unease about how long the relatively advantageous position can be maintained'[1].

We can accept the existence of this intuitive knowledge (or something answering to that description) without accepting Dr Jaques's ascription of it to a single variable—the 'time span of discretion'. In practice, workers seize on to scraps of information pertaining to the pay of others in their occupation and in other occupations of similar status, the Ministry of Labour conducts an elaborate service for publicizing pay rates, levels of earnings and their rate of change and the collection and interpretation of such data is a major pre-occupation of trade unions and professional organizations, large firms belong to networks for the exchange of information, the Civil Service has its Pay Research Unit and at employment exchanges there is readily available information relating to a multitude of vacancies and their rates of pay.

It then becomes extraordinarily difficult to gain anything more than a temporary relative improvement in the pay of any occupation. In the words of Lady (then Professor) Wootton,

'Change—always, everywhere—requires justification: the strength of conservatism is that it is held to justify itself. It is not therefore surprising that the maintenance of standards, absolute or comparative, should be woven as warp and woof into the texture of wage discussions; or, to change the metaphor, that history should be summoned to fill the void when moral actions must be performed without moral principles to guide them.

'This lack of guiding principle affects, moreover, equally those who pay and those who receive wages. Conservatism does duty on both sides. On the one side, the unions, as we have seen, appeal to precedent, and defend their proposals as necessary to restore the *status quo*—if not literally *ante bellum*, at least before some selected date-line; whilst employers, on the other hand, take their stand on the simple rule of "no change". The dispute between them turns, not so much on the choice of the direction in which to move, as on rival interpretations of what is meant by standing still'[2].

There is something elemental in this attachment of a person to his level of income, measured in terms of its purchasing power (the maintenance of a standard of living) and in terms of the earnings of other occupations, that is not unlike the attachment of an animal to its young. It applies to the individual and leads individuals to act in concert with or without trade union organization; a sense that their work has been devalued can turn a disciplined work force

---

[1]'An Objective Approach to Pay Differentials', *The New Scientist*, vol. 4, no. 85, 3 July 1958, p. 313. See also Elliott Jaques, *Measurement of Responsibility* (London, Tavistock Publications, 1956).

[2]Barbara Wootton, *The Social Foundations of Wage Policy* (London, Allen and Unwin, 1954), p. 162.

into a surly, disgruntled mob.   In the phrase of Adam Smith, they are 'desperate men'.

And there is justification for this frame of mind, for the devaluation of a man's labour, through no fault of his own, is a form of confiscation of property.

The *status quo* is constantly being disturbed, however, by trade unions or professional associations getting better terms for the occupations they represent or by employers unilaterally or by individual bargaining raising the pay of all or some of the occupations or individuals they employ.   This is a never-ending process, though the speed at which it operates may show great variation from time to time, and, since there are always some occupations whose members feel aggrieved or that they deserve upgrading in the pay structure, it is unlikely that equilibrium can ever be attained.   So the process draws its energy from an endless stock of hope and envy, of which trade unionism is in part an expression. But trade unionism is only the outward expression of a general tendency for people with common interests to ally themselves for their mutual advancement. In non-union shops or unorganized sectors, discontent will show itself if they are left behind; and if rising activity is at the same time increasing profits and the need of the employer for his workers, he will have to raise his rates as well, simply to keep his workers happy.

Thus it would be quite mistaken to regard the pay structure as unchanging: it is in an almost constant state of change.   It is by its nature incapable of reaching a state of rest, because it is made up of a multitude of units (that is, units for purposes of determining rates of pay) who have different ideas as to what their relationships to one another should be.   Group A may claim parity with group B, which may claim a differential of x per cent over group A.   Both groups cannot then be at rest at the same time[1].

From chapter III, we can describe the circumstances in which major changes in pay structure are brought about.   There were three periods between 1913 and 1960 when this occurred, in the form of a general narrowing of differentials: 1914 to 1920, 1934 to 1944 (in particular, 1938 to 1940) and 1951 to 1955. Between 1920 and 1924, there was a drastic widening of differentials so that, by the latter year, the pre-war position had generally been regained.   After 1955, there was again a reversal of the narrowing process.

The common characteristic of the periods of narrowing differentials is their high rate of inflation.   For the period 1914 to 1920, the average annual rise in the cost of living index was nearly 17 per cent; for 1935 to 1942, 6·2 per cent;

---

[1]This was the case in recent disputes about the salaries of Civil Service clerical officers, on the one hand, and postal and telegraph officers on the other, though the model is not often as simple as this.   More generally, it happens with Civil Service rates, which by an elaborate process are made to follow rates outside the Civil Service and are thus regarded as a good indicator of what outside rates are doing when these outside rates are themselves revised.

for 1950 to 1955, 5·1 per cent. In the periods 1944 to 1950 and 1956 to 1960, when dispersion was stable or widening, the rise in prices was more moderate: 3·7 per cent and 2·7 per cent per year, respectively.

What is the connexion between rapidly rising prices and reduced differentials? Sometimes it is felt that the change is temporary and that, pending a general reassessment that must be postponed until a new period of stability is reached, lower-paid workers should be compensated in whole or in part so that they may avoid real hardship. This, at any rate, was the basis of cost of living bonuses in the public service in the two wars, when the degree of compensation for price rises diminished as the income range was ascended.

Another cause is the frequency of claims for flat-rate rather than percentage increases during periods of rapidly rising prices; and even when the increase is in percentage form, it is generally a percentage of the standard rate so that it forms a lower percentage for those whose rates are above the standard. In periods of rapid change, with social relationships under strain, flat-rate claims are made because they express and generate a sense of solidarity between occupations at different levels in the same union or federation of unions. The employers are offered a package deal: the proportions of skilled and unskilled labour are fixed by technique or custom and, though they could buy their unskilled labour more cheaply, they are prevented from doing so by the fact that the craftsmen stipulate not only their own rate, but that for their helpers.

For the reductions in differentials between manual and non-manual workers, the greater stability of salaries appears to be the immediate cause. We noted in chapter III that their rise began later and moved more slowly between 1914 and 1920 and that, when wages tumbled in 1921 and 1922, salaries remained almost unscathed. Part of this greater stability may stem from the difference in social relationships between non-manual workers and their employers, part from the greater stability of their employment (for revisions of pay tend to be delayed until new appointments are made) and part from the fact that they are frequently on incremental scales so that inflation is mitigated by the annual rise.

From the contrasting pay history of the years 1921 to 1923 and 1924 to 1934, we may deduce some of the conditions necessary for a reduction in wage rates. The reductions of 1921 and 1922 were achieved in a period in which retail prices were halved and unemployment reached 23 per cent and did not fall below 12 per cent. More than half the reductions in 1921 and nearly 40 per cent of those in 1922 were brought about 'automatically' in terms of cost of living sliding scale agreements, but even so, there was great industrial unrest and the loss, through strikes, of more than a hundred million man-days[1].

Between 1924 and 1934, we have noted an almost equal fall in retail prices and rise in unemployment, but these were accompanied by a fall in wage rates

[1]See chapter III, p. 115.

of only 6 per cent, compared with 38 per cent in 1921 and 1922. For the 'ratchet effect' to be overcome, then, it is not enough for a price fall and unemployment to be substantial: they must be both drastic and sudden.

What is the role of the trade unions in the process of change? There has been considerable controversy on this subject, some writers conceding them great power to reshape pay structure, others an ability merely to rubber-stamp what would have happened anyway[1]. To some extent, this controversy has been caused by a misconception, by the notion that pay structure is static instead of in a constant state of movement. As with Alice, it is sometimes necessary to run faster and faster to stay in the same place; the object of the race is not to win, for it is one without an end, but to get closer to those ahead or farther away from those behind; the unions then act as agents for hurrying things along.

In the race, transient advantages may be of considerable importance to the parties concerned, and may give groups of workers advantages that are obscured in long-term comparisons[2]. Their neglect by those theorists who stress the self-defeating nature of wage increases is one reason why their arguments fail to get across. An increase in pay may give real and immediate relief to those who get it, even though in due course it will work its way round to retail prices and they will be no better off than they were before.

It is possible that trade unions may be responsible for the upward movement of money wage rates in the face of high unemployment at the upward turn in the trade cycle. Why do employers raise rates when there are still large numbers of unemployed workers who would be delighted to take employment at prevailing rates? Part of the reason may be found in the relationship of the employer to his workers: profits are rising, orders accumulating, the losses of the depression are being recouped. But his employees have also suffered in the depression and feel they have a right to some share in the new prosperity. The avoidance of ill-feeling might in itself be sufficient reason for granting increases, but the existence of a union that might close the factory at this crucial moment, when customers have alternative sources of supply, is likely to hasten and augment the share-out.

The proximity of foremen and managers to the manual workers whom they control may explain their immunity from the sort of reductions, relative to manual pay, from which professional workers have suffered. An increase for manual workers necessitates one for foremen, which sends the impulse up

[1]See, for example, A. M. Ross, *Trade Union Wage Policy* (Berkeley and Los Angeles, University of California Press, 1948); Paul H. Douglas, *Real Wages in the United States, 1890–1926* (Boston, Houghton Mifflin, 1930); R. Ozanne, 'Impact of Unions on Wage Levels and Income Distribution', *Quarterly Journal of Economics*, vol. 73, no. 2, May 1959, p. 177; J. E. Maher, 'Union, Non-union Wage Differentials', *American Economic Review*, vol. 46, no. 3, June 1956, p. 338.

[2]See D. Robinson, 'Wage Differentials over Time', *Bulletin of the Oxford University Institute of Statistics*, vol. 23, no. 4, November 1961, p. 367.

the hierarchy. Managers have a second source of increase: if profits rise, the pay of directors and general managers will tend to follow and this movement will tend to be transmitted downward.

It is a mistake to imagine that there is a sharp division between unionized and un-unionized workers, for trade unions cannot do much more than institutionalize and direct drives and aspirations that are already present in the individual workers. Unions protect individual workers against arbitrary acts; they give collections of workers more control over their own destiny than they would have as individuals and present the possibility of pursuing social ends that might not otherwise be attainable. It is in pursuit of such ends that unions set about reducing differentials by extracting flat-rate increases from employers for different levels of skill. It does not follow that they always succeed in changing established patterns. For example, we may watch the movement of negotiated increases and earnings in the engineering industry when, between 1934 and 1940, flat-rate increases were claimed and conceded regardless of skill[1]:

	Changes in standard hourly rate	Change in hourly earnings		
		Skilled	Semi-skilled	Unskilled
	Pence	Pence	Pence	Pence
October 1934—October 1935	0·50	0·81	0·76	0·65
October 1935—October 1936	0·50	0·94	1·02	0·58
October 1936—October 1937	0·625	1·16	0·86	0·84
October 1937—July 1938	0·375	0·58	0·43	0·36
July 1938—October 1939	0·50	2·17	1·41	1·08
October 1939—July 1940	1·25	3·51	3·02	2·11

Notes: Time-workers and payment by results workers combined. Skilled includes skilled fitters (not toolroom), turners, machinemen rated at or above fitters' rate, platers, riveters and caulkers, moulders, sheet metal-workers. Semi-skilled: machinemen rated below fitters' rate. Unskilled: labourers.

Although, between October 1934 and July 1940, standard hourly rates for all classes had risen by 2·75*d.*, hourly earnings for skilled workers had increased by 9·17*d.*, for the semi-skilled by 7·50*d.* and for the unskilled by 5·62*d.* It was union policy to extract the same increases for all and, *ipso facto*, to narrow differentials, but resistances were such that the end result was a stalemate, with unskilled hourly earnings 66·0 per cent of skilled in October 1934 and 64·4 per cent in July 1940.

By June 1959, the differential in standard rates had narrowed still further: the labourer's rate was 84·25 per cent of the fitter's. But the hourly earnings differential for time-work was almost identical: the labourer 73·7 per cent of

[1]See *Proceedings at a Special Conference between the Engineering and Allied Employers' National Federation, the Amalgamated Engineering Union, the National Union of Foundry Workers and the Engineering Joint Trades Movement, London, 5th November 1940: Wages and Working Conditions* (London, 1940).

the fitter in July 1940 and 73·6 per cent in June 1959[1]. Both fitters and labourers had developed an earnings gap[2], but while this was 11·8 per cent for labourers in June 1959, it was 18·6 per cent for fitters.

Of course, the above is only an hypothesis; but it appears to make the facts intelligible, whereas demand and supply theory does not. It suggests that attempts to formulate a national pay policy or to manipulate pay structure are misconceived if they are based on a belief in the effectiveness of price in the regulation of supply and demand. Bishops, judges and cabinet ministers have had their real pay drastically reduced in the last fifty years, yet there is still no shortage of candidates for those positions; the substantial increases paid in recent years to Civil Servants, police and railwaymen to restore their place in the pay hierarchy are a demonstration of the fact that these services could continue for a considerable time with levels of pay inferior to those of comparable workers elsewhere.

Pay structure cannot easily be varied by design nor undermanned industries manned up by a simple increase in pay, for if one class of workers is advanced beyond their conventional position, forces will be generated that in due course will be likely to restore the former position. It seems that it is easier, on the whole, to correct great inequalities in pay by more extensive education, by training people for higher jobs rather than raising the pay for the lower ones, and by the improvement of non-pecuniary conditions, including job security and holidays.

A change in pay structure, to have lasting effect, would require careful preparation, much public education, support of trade unions and employers, and consent of those to whom it was to apply.

[1]Note that the previous calculation related labourers to the average for all skilled men, while this one relates them to fitters only.
[2]The difference between standard rates and earnings.

OCCUPATIONAL COMPOSITION OF THE OCCUPATIONAL CLASSES

For a complete list of occupations in each occupational class reference must be made to the *Census 1951: Classification of Occupations*[1]. From the 'Alphabetical index of occupational terms' contained in that volume, the classification of any of a great multitude of occupations can be found[2]. The classification also shows the Registrar General's allocation of the occupations to five social classes and it is on this, in general, that our allocation to occupational classes has been based. But social classes II and III have been further subdivided in the present study, so that the line-up is as follows:

Description	Social class	Occupational class
Higher professional	I	1A
Lower professional	II	1B
Employers and proprietors	II	2A
Managers and administrators	II	2B
Clerical workers	III	3
Foremen, supervisors, inspectors	III	4
Manual		
Skilled	III	5
Semi-skilled	IV	6
Unskilled	V	7

The rules are simply applied: a professional worker allocated in the Census to social class I goes to our occupational class 1A; one in social class II goes to occupational class 1B. All employers and proprietors[3] have been put in occupational class 2A, except those following one of the professions of occupational class 1A or 1B to which *all* professionals, of whatever industrial status, have been allocated. Likewise, all managers and administrators go to occupational class 2B, all clerical workers to class 3, all foremen and supervisors to class 4.

Manual workers in social class III go to occupational class 5, those in social class IV to occupational class 6, those in social class V to occupational class 7. There are some exceptions to these rules, however, and in the list that follows these have been indicated by placing the social class number in brackets after the relevant occupation.

---

[1]H.M. Stationery Office, 1956.

[2]Brief job descriptions are given in *A Dictionary of Occupational Terms*, Ministry of Labour (H.M. Stationery Office, 1927).

[3]Here defined as a self-employed person whose employment requires the use of sufficient capital to make entry to the employment difficult, for example a self-employed shopkeeper is allocated to occupational class 2A; a self-employed window-cleaner is not.

The list that follows is not exhaustive but shows the general scope of each class, those occupations whose allocation might otherwise be in doubt and those whose occupational class and social class do not line up in the way described above.

Occupational class 1A (Higher professions)

Accountants (professional)
Architects and town planners
Authors, editors, journalists
Clergy, priests, nuns
Engineers (professional)

Lawyers, judges, stipendiary magistrates
Medical and dental practitioners
Officers in the armed forces
Scientists

Occupational class 1B (Lower professions)

Actors (III)
Aircrew (III)
Artists
Draughtsmen
Engineering officers and electricians on board ship
Librarians
Medical auxiliaries, including chiropodists (III), opticians and physiotherapists

Musicians (III)
Navigating officers and pilots
Nurses, including assistant (III), student (III) and nursery (III) nurses
Officials of associations
Pharmacists
Sportsmen (professional) (III)
Teachers, including university teachers

Occupational class 2A (Employers and proprietors)

All employers except those in the professions (Occupational classes 1A and 1B)
Proprietors, as defined above
Farmers
Restaurant, boarding-house, hotel and public house proprietors
Retail and wholesale traders
Road transport proprietors

Occupational class 2B (Administrators and managers)

Managers and administrators in mining, manufacturing, trade, transport, finance, and public administration, including the following:

Auctioneers, estate agents, appraisers, valuers
Bankers, inspectors (I)
Bus and tram managers (I)
Civil Service administrative and other higher officers (I)
Civil Service and local government executive and higher clerical officers
Clerks of works
Company directors (business not specified) (I)

Government officials n.e.s. (not clerks) (III)
Inspectors and superintendents in gas, water and electricity distribution (III)
Insurance managers, underwriters (I)
Police inspectors, superintendents, chief constables
Railway officials
Secretaries and registrars of companies, institutions and charities
Shipbrokers, agents, managers (I)
Stockbrokers (I)

Occupational class 3 (Clerical workers)

Clerks n.e.s.
Costing, estimating and accounting clerks, including book-keepers (II)

Insurance agents and canvassers
Office machine operators
Typists and shorthand typists

Occupational class 4 (Foremen, supervisors, inspectors)

All foremen, supervisors and inspectors, including the following:

Farm bailiffs
Haulage and cartage contractors, master carmen (employees)

Inspectors, viewers, testers
Overmen, coalmining

Occupational class 5 (Skilled manual workers)
All craftsmen and skilled process workers in social class III, as well as the following:

Fire brigade officers and men
Hairdressers
Photographers
Police, other ranks
Radio operators

Railway transport: engine drivers, guards, signalmen, pointsmen and level crossing men
Sea transport: petty officers, seamen and deckhands; pursers, stewards and domestic staff
Warehousemen
Stationary engine drivers

Occupational class 6 (Semi-skilled manual workers)
Semi-skilled process workers in social class IV, as well as the following:

Agricultural workers
Armed forces, other ranks (III)
Conductors, bus and tram
Domestic servants, including chefs (III) and kitchen hands (V)
Drivers of self-propelled passenger and goods vehicles (III)
Laundry workers
Machine minders

Packers
Postmen and sorters (III)
Railway engine firemen, running-shed workers, ticket collectors
Salesmen, shop-assistants (III)
Storekeepers (III)
Telephone and telegraph operators (III)
Waiters (III)

Occupational class 7 (Unskilled manual workers)
Boiler firemen and stokers (IV)
Builders' labourers and navvies
Charwomen, office cleaners
Door-keepers (IV)

Labourers and other unskilled workers n.e.s.
Porters
Watchmen

(Figures in brackets denote the Registrar General's social class where this does not align with the occupational class as suggested in the rules stated above.)

APPENDIX B

OCCUPATIONAL GROUPS BY INDUSTRY, ENGLAND AND WALES, 1951

Order	Industry		1A	1B	Occupational class 2	3	4	5	6	7	Total
I	Agriculture, forestry, fishing	M	239	708	256,984	2,094	17,496	73,384	510,507	1,943	863,355
		%	0·03	0·08	29·77	0·24	2·03	8·50	59·13	0·23	100
		F	44	123	18,585	4,849	167	492	75,310	375	99,945
		%	0·04	0·12	18·60	4·85	0·17	0·49	75·35	0·38	100
		Total	283	831	275,569	6,943	17,663	73,876	585,817	2,318	963,300
		%	0·03	0·09	28·61	0·72	1·83	7·67	60·81	0·24	100
II	Mining and quarrying	M	4,791	2,609	6,671	15,744	42,183	295,278	353,308	14,684	735,268
		%	0·65	0·35	0·91	2·14	5·74	40·16	48·05	2·00	100
		F	45	320	118	7,659	18	95	2,775	1,118	12,148
		%	0·37	2·63	0·97	63·05	0·15	0·78	22·84	9·20	100
		Total	4,836	2,929	6,789	23,403	42,201	295,373	356,083	15,802	747,416
		%	0·65	0·39	0·91	3·13	5·65	39·52	47·64	2·11	100
III	Treatment of non-metalliferous mining products other than coal	M	1,447	3,437	11,296	8,309	7,831	77,956	42,807	68,019	221,102
		%	0·65	1·55	5·11	3·76	3·54	35·26	19·36	30·76	100
		F	39	500	511	11,386	822	32,623	13,739	10,829	70,449
		%	0·06	0·71	0·73	16·16	1·17	46·31	19·50	15·37	100
		Total	1,486	3,937	11,807	19,695	8,653	110,579	56,546	78,848	291,551
		%	0·51	1·35	4·05	6·76	2·97	37·93	19·39	27·04	100
IV	Chemicals and allied trades	M	14,385	14,577	26,628	22,620	12,879	58,121	70,249	70,773	290,232
		%	4·96	5·02	9·17	7·79	4·44	20·03	24·20	24·38	100
		F	805	5,121	1,268	40,960	1,333	2,722	36,896	17,473	106,578
		%	0·76	4·80	1·19	38·43	1·25	2·55	34·62	16·39	100
		Total	15,190	19,698	27,896	63,580	14,212	60,843	107,145	88,246	396,810
		%	3·83	4·96	7·03	16·02	3·58	15·33	27·00	22·24	100
V	Metal manufacture	M	6,080	7,798	13,547	22,549	23,942	188,223	82,491	105,900	450,530
		%	1·35	1·73	3·01	5·00	5·31	41·78	18·31	23·51	100
		F	171	1,628	350	22,418	3,291	7,038	11,686	10,258	56,840
		%	0·30	2·86	0·62	39·44	5·79	12·38	20·56	18·05	100
		Total	6,251	9,426	13,897	44,967	27,233	195,261	94,177	116,158	507,370
		%	1·23	1·86	2·74	8·86	5·37	38·48	18·56	22·89	100

Order	Industry		1A	1B	2	3	4	5	6	7	Total
							Occupational class				
VI	Engineering, shipbuilding and electrical goods	M	25,114	54,934	62,382	69,207	77,290	604,290	191,413	155,016	1,239,646
		%	2·03	4·43	5·03	5·58	6·23	48·75	15·44	12·50	100
		F	425	7,797	2,229	108,522	24,185	39,125	105,290	35,730	323,303
		%	0·13	2·41	0·69	33·57	7·48	12·10	32·57	11·05	100
		Total	25,539	62,731	64,611	177,729	101,475	643,415	296,703	190,746	1,562,949
		%	1·63	4·01	4·13	11·37	6·49	41·17	18·98	12·20	100
VII	Vehicles	M	7,892	20,374	41,893	38,722	50,223	428,199	122,810	89,844	799,957
		%	0·99	2·55	5·24	4·84	6·28	53·53	15·35	11·23	100
		F	197	2,546	1,852	51,896	6,434	9,498	31,662	12,711	116,796
		%	0·17	2·18	1·59	44·43	5·51	8·13	27·11	10·88	100
		Total	8,089	22,920	43,745	90,618	56,657	437,697	154,472	102,555	916,753
		%	0·88	2·50	4·77	9·88	6·18	47·74	16·85	11·19	100
VIII	Metal goods not elsewhere specified	M	1,751	1,228	20,343	11,854	15,915	145,583	53,167	41,405	291,246
		%	0·60	0·42	6·98	4·07	5·46	49·99	18·26	14·22	100
		F	34	900	1,093	26,384	7,285	18,375	73,455	22,317	149,843
		%	0·02	0·60	0·73	17·61	4·86	12·26	49·02	14·89	100
		Total	1,785	2,128	21,436	38,238	23,200	163,958	126,622	63,722	441,089
		%	0·40	0·48	4·86	8·67	5·26	37·17	28·71	14·45	100
IX	Precision instruments, jewellery, etc.	M	1,255	2,724	7,896	4,110	4,820	61,081	10,445	5,626	97,957
		%	1·28	2·78	8·06	4·20	4·92	62·35	10·66	5·74	100
		F	61	605	599	11,513	2,027	13,775	11,197	4,801	44,578
		%	0·14	1·35	1·34	25·83	4·54	30·90	25·12	10·77	100
		Total	1,316	3,329	8,495	15,623	6,847	74,856	21,642	10,427	142,535
		%	0·92	2·34	5·96	10·96	4·80	52·52	15·18	7·32	100
X	Textiles	M	2,781	4,112	26,111	15,717	22,736	155,961	95,110	70,589	393,117
		%	0·71	1·05	6·64	4·00	5·78	39·67	24·19	17·96	100
		F	107	2,548	1,798	28,892	3,893	282,152	106,097	49,087	474,574
		%	0·02	0·54	0·38	6·09	0·82	59·45	22·36	10·34	100
		Total	2,888	6,660	27,909	44,609	26,629	438,113	201,207	119,676	867,691
		%	0·33	0·77	3·22	5·14	3·07	50·49	23·19	13·79	100
XI	Leather, leather goods and fur	M	267	263	4,561	1,293	1,829	29,646	2,008	6,876	46,743
		%	0·57	0·56	9·76	2·77	3·91	63·42	4·30	14·71	100
		F	12	94	412	3,093	245	18,382	1,239	2,315	25,792
		%	0·05	0·36	1·60	11·99	0·95	71·27	4·80	8·98	100
		Total	279	357	4,973	4,386	2,074	48,028	3,247	9,191	72,535
		%	0·38	0·49	6·86	6·05	2·86	66·21	4·48	12·67	100

Order	Industry		1A	1B	2	3	4	5	6	7	Total
						Occupational class					
XII	Clothing	M	281	590	24,418	7,001	6,577	119,722	56,639	9,697	224,925
		%	0·12	0·26	10·86	3·11	2·92	53·23	25·18	4·31	100
		F	19	543	4,774	25,241	7,078	126,889	267,182	16,550	448,276
		%	0·00	0·12	1·06	5·63	1·58	28·31	59·60	3·69	100
		Total	300	1,133	29,192	32,242	13,655	246,611	323,821	26,247	673,201
		%	0·04	0·17	4·34	4·79	2·03	36·63	48·10	3·90	100
XIII	Food, drink and tobacco	M	3,191	2,218	41,868	26,497	18,389	127,060	96,749	90,886	406,858
		%	0·78	0·55	10·29	6·51	4·52	31·23	23·78	22·34	100
		F	427	2,453	2,925	43,017	3,095	40,582	102,099	44,058	238,656
		%	0·18	1·03	1·23	18·02	1·30	17·00	42·78	18·46	100
		Total	3,618	4,671	44,793	69,514	21,484	167,642	198,848	134,944	645,514
		%	0·56	0·72	6·94	10·77	3·33	25·97	30·80	20·90	100
XIV	Manufactures of wood and cork	M	365	1,718	13,504	5,779	8,138	159,468	17,594	32,599	239,165
		%	0·15	0·72	5·65	2·42	3·40	66·68	7·36	13·63	100
		F	6	248	763	10,339	504	22,382	7,539	5,516	47,297
		%	0·01	0·52	1·61	21·86	1·07	47·32	15·94	11·66	100
		Total	371	1,966	14,267	16,118	8,642	181,850	25,133	38,115	286,462
		%	0·13	0·69	4·98	5·63	3·02	63·48	8·77	13·31	100
XV	Paper and printing	M	14,153	4,525	29,608	19,899	9,195	152,262	38,299	34,508	302,449
		%	4·68	1·50	9·79	6·58	3·04	50·34	12·66	11·41	100
		F	2,139	1,486	2,205	37,624	3,688	55,326	26,085	31,832	160,385
		%	1·33	0·93	1·37	23·46	2·30	34·50	16·26	19·85	100
		Total	16,292	6,011	31,813	57,523	12,883	207,588	64,384	66,340	462,834
		%	3·52	1·30	6·87	12·43	2·78	44·85	13·91	14·33	100
XVI	Other manufacturing industries	M	1,961	5,085	14,471	8,228	6,528	66,764	15,112	25,388	143,537
		%	1·37	3·54	10·08	5·73	4·55	46·51	10·53	17·69	100
		F	104	1,421	1,029	18,560	1,840	34,783	21,134	18,892	97,763
		%	0·11	1·45	1·05	18·98	1·88	35·58	21·62	19·32	100
		Total	2,065	6,506	15,500	26,788	8,368	101,547	36,246	44,280	241,300
		%	0·86	2·70	6·42	11·10	3·47	42·08	15·02	18·35	100
XVII	Building and contracting	M	15,028	4,707	46,227	22,351	46,712	711,425	51,582	304,509	1,202,541
		%	1·25	0·39	3·84	1·86	3·88	59·16	4·29	25·32	100
		F	48	290	1,699	25,976	62	1,121	2,299	2,106	33,601
		%	0·14	0·86	5·06	77·31	0·18	3·34	6·84	6·27	100
		Total	15,076	4,997	47,926	48,327	46,774	712,546	53,881	306,615	1,236,142
		%	1·22	0·40	3·88	3·91	3·78	57·64	4·36	24·80	100

Order	Industry		1A	1B	Occupational class 2	3	4	5	6	7	Total
XVIII	Gas, electricity and water	M	12,018	4,794	15,865	30,688	7,639	90,996	56,362	82,871	301,233
		%	3·99	1·59	5·27	10·19	2·54	30·21	18·71	27·51	100
		F	56	585	252	20,755	64	217	3,889	3,275	29,093
		%	0·19	2·01	0·87	71·34	0·22	0·75	13·37	11·26	100
		Total	12,074	5,379	16,117	51,443	7,703	91,213	60,251	86,146	330,326
		%	3·66	1·63	4·88	15·57	2·33	27·61	18·24	26·08	100
XIX	Transport and communication	M	5,023	25,462	60,849	115,325	47,812	297,036	569,783	221,974	1,343,264
		%	0·37	1·90	4·53	8·59	3·56	22·11	42·42	16·52	100
		F	83	1,239	8,496	84,232	5,533	3,279	69,848	13,701	186,411
		%	0·04	0·66	4·56	45·19	2·97	1·76	37·47	7·35	100
		Total	5,106	26,701	69,345	199,557	53,345	300,315	639,631	235,675	1,529,675
		%	0·33	1·75	4·53	13·05	3·49	19·63	41·81	15·41	100
XX	Distributive trades	M	3,471	17,421	556,623	81,793	11,389	108,941	474,094	124,493	1,378,225
		%	0·25	1·26	40·39	5·93	0·83	7·90	34·40	9·03	100
		F	248	7,555	166,480	214,558	613	24,144	568,108	39,941	1,021,647
		%	0·02	0·74	16·30	21·00	0·06	2·36	55·61	3·91	100
		Total	3,719	24,976	723,103	296,351	12,002	133,085	1,042,202	164,434	2,399,872
		%	0·15	1·04	30·13	12·35	0·50	5·55	43·43	6·85	100
XXI	Insurance, banking and finance	M	5,181	475	72,009	151,586	796	9,058	9,072	15,477	263,654
		%	1·97	0·18	27·31	57·49	0·30	3·44	3·44	5·87	100
		F	89	186	4,324	117,344	98	123	6,544	10,052	138,760
		%	0·06	0·13	3·12	84·57	0·07	0·09	4·72	7·24	100
		Total	5,270	661	76,333	268,930	894	9,181	15,616	25,529	402,414
		%	1·31	0·16	18·97	66·83	0·22	2·28	3·88	6·34	100
XXII	Public administration and defence	M	75,602	31,225	104,776	146,103	17,938	157,863	582,914	204,550	1,320,971
		%	5·72	2·36	7·93	11·06	1·36	11·95	44·13	15·48	100
		F	2,756	15,317	19,150	140,079	598	2,921	38,666	27,973	247,460
		%	1·11	6·19	7·74	56·61	0·24	1·18	15·63	11·30	100
		Total	78,358	46,542	123,926	286,182	18,536	160,784	621,580	232,523	1,568,431
		%	5·00	2·97	7·90	18·25	1·18	10·25	39·63	14·83	100
XXIII	Professional services	M	150,465	195,071	26,694	57,889	1,721	33,304	81,875	19,504	566,523
		%	26·56	34·43	4·71	10·22	0·30	5·88	14·45	3·44	100
		F	22,202	414,659	12,417	130,941	211	2,777	161,618	45,252	790,077
		%	2·81	52·48	1·57	16·57	0·03	0·35	20·46	5·73	100
		Total	172,667	609,730	39,111	188,830	1,932	36,081	243,493	64,756	1,356,600
		%	12·73	44·95	2·88	13·92	0·14	2·66	17·95	4·77	100

Order	Industry		Occupational class								
			1A	1B	2	3	4	5	6	7	Total
XXIV	Miscellaneous services	M	5,508	28,994	129,192	16,690	1,969	98,132	305,036	38,810	624,331
		%	0·88	4·64	20·69	2·67	0·32	15·72	48·86	6·22	100
		F	1,209	26,569	112,556	69,544	263	58,274	899,306	59,178	1,226,899
		%	0·10	2·17	9·17	5·67	0·02	4·75	73·30	4·82	100
		Total	6,717	55,563	241,748	86,234	2,232	156,406	1,204,342	97,988	1,851,230
		%	0·36	3·00	13·06	4·66	0·12	8·45	65·06	5·29	100
	ALL	M	358,249	435,049	1,614,416	902,048	461,947	4,249,753	3,889,426	1,835,941	13,746,829
		%	2·61	3·16	11·74	6·56	3·36	30·91	28·29	13·35	100
		F	31,326	494,733	365,885	1,255,782	73,347	797,095	2,643,663	485,340	6,147,171
		%	0·51	8·05	5·95	20·43	1·19	12·97	43·01	7·90	100
		Total	389,575	929,782	1,980,301	2,157,830	535,294	5,046,848	6,533,089	2,321,281	19,894,000
		%	1·96	4·67	9·95	10·85	2·69	25·37	32·84	11·67	100

163

APPENDIX C

DERIVATION OF DATA ON INCREASES IN CERTAIN PROFESSIONS BETWEEN 1951 AND 1960

Since the Occupational Tables of the 1961 Population Census were not yet available, we had to use other sources to get an idea of changes between 1951 and 1960. These refer to particular sections of the relevant occupations and, because of their less embracing nature, cannot be reconciled with numbers shown in the Census. However, they do afford a good guide to the rate of growth of the occupations concerned.

Doctors

The Report of the Royal Commission on Doctors' and Dentists' Remuneration, 1957-1960, Cmnd 939 (H.M. Stationery Office, 1960), gives hospital staff, presumably 1 July 1951 (p. 56). General practitioners (principals) on the National Health Service list are given annually for Scotland (from 31 December 1951) and England and Wales (from 1 July 1952) in *Annual Abstract of Statistics, 1957*, (H.M. Stationery Office, 1957), pp. 60-1. To approximate to numbers in England and Wales in 1951, it was assumed that the rate of change between 1952 and 1953 had also been effective between 1951 and 1952. Numbers were extended to 1958 from the Royal Commission report, pp. 56 and 106, and projected to 1960 *pari passu* with whole-time hospital medical staff (*Annual Abstract of Statistics, 1961*, pp. 55-6) plus numbers of principals on National Health Service lists, England, Wales and Scotland.

Dentists

Dentists in general practice on general list: *Annual Abstract of Statistics, 1957*, pp. 60-1 and *1961*, pp. 55-6.

Engineers and scientists

A report of the Advisory Council on Scientific Policy, *Scientific and Engineering Manpower in Great Britain, 1959*, Cmnd 902 (H.M. Stationery Office, 1959), p. 16, gives stock in 1956 and 1959. A further report, *The Long-Term Demand for Scientific Manpower*, Cmnd 1490 (H.M. Stationery Office, 1961), pp. 22-3, gives those qualifying at universities and technical colleges or gaining admission to professional institutions, 1955/6 to 1958/9, with estimates for later years, and estimated losses 1956 to 1959. It was assumed that net intake for 1951/5 was the same each year as in 1956, since it was only from 1955/6 that there was an increase in the number of full-time students in science and technology faculties in universities in Great Britain.

Full-time students in science and technology faculties

	1950/1	1954/5
Pure science	17,168	17,327
Technology	10,591	10,586

The stock in 1951 was estimated accordingly. For 1960, estimated intake for 1959/60 (Cmnd 1490, p.22) less estimated loss for 1959, was added to stock for 1959 (shown in Cmnd 902).

Nurses and midwives

Whole-time and part-time, employed in National Health Service, from *Annual Abstract of Statistics* for relevant years.

Others in medicine

Whole-time, hospital service, from *Annual Abstract of Statistics*.

Teachers

Full-time, Great Britain, *Annual Abstract of Statistics, 1960*, table 93, p. 84 and table 124, p. 99.

Laboratory technicians and draughtsmen

Table 7 of the *Census 1951, England and Wales: Industry Tables* (H.M. Stationery Office, 1957) shows that in the chemical, metal and engineering industries, laboratory technicians formed 0·87 per cent and draughtsmen and design technicians 2·00 per cent of all those employed in those industries. A Ministry of Labour survey in 1960 showed 1·36 per cent for laboratory technicians and 4·01 per cent for design and drawing office staff[1]. These percentages have been applied to the Ministry's estimates for total manpower in this group of industries for the relevant years. The Ministry's sample was limited to firms with 100 or more employees and three-quarters of the firms approached had over 3,000 workers each. It seems probable, for this reason, that the sample somewhat overstates the proportion of laboratory and drawing office staff.

[1] *Ministry of Labour Gazette*, vol. 68, no. 12, December 1960 p. 464 *et. seq.*

INCOME DISTRIBUTION, 1911/12 AND 1958/9 (TABLE 24)

For 1958/9, the figures are derived from table 63 of the *103rd Report of the Commissioners of H.M. Inland Revenue for the year ended 31st March 1960*, Cmnd 1258 (H.M. Stationery Office, 1961). This gives a classification in thirteen ranges of Schedule E income from the principal source before the deduction of National Insurance contributions and other allowable expenses. It relates to individuals for whom pay-as-you-earn cards have been issued and thus accounts separately for wives and husbands even though they may be assessed as one unit. But it excludes cases with annual remuneration of below £190: that is, those for whom no tax deduction card was issued because their weekly or monthly pay never rose to the annual rate of £190, and whose weekly or monthly rate was at or above this level, but who did not work long enough during the year to earn £190.

Thus the number accounted for in the Inland Revenue table is less than the total number of employees estimated from the count of National Insurance cards. This showed for Great Britain in May 1958:

	Thousands
Males	14,220
Females	7,600
Total	21,820

To these must be added 600,000 men and 14,000 women in the armed forces[1]. The difference between the total from Inland Revenue table 63 and that from the card count approximates to the number of employees who earned below £190 in the year.

From the data in the Inland Revenue table 63, 400,000 Northern Irelanders had to be eliminated. Their average income, derived from the data in Inland Revenue table 60, was £445, compared with £514 for Scotland, £562 for England and Wales and £557 for the United Kingdom. They were extracted on the assumption that their distribution between the ranges accorded with that for the United Kingdom lowered by 20 per cent.

The Inland Revenue table includes an unspecified number of retired people in receipt of pensions of £190 or more from their ex-employers. Thus table 24 underestimates the total number of employees (1,820,000) who earned less than £190 in the year. We also have no record of and make no allowance for employees whose earnings were not declared and who were not insured.

[1]See *Ministry of Labour Gazette*, vol. 67, no. 2, February 1959, p. 43 and vol. 66, no. 7, July 1958, p. 261.

M

In 1911/12 only 451,000 employees out of a total of 16,658,000 paid income tax, so that the income distribution for those below this level (£160 per year) had to be constructed from earnings data from other sources. These were:

(a) The Board of Trade earnings and hours inquiry of 1906[1], embracing manual workers in the following industries: textiles; clothing; building and woodworking; public utility services; agriculture (1907); metal, engineering and shipbuilding; railways, paper and printing; pottery, bricks, glass and chemicals; food, drink and tobacco; miscellaneous trades. For all of these except agriculture, earnings were analysed by sex, adult and juvenile in shilling ranges, so that there was no obstacle to the construction of a frequency distribution. For agriculture, only average earnings for men by county were given. This gives a fairly wide dispersion about the average, but the effect must be to compress the range of earnings.

(b) The dispersion of coalminers (who were not included in the earnings census) was estimated from the data for occupational earnings per shift for June 1914 given by Finlay A. Gibson in *The Coal Mining Industry of the United Kingdom*[2].

(c) Domestic servants were allocated to income ranges on the basis of the information presented by W. T. Layton, supported by what scraps of information can be collected from household accounts, government estimates and the Booth and Rowntree surveys[3].

(d) For other occupations below the tax level, representative of a group of about 1,730,000 employees, we use the estimates presented in a report to the British Association in 1910[4].

The numbers in each range for each industry were raised so that the total equalled that given in the Census Industry Tables for 1911[5]. The aggregates for the industries included in the 1906 earnings inquiry, with agriculture and coal, were then raised again so that, together with domestic servants, shop-assistants, clerks and others included in the Cannan Committee investigation, the totals for males and females equal those shown for employees in the 1911 Population Census.

[1] *Report of an Enquiry by the Board of Trade into Earnings and Hours of Labour of Workpeople of the United Kingdom in 1906*, 8 parts, Cd 4545, 4844, 5086, 5196, 5460, 5814, 6053, 6556 (H.M. Stationery Office, 1909-13).

[2] *Op. cit.* (Cardiff, The Western Mail, 1922).

[3] W. T. Layton, 'Changes in the Wages of Domestic Servants during Fifty Years', *op. cit.*, *Journal of the Royal Statistical Society*, September 1908, p. 515; C. Booth, *Life and Labour of the People in London* (London, Macmillan, 1902); B. S. Rowntree, *Poverty: A Study of Town Life* (London, Macmillan, 1902).

[4] 'The Amount and Distribution of Income (other than wages) Below the Tax Exemption Limit in the United Kingdom', *loc. cit.* The Committee, which collected information from a large number of employers, included Professors Cannan (in the chair), Bowley and Edgeworth.

[5] *Census of England and Wales, 1911: vol. X, Occupations and Industries*, Cd 7018, 7019 (H.M. Stationery Office, 1913-14).

The 1906 earnings were raised by 4 per cent to approximate to the level of 1911/12, this being about the average rise in industrial wage rates. Agricultural earnings were raised by 2·66 per cent (the approximate rise in rates between 1907 and 1911/12). Coal earnings were reduced to 91·18 per cent of their 1914 level (to offset the rise in rates between 1911/12 and 1914).

But the data for 1958/9 represent actual earnings of individual employees for the year, so they include payments for overtime and are net of deductions for short-time and periods of unemployment.

The tax figures for 1911/12 are, of course, directly comparable with those for the later year; clerks, domestic servants, agricultural workers and shop-assistants enjoyed stability of employment, so that their annual average was probably not far from 52 times their weekly average; but the same did not apply to manual workers in other industrial sectors.

Allowance for overtime and short-time presents no difficulty, for the 1906 reports present two sets of tables; one refers to workers who worked the full standard week, and the other to all workers, however many hours they worked in the week. It is the latter that we have used in compiling the income distribution.

Unpaid holidays present a greater difficulty. Most employers, the 1906 reports tell us, paid their foremen for public or annual holidays; some, especially in the printing, soap and candle, food, drink and tobacco industries, paid all their workers; but the general rule was that holidays were unpaid. They amounted, in all, to about two weeks out of fifty-two. In calculating annual income, weekly earnings were thus multiplied by 50 and not by 52.

The final adjustment concerned unemployment. Trade union unemployment benefit funds returned an average rate of 3·56 per cent for the period April 1911 to March 1912, which is reduced to 2·9 per cent if the effect of the coal stoppage of March 1912 is eliminated. Unemployment for all insured workers was calculated only from September 1912[1]. For the last four months of that year, it was 2·17 times the trade union rate. In chapter III we saw that the rate for all insured workers approximates to that for semi-skilled workers while, in 1931, the rate for the unskilled is 1·78 times that for the semi-skilled.

These ratios give an approximation adequate for this rough calculation. According to them, unemployment in 1911 would have been:

	Percentages
Skilled workers	3
Semi-skilled workers	6·5
Unskilled workers	11·5

[1]The comparison is rough, for the trade union figures refer to a limited number of occupations and the National Insurance figures to a limited number of industries. However, engineering, building and woodworking are heavily represented in each.

APPENDICES

The income ranges for those covered in the 1906 inquiries were then reduced by 11.5 per cent for the first range; 6.5 per cent for the next range for women and for the next two ranges for men and 3 per cent for the remaining ranges.

In all relevant cases, the money equivalent of board and lodging or payment in kind was included in earnings.

EMPLOYEE INCOME AFTER TAX (TABLE 25)

The Inland Revenue tables show personal income before and after tax, but, because tax is assessed on income units, not individuals, they cannot isolate employee incomes from other personal incomes after tax.

For 1911/12, this operation could be done fairly simply (if crudely) because the income level at which tax was paid was high (£160) and must have largely been earned by married men. Beyond £160, tax was 1s. 2d. in the £, with a maximum 9d. per £ of income up to £2,000 of income, and 1s. for incomes above £2,000 to £3,000. Supertax was charged when income exceeded £5,000 at 6d. in the £ on the amount by which the income exceeded £3,000.

On incomes up to £500, an abatement was allowed of £10 for each child under the age of 16. On Schedule E incomes, this averaged £3·56 per assessment. Insurance abatement averaged £7·57 per assessment.

On this basis, employee income in the average for each range was taxed, curves plotted on semi-logarithmic paper and the deciles, etc., in table 25, read.

For 1958/9, income after tax was calculated as a percentage of income before tax for each range of personal income before tax (table 64 of the *103rd Inland Revenue Report, loc. cit.*). But tax on earned income is lower than that on unearned income, so that on earned income it was 8·35 per cent in 1958/9, and on all personal income it was 12·1 per cent. Personal income after tax was proportionately raised to approximate employee income after tax, a curve plotted and the decile, etc., points read off.

M*

DISPERSION OF MANUAL EARNINGS

The Ministry of Labour's 1960 report on the dispersion of manual earnings[1] is confined to men aged 21 and over and women aged 18 and over, while those for the earlier years also give information for juveniles[2]. It also excludes part-time workers[3], and 'full-time workers who for any reason, e.g., sickness, accident, voluntary absenteeism, worked in total less than their recognized hours in the pay-week of the return'[4]. However, full-time workers working overtime were included, so that the average hours worked by men were 48·0 at a time when the standard week was between 42 and 43 hours. For women, on the other hand, hours averaged 40·5, indicating that 'normal hours' for women are, on average, substantially below those for men. The *Gazette* comments, 'numbers of employers, partly because of the shortage of labour, are prepared to accept the service of many of their women workers on such terms'[4].

It seems reasonable to suppose that the chronic labour shortage of the war and after should have made employers more willing to adapt hours of work so as to make it possible for more women to take employment, but the phenomenon antedates the war. In 1938, 31·2 per cent of the women covered by the inquiry worked less than 44 hours, and average hours for women were 43·5, compared with 47·7 for men. If women part-time workers are included in the 1960 average (those regularly working 30 hours or less) the average for women in manufacturing industry is reduced to 38·0 hours, so that, on average, the gap between men's and women's working hours has increased considerably since 1938.

What the position was before that, it is impossible to tell, because hours data were not shown separately for men and women. However, in 1906, about 20 per cent of the workers in the clothing trades for whom particulars relating to hours were obtained were working a normal week of less than 50 hours, at a time when the standard week was about 55. In 1924, the percentage normally working less than 44 hours, when the standard week was 47 or 48 hours, was 16·2.

In addition, hours of work may be cut by short-time or absence for some other cause, or prolonged by overtime. In 1906, short-time was more usual

---

[1]*Ministry of Labour Gazette*, vol. 69, nos. 4 and 6, April and June 1961.
[2]Adult men in 1906 were those aged 20 and over; in 1938 and 1960, those aged 21 and over.
[3]Here embracing all those who 'by agreement regularly work less than the full normal hours of their class'.
[4]*Ministry of Labour Gazette*, April 1961, p. 138.

M2*

than overtime, but the distribution of earnings is given both for workers who worked the normal week and for all workers, including those on overtime or short-time. For 1938, distribution is given in range of hours: under 44, 44 and under 47, 47 to 48, and over 48.

172

DERIVATION OF PROFESSIONAL EARNINGS DATA
(TABLE 30)

1. BARRISTERS, SOLICITORS, DENTISTS, GENERAL MEDICAL PRACTITIONERS

For 1913/14 and 1922/3, we have material derived by the department of Inland Revenue from tax returns. Initially, this was collected for the Committee on Pay, etc. of State Servants (Anderson Committee, *loc. cit.*), whose report was made in July 1923.

The analysis was based on all the assessments for each profession in selected areas without distinction between Schedule D (income of independent practitioners) or Schedule E (salaries)[1].

One difficulty in using income tax returns for pre- and post-World War I comparisons is the comparatively high exemption limit of the first period, so that the group represented in the tax returns of 1913/14 is from a higher segment of the pay hierarchy than that of the post-war years. Thus a comparison of median, quartiles, etc., gives the impression that rates have risen less than they really have. The Inland Revenue statistician accordingly made a further calculation: he compared the incomes at particular points of rank order, correcting the figure of rank for the post-war year only by the percentage increase in male population. Thus he compared the income 200th in rank in 1913/14 (in the selected areas) with the 206th in rank in 1922/3 (in the same area) and so on.

The *Occupation Tables* of the 1921 Census would not have been available at that time, but a finer adjustment can now be made by using the change in numbers for each profession instead of in the male population as a whole. The number of doctors increased from 26,086 in 1911 to 26,264 in 1921. The median would have come at 13,043/4 in 1911 and 13,132/3 in 1921. Likewise, the 1,000th (from top or bottom) in 1911 would be appropriately paired with the 1,007th in 1921. The other professions were treated similarly.

In using the material, thus adjusted, for 1913/14 and 1922/3, we assume that numbers did not change much, or changed *pari passu*, between the census years and the tax years, and that numbers in the relevant professions in the sample areas did not change much as a result of migration to other areas.

We have sufficient data to construct frequency distributions for both years. This was plotted on a semi-logarithmic graph and from this the readings shown in table 29 were made.

[1] In 1913/14, Schedule E was limited to the salaries of officials of the government, public bodies and public companies. Other employees above the exemption limit were assessed under Schedule D. For 1922/3, all employees were assessed under Schedule E.

For 1955/6, we have the survey conducted for the Royal Commission on Doctors' and Dentists' Remuneration, 1957-1960, and described in Appendix A of the *Report*. A detailed statistical analysis is given in the *Supplement to Report: Further Statistical Analysis*, Cmnd 1064 (H.M. Stationery Office, 1960). Like the earlier figures, these represent income net of expenses as accepted by the tax authorities.

For medical and dental practitioners we have, in addition, information for the years 1935-7. See 'Tables and notes extracted from the Report made to the British Medical Association by Professor A. Bradford Hill', Appendix II, p. 17, of the *Report of the Inter-Departmental Committee on Remuneration of General Practitioners*, Cmd 6810 (H.M. Stationery Office, 1946) and the *Report of the Inter-Departmental Committee on the Remuneration of General Dental Practitioners*, Cmd 7402 (H.M. Stationery Office, 1948).

2. THE CLERGY

For the Church of England, a sample of 300 taken from *Crockford's Clerical Directory* (the first 100, the last 100 and 100 whose names began with the letter L).

For the Presbyterian Church of Scotland, a sample of 700 taken from the *Church of Scotland Year-Book* for 1912, 1926 and 1957, and *Reports of the General Assembly of the Church of Scotland* for 1936. The sample consisted of the first 300, the last 300 and 100 from the middle.

Comparisons over time of the income of the parochial clergy also require some qualifications. Until 1927 a retired clergyman of the Church of England could claim up to a third of the income of his last living and an incumbent might be in the unfortunate position of having to pay a pension to one (or possibly more!) retired predecessors. However, not all those who were entitled to a pension in fact claimed it, and not all those who claimed would necessarily have claimed the full amount. As there were approximately 900 retired clergymen in 1912[1] to something over 12,000 in office, a deduction of 2 per cent from the 1912 stipend would probably be adequate to cover this item. The figure for 1912 shown in table 54 is therefore 2 per cent below the estimate from *Crockford*, while figures for 1924 are given in *Crockford* net of pension payments.

The figures for 1957 were net of dilapidation payments, those for the other years were not. Up to 1924 every incumbent was responsible for repairs to his parsonage house and was supposed to leave it in a good state of repair. This arrangement was replaced by a scheme whereby a five-yearly survey was carried out by the diocesan surveyor who assessed the cost of the work needing to be done. The parson then paid an annual amount based on this assessment. Basically the same scheme operates today but in about three cases out of four

[1]The 1911 Census shows 941.

the parochial church councils make good the outlay to their clergy. In order to make the 1957 figures more nearly comparable with the figures for the other years in this respect the sum of £45[1] has been added to the average income figure derived from the sample from *Crockford's Directory*.

For purposes of inter-professional comparison, a further adjustment must be made for business expenses—stationery, postage, travelling, official hospitality, etc.—that a vicar must pay from his own income. The Church Assembly estimated these expenses to have amounted, in 1958/9, to about £122 for a vicar in the suburbs of London and £156 for a country vicar[2]. Estimates for the earlier years are not available, and the best that can be done is to deflate the 1958/9 figures by the cost of living index[3] assuming for that year a weighted average for town and country of about £135[4]. The *Crockford* figures for the various years have been reduced as follows:

	£
1912	32
1924	56
1935	46
1957	131

3. ARMY OFFICERS

Ten-year scale averages for those living in, with major-generals, majors and lieutenants weighted as follows:

1913	1 : 15 : 45
1924 and 1936	1 : 11 : 49
1955 and 1960	1 : 30 : 30

4. ENGINEERS

For 1923, from an inquiry by the Society of Technical Engineers reported in the International Labour Office, *Engineers and Chemists: Status and Employment in Industry*[5]. Average salaries are shown at 15 age points in the range 22 to 50. 1913/14: the average for those aged under 45 and 45 to 54 for 1923, reduced *pari passu* with the average for executive engineers in the Post Office Engineering Department and Lloyd's engineering surveyors.

For 1955/6, average from the Royal Commission on Doctors' and Dentists' Remuneration (the Pilkington Commision), *loc. cit.* For 1959/60, from the *Professional Engineer*, January 1961. The arithmetic mean is not given for this year, so the same relationship has been assumed between it and the average of the quartiles and median and this raised accordingly to represent the arithmetic mean.

[1] *Annual Report* of the Church Commissioners for England, 1957-58 (London, 1958).
[2] *The Stipends and Expenses of the Clergy* (1959).
[3] See notes to table 49.
[4] That is assuming weights of 5 for numbers at work in towns to 3 in the country.
[5] Studies and Reports, series L, no. 1 (Geneva, 1924).

5. CHEMISTS

The average for 1955/6 as shown in the Pilkington Report. This has been reduced for earlier years *pari passu* with relatives for those aged 20 to 40. Earlier years are from censuses of the Royal Institute of Chemistry for 1938/9 and 1930/1[1]. 1913/14: average for 1930/1 reduced *pari passu* with Civil Service analysts, 2nd class.

[1]*Institute of Chemistry Journal and Proceedings*, part 3, 1931, p. 197 and part 2, 1939, p. 207.

176

DERIVATION OF MANAGERS' AND ADMINISTRATORS' EARNINGS

For the years 1913/14 and each year from 1920/1 to 1924/5, we have the extracts from tax returns made by the Inland Revenue initially for the Anderson Committee[1]. This enables us to compare the income of employees in various industries who were receiving £200 and £500 in 1913/14 with employees in the same rank order (by level of pay) in the same collections of companies in the later years[2]. For example, in coal, metals and engineering, the individual at £500 in 1913/14 was ranked 1,982nd in the salary hierarchy. In the same companies in 1924/5, the 1,982nd highest paid employee was getting £1,195.

In the returns we are given additional information, including the average income of those in the sample who were getting more than £2,000 in 1913/14 and the average pay for the same number (counting from the top) in 1924/5; and also the rank position of individuals at £2,000 and £1,000 in 1913/14 and the income of the individuals in the same rank positions in the later years.

---

[1]See Appendix G above.

[2]In 1909/10, the Cannan Committee, in 'The Amount of Distribution of Income (other than wages) below the Income-Tax Exemption Limit in the United Kingdom', *loc. cit.*, calculated that only about 94,000 out of 483,000 clerks were above the income tax exemption level of £160. Thus it is probable that most employees in industry at £200 in 1913/14 were employed in some sort of managerial or managerial/professional capacity.

INDEX

n. = footnote

Abel-Smith, Brian, 69
Accountant, chief, 75–6
Accountants, Civil Service, 66
Acrobats, 17
Actors, 17 *et seq.*, 121
Administrators, *see* Managers and admini-
   strators
Advertising agents, 23
Advisory Council on Scientific Policy, 163
Agricultural labourers, workers, 13, 14, 31,
   33, 34, 36, 91 *et seq.*, 108, 113 n., 115,
   122, 148, 167
Agricultural machine drivers, 29, 30
Agricultural Wages Board, 100
Agriculture, 9, 20 *et seq.*, 35, 36, 39, 40,
   48, 92, 103, 126, 166, 167
Ainsworth, R. B., 56
Amalgamated Engineering Union, 153
Analysts, Civil Service, 66, 67
Anderson Committee, *see* Committee on
   Pay, etc., of State Servants
Aquinas, St Thomas, 148
Architects, 8, 14 *et seq.*, 65 n., 66
Armed services, 33
Armed services, other ranks, 34, 91
Auctioneers, 23
Australia, 12
Authors, *see* Writers

Baggagemen, 12
Bakers, 31, 32, 86 *et seq.*, 122
Bank clerks, 79, 81
Bank managers, 10, 24, 74
Bank tellers, 13 n.
Banking, 26, 117
Bargemen, 35
Barmaids, 131
Barristers, 62 *et seq.*, 67, 116, 118, 172
Battery chargers, 29
Bellerby, J. R., 93
Bendix, R., 139
Bishops, 65, 70, 154
Blacksmiths, 31, 86, 122
Board of Trade, 4, 6, 81, 91, 96, 97, 166
Boarding-house keepers, 19, 21
Boarding-houses, 20, 23
Boatmen, 35
Boiler attendants, 91
Boiler firemen and stokers, 38
Bookbinders, 89
Book-keepers, 13 n., 24 *et seq.*, 130, 136,
   146

Boot and shoe clickers, 86, 88; closers,
   89, 90; boot and shoe industry, 119,
   131
Booth, C., 166
Bowley, A. L., 55, 74, 75, 78, 80, 93, 95,
   103 n., 111 *et seq.*, 120, 166 n.
Branch managers, 24
Brazil, 12
Bricklayers, 87, 88, 107, 112, 122, 130, 146
Brickmaking, 58, 59, 84, 120, 123, 166
Britain, J. A., 73 n.
British Medical Association, 1, 126
British Transport Commission, 78, 88,
   92, 98
Brokers, agents, 23, 73
Buffers and polishers, 86
Building, 20, 39, 40, 48, 57 *et seq.*, 84, 102,
   107, 119, 120, 123, 127, 147, 166, 167
   n.; craftsmen, 20, 29, 30, 32, 112 n.;
   workers, 31; labourers, 38, 112 n.,
   122, 127
Bus conductors, 9, 12, 35, 91, 92, 130, 131,
   146
Bus drivers, 9, 35, 91, 92, 94, 130, 146
Buyers, 23

Cabinet-makers, 31, 86
Cadbury, E., 89, 99, 100
Cadbury Brothers, 80, 85
Cairnes, J. E., 2, 135, 136, 138, 139, 141
Campion, H., 74, 75, 93, 95, 121, 123
Canada, 12
Cannan Committee, 78, 166, 176 n.
Cantillon, Richard, 135 *et seq.*
Caradog Jones, D., 95 n.
Caretakers, 12
Carpenters, 31, 87, 88, 119, 122, 130, 136
Carters, 91, 92
Cashiers, 13 n., 36, 130, 136, 146
Catering, 9, 20 *et seq.*, 33, 35, 36, 77, 130,
   131
Catering Wages Boards, 100
Caulkers, 86
Cement, 58
Central Statistical Office, 40, 47, 128
Ceramics, 39, 40, 48
Chain makers (goldsmiths), 89
Chamberlin, E. H., 135
Chancellor of the Exchequer, 70
Charrington and Co., 73
Chartered accountants, 10, 14 *et seq.*, 24
Chartered secretaries, 10

Charwomen, 37, 38, 100, 116
Chemicals, chemical industry, 18, 21 *et seq.*, 26 *et seq.*, 30, 36, 39, 40, 48, 58, 59, 84, 117, 120, 123, 164, 166
Chemists, 64 *et seq.*, 68, 71, 121, 175
Chiropodists, 10, 19
Church Commissioners, 174
Church of Scotland, 173
Civil Service, 12, 65 *et seq.*, 79 *et seq.*, 123, 124; administrative class, 10, 24, 70, 71, 78, 113, 116, 121, 124; executive class, 10, 24, 70, 71, 113, 116, 124; Pay Research Unit, 66, 83; clerical officers, 79, 124, 125, 146 n., 150 n.; Arbitration tribunal, 83
Cleaners, 99
Clergy, *see* Ministers of religion
Clerical Salaries Analysis, 26, 27, 124, 128
Clerical workers, clerks, 3 *et seq.*, 8, 10 *et seq.*, 24 *et seq.*, 39, 41 *et seq.*, 49, 78 *et seq.*, 104 *et seq.*, 109, 115, 116, 121, 123, 124, 127, 128, 130, 131, 142, 143, 146, 155 *et seq.*, 166, 167, 170
Clothing industry, 21, 22, 39, 40, 48, 49, 58, 59, 84, 85, 89, 102, 120, 123
Coachmakers, 86, 87
Coal, 117, 176
Coalface workers, 31, 32, 86 *et seq.*, 103
Coalminers, 113 *et seq.*, 125 n., 126, 148, 166, 167
Commercial travellers, 23
Committee of London Clearing Bankers, 74, 78
Committee on Pay, etc., of State Servants, 23, 62, 84, 116, 117, 172, 176
Committee on Remuneration of General Practitioners, Inter-Departmental, 63, 67, 173
Companies Act, 72
Company directors, 72, 73
Compositors, 87, 88, 120, 122
Confectioners, 86
Construction, *see* Building
Co-operative societies, 75, 95
Copeman, George, 77
Copyists, 24
Cost of living, *see* Prices
Cost of living bonus, 68 n., 112, 115, 120, 151
Costermongers, 38
Cotton frame tenters, 95
Craftsmen, self-employed, 30, 31
Crane drivers, 29
Crockford's Clerical Directory, 173, 174
Cutters, clothing, 86, 89, 90

Danckwerts Tribunal, 126

Dealers, wholesale and retail, 12, 23
Dentists, 14 *et seq.*, 62 *et seq.*, 67, 116, 118, 163, 172, 173
Design technicians, *see* Draughtsmen
Directory of Directors, 72
Dispatchers, 13 n.
Distributive trades, 20 *et seq.*, 24, 35, 36, 39, 40, 48, 74, 75, 117, 121
Dock labourers, 37, 38, 122, 127
Doctors, *see* Medical practitioners
Domestic servants, 33, 34, 36, 89, 94 *et seq.*, 115, 122, 125 n., 127, 167
Domestic service, 21, 35, 49
Douglas, Paul H., 152 n.
Drapery, 74
Draughtsmen, 10, 17, 18, 68, 69, 71, 121, 124, 125, 141 *et seq.*, 164
Draughtsmen's and Allied Technicians' Association, 69, 121, 124
Dressmakers, 31, 32, 85, 90, 91
Drink manufacture, *see* Food, drink, tobacco
Drivers, 10, 17, 18, 29, 69, 71, 122, 129, 130, 131

Earnings censuses, inquiries, 6 n., 27, 36, 51, 56 *et seq.*, 61, 100 *et seq.*, 125 n., 126, 128, 166 *et seq.*, 170, 171
Edgeworth, F. Y., 78 n., 166 n.
Editors, *see* Writers
Education, 8 *et seq.*, 136 *et seq.*, 154
Education, Ministry of, 69
Edwards, Alba M., 12
Electrical goods, 36
Electrical industry, 15
Electricians, 31, 87, 122, 130
Electricity supply, *see* Gas, electricity and water
Employers and proprietors, 3 *et seq.*, 10, 14, 19 *et seq.*, 39, 41 *et seq.*, 49, 125 n., 147, 155 *et seq.*
Employment exchanges, 93, 95, 99, 129
Engels, F., 137
Engine cleaners, 97
Engine drivers, 87, 88, 107, 108, 122
Engineering and Allied Employers' National Federation, 88, 92, 95, 98, 129, 146, 153
Engineering and shipbuilding, 9, 18, 21 *et seq.*, 26, 28, 30, 36, 39, 40, 48, 58, 59, 84, 88, 102, 115, 117, 118, 120, 123, 127, 129, 131, 153, 164, 166, 167 n., 176
Engineering craftsmen, 112, 125, 153; labourers, 112, 129, 153, 154
Engineering machinists, 91 *et seq.*, 153
Engineering officers, 17

Engineers, 8, 10, 14 *et seq.*, 64, 66, 67, 76 n., 163, 174
Engravers, 86
Erectors, 86, 130
Estate agents, 23
Expectation of life, 45

Farm bailiffs, 28
Farm labourers, *see* Agricultural labourers
Farmers, 13, 14, 19, 20
Financial services, 24, 26, 39, 40, 48, 49, 121
Financial Times, 73
Finishers, textile, 91
Firemen, 34
Fishermen, 34
Fitters, 8, 31, 86 *et seq.*, 106, 122, 129, 130, 146, 153, 154
Fogarty, Michael, 148
Folders (printing), 99
Food, drink, tobacco, 21, 39, 40, 48, 49, 58, 59, 84, 85, 102, 117, 120, 123, 131, 166, 167
Foremen, inspectors, supervisors, 3 *et seq.*, 9, 10, 14, 22, 27 *et seq.*, 39, 41 *et seq.*, 49, 81 *et seq.*, 102, 104 *et seq.*, 109, 116, 122, 123, 142, 143, 148, 152, 155 *et seq.*, 167
Foresters, 34
Foundry Workers, National Union of, 153
France, 11, 12
French polishers, 32, 86, 89
Furniture industry, 119

Gangers, 83, 84
Garages, 21
Gas, electricity and water, 39, 40, 48, 57, 84, 92, 120, 123, 166
General managers, 24
German Federal Republic, 11, 12
Gibson, Finlay A., 88, 166
Glass, D. V., 143
Glass industry, 58, 84, 120, 123, 166
Government industrial establishments, 57
Grain millers, 86
Gray, F. M., 95
Grinders and mixers, chemicals, 122
Grocery trade, 74, 75, 95
Guards, 87, 88
Guillebaud Committee, 128
Guinness, 98

Hairdressers, 29 *et seq.*
Hairdressing, 21
Hawkers, 38
Headmasters, 70
Health, Minister of, 126

Hewers and getters, coal, 29, 30, 122, 127
Higgs, Henry, 135
Higher clerical officers, 24
Hill, Sir Austin Bradford, 63, 67, 173
Holidays, 60, 61, 154, 167
Hosiery, 85, 89, 90
Hospital service, 18
Hotels, 20, 23, 24, 130, 131
Hours of work, 53, 56, 57, 60, 61, 113, 126, 170

Income tax, 112, 113, 117, 125, 126, 165 *et seq.*
Incorporation, 21, 22
India, 12
Industrial distribution, 39, 59
Industry Orders, 59
Inflation, 132, 150
Inland Revenue, 51, 62, 71 *et seq.*, 112, 117, 118, 126, 165 *et seq.*, 169, 172, 173, 176
Inspectors, *see* Foremen, inspectors, supervisors
Institute of Chemistry, 175
Institute of Office Management, 26, 78, 124, 128, 146
Institute of Personnel Management, 76 n., 77, 83
Institution of Works Managers, 76, 77
Insurance, 26, 117; managers, 10, 24; agents, 25
International Labour Office, 11, 174
International Standard Classification of Occupations, 11

Japan, 12
Jaques, Elliott, 148, 149
Jevons, Stanley, 135
Jewellers, 136
Jewkes, J., 95
Jointers' mates, 91
Journalists, *see* Writers
Judges, 65, 70, 154

Keynes, J. M., 135, 144
Klingender, F. D., 80
Korean war, 61

Laboratory assistants, technicians, 12, 17, 18, 68, 69, 121, 164
Labour, Ministry of, 3, 9, 15, 18, 51, 56, 75, 85, 88, 90, 93, 95, 111 *et seq.*, 118, 119, 120, 125 n., 126, 127, 128, 129, 145, 146, 149, 155, 164, 165, 170, 171
Labourers, *see* Unskilled manual workers
Laundries, 21, 36, 84, 85, 89, 95, 96, 120
Layton, W. T., 95, 166
Leather industry, 23, 24, 30, 39, 40, 48

Lees Smith, H. B., 78
Legal adviser, 66, 67
Legerdemain, professors of, 17
Lehmkuhl, A., 148
Letterpress assistants, 91
Librarians, 17, 68, 69, 71
Liepmann, Kate, 9
Lift attendants, 38
Lipset, S. M., 140
Lloyd's, 174
Local authorities, 57, 121
Lock-keepers, 35
London and Cambridge Economic Service, 55
Lorry-drivers' mates, 38
Lydall, H. F., 73 n.

Machine erectors, 8
Machine minders, 30
Machine-tool setters, 31, 122, 129, 130, 146
Machinists, clothing, 91, 94, 95
Maher, J. E., 152 n.
Maintenance workers, 30, 130
Malthus, T. R., 137
Managers and administrators, 3 et seq., 8, 10, 12, 14, 19, 22 et seq., 26, 39, 41 et seq., 49, 60, 66, 104 et seq., 122, 123, 128, 142, 143, 145, 147, 148, 152, 153, 155 et seq.
Manipulative workers, P.O., 35, 91, 116, 125
Manual workers, see Skilled manual workers; Semi-skilled manual workers; Unskilled manual workers
Manufacturing, manufacturing establishments, 21 et seq., 57, 59, 60, 92, 103, 121, 128, 147, 148
Marley, J. G., 74, 75, 93, 95, 121, 123
Marshall, Alfred, 2, 135, 136, 139
Marx, Karl, 135, 137
Masons, 87
Masseurs, 19
Matheson, M. C., 89, 99
Meat trade, 75
Mechanics, 31, 87, 122
Medical Officers, Civil Service, 66, 67
Medical practitioners, 9, 14, 15, 62 et seq., 67, 116, 118, 121, 163, 172, 173; auxiliaries, 18, 121, 164; medical service, subordinate, 19
Messengers, 12, 37, 38, 116
Metal goods n.e.s., 39, 40, 48
Metal manufacture, 9, 18, 23, 26, 28, 30, 39, 48, 58 et seq., 84, 102, 117, 118, 120, 123, 164, 166, 176
Metallurgists, 17, 121
Metal-makers, 29, 30, 32

Meux's Brewery, 97, 98
Mill, John Stuart, 2, 138
Millinery, 85, 89
Millwrights, 31, 86
Minimum list headings, 59
Mining, 20 et seq., 35, 39, 48, 57, 115, 127
Ministers of religion, 8, 14, 15, 64, 65, 121, 173, 174
Miscellaneous services, 39, 40, 48, 49
Mobility, 138 et seq., 147
Mortality ratio, 61 n.
Motor industry, 15
Motor mechanics, 31
Moulders, 86, 153
Mounters (jewellery), 86
Music teachers, 17, 19
Musicians, 17 et seq., 121

National Health Service, 16, 164
National income, 125
National Institute of Economic and Social Research, 71 n., 76
National Institute of Industrial Psychology, 10, 82, 85
National Insurance, 118, 119, 165
Navigating officers, aircrew, 17
New Survey of London Life and Labour, 78 et seq., 90, 95
Newspaper sellers, 38
Nove, Alec, 11
Nurses, 16 et seq., 69, 70, 121, 164

Occupational class, 3 et seq., 138 et seq., 155 et seq.
Office machine operators, 13 n., 24, 25, 27, 130
Office Management Association, see Institute of Office Management
Office managers, 24; workers, 36, 130, 131; cleaners, 38
Officers, armed services, 14 et seq., 64, 65, 174
Outfitting, 74
Overmen, coalmining, 28
Overtime, 60, 61, 167, 170, 171
Ozanne, R., 152 n.

Packers, 33, 34
Painters, 17, 19, 87
Painters, decorators, 31, 129, 130
Paper and printing industry, 39, 40, 48, 58, 59, 84, 85, 102, 117, 119, 120, 123, 166, 167
Participation rates, 43 et seq.
Partnership, 21, 126
Pastry-cooks, 32

Patternmakers, 86
Paviours, 35
Personnel managers, 77
Petty, Sir William, 135
Pharmacists, 17, 19
Photographers, 31
Physicists, 17
Physiotherapists, 19
Pilkington Commission, *see* Royal Commission on Doctors' and Dentists' Remuneration
Pilots, 17
Platelayers, 35
Platers, 86, 153
Plumbers, 31, 87, 119
Police, 29, 113 n., 154
Polishers (jewellery), 89
Population census, 1, 3, 6, 8, 12, 24, 27, 39, 43 n., 47, 48, 61, 120, 155, 164, 166, 172
Porters, 37, 38, 96, 97, 107, 136
Post Office, 85, 91, 92; Engineering Department, 84, 116, 121, 124, 125, 174
Postal and telegraph officers, 17
Postmen, 9, 12, 35, 91 *et seq.*, 113, 116, 124
Pottery, 58, 84, 120, 123, 131, 166
Pottery Manufacturers' Federation, British, 88, 90, 92
Pottery workers, 86, 88 *et seq.*, 94, 122, 131; packers, 91, 92, 94
Precision instruments, 39, 40, 48
Prices, 109, 110, 111, 114, 119, 120, 123, 132, 151, 152
Priestley Commission, *see* Royal Commission on the Civil Service, 1953–55
Process workers, 28, 130, 131
Producers, 17
Production managers, 77
Professional services, 39, 40, 48, 49
Professional workers, 60, 116, 126, 128, 137, 139, 143, 144, 147, 152, 163 *et seq.*, 172 *et seq.*
Professions, higher, 3 *et seq.*, 12, 14, 16 *et seq.*, 39, 41 *et seq.*, 49, 68 *et seq.*, 104 *et seq.*, 109, 121, 123, 126, 127, 128, 141, 142, 143, 155 *et seq.*
Professions, lower, 3 *et seq.*, 12, 14, 16 *et seq.*, 39, 41 *et seq.*, 49, 68 *et seq.*, 104 *et seq.*, 109, 121, 123, 127, 128, 141, 142, 143, 155 *et seq.*
Proprietors, *see* Employers and proprietors
Public administration, 39, 40, 48
Public houses, 20, 23, 24

Radio operators, 12
Rag sorters, cutters, 99
Railway clerks, 79

Railway firemen, 91, 92, 94, 108
Railway Pay Committee of Inquiry, 128
Railway platelayers, 91, 92, 94
Railwaymen, 113, 154
Railways, 24, 107, 117, 121, 126, 128, 166
Real income, 55, 56
Registrar General, 1, 61 n., 143 n., 155
Registrars, company, 24
Restaurants, 20, 23, 24
Retail distribution, 9, 77, 78, 103
Retail Food Wages Council, 93
Ricardo, David, 135
Riveters, 86, 153
Robinson, D., 152 n.
Ross, A. M., 152 n.
Routh, Guy, 116, 121, 142
Rowntree, B. S., 166
Royal Commission on Doctors' and Dentists' Remuneration, 61, 62, 67, 77, 163, 173, 174, 175
Royal Commission on the Civil Service, 1929–31, 23; 1953–55, 66, 83
Running-shed workers, 35

Sales managers, 23, 76
Salesmen, 8, 36
Scientists, 14 *et seq.*, 76 n., 163
Scott, W. R., 78
Sculptors, 17, 19
Secretaries, company, 24
Semi-skilled manual workers, 3 *et seq.*, 9, 14, 32 *et seq.*, 39, 41 *et seq.*, 49, 91 *et seq.*, 102 *et seq.*, 109, 118, 122, 123, 127, 128, 129, 130, 131, 133, 142, 143, 145, 147, 148, 155 *et seq.*, 167
Shann, G., 89, 99
Sheet metal-workers, 153
Shift superintendents, 76
Shift-charge engineers, 84
Shipbrokers, 23
Shipbuilding, *see* Engineering and shipbuilding
Shipbuilding drillers and hole cutters, 91; platers' helpers, 91
Shipping, 117
Shipping clerks, 13 n.
Shipwrights, 86, 129, 130
Shoemakers, 31
Shop assistants, 8, 36, 75, 89, 91 *et seq.*, 108, 113 n., 115, 122, 125 n., 130, 131, 146, 167
Shop Assistants, National Union of, 93, 95
Shop managers, 74, 75
Shopkeepers, 19
Shorthand-typists, 24 *et seq.*, 79, 130, 131, 146
Short-time, 57 n., 60, 61, 167

Showmen, 17
Signalmen, 87
Signwriters, 31, 89
Skill coefficients, 30, 39 *et seq.*
Skilled manual workers, 3 *et seq.*, 9, 10,
    14, 28 *et seq.*, 39, 41 *et seq.*, 49, 86
    et seq., 102 *et seq.*, 109, 122, 123, 127,
    129, 130, 131, 142, 144, 145, 147, 148,
    151, 155 *et seq.*, 167
Smith, Adam, 2, 136, 137, 138, 139, 141,
    147, 150
Social welfare workers, 17, 121
Society of Technical Engineers, 174
Solicitors, 62 *et seq.*, 66, 67, 116, 118, 172
Sorokin, P. A., 140
Sorters, P.O., 91, 116
Spain, 12
*Special Areas in England and Wales,
    Report of the Commissioners, 1937,* 127
Spinners, weavers, 32, 86, 89 *et seq.*, 122,
    130
Stamp, Sir J., 74, 80
Standard Industrial Classification, 35
Stationary engine drivers, 29
Station-masters, 121, 128
Stock Exchange Official Yearbook, 72
Stockbrokers, 23
Stokers, 38
Storekeepers, 33, 34; assistants, 38
Street traders, sellers, 37, 38
Supervisors, *see* Foremen, inspectors,
    supervisors
Surveyors, 14, 15, 65, 66
Sweden, 12
Switchboard attendants, 29

Tailors, 20, 86
Taxation, effect of, 21, 55, 56, 169, 172
Teachers, 8, 10, 16 *et seq.*, 69 *et seq.*, 116,
    118, 121, 141, 164
Teachers, National Union of, 1
Technical changes, 39
Telegraphists, 12, 33, 35
Telephonists, 9, 12, 33, 35, 91
Textile goods, 23, 30, 34
Textile industry, 9, 23, 24, 28, 30, 39, 49,
    58, 59, 84, 102, 117, 120, 123, 166;
    workers, 91, 113, 114
Textile printers, 86
Ticket examiners, collectors, 9, 13, 35, 91,
    92, 94
Titmuss, Richard, 73 n.
Tobacco, *see* Food, drink, tobacco
Tool setters, *see* Machine-tool setters
Trade boards, 75, 93, 95, 100
Trade unions, 1, 2, 110, 111, 118, 119, 139,
    149, 150 *et seq.*

Transport, 20, 21, 24, 39, 40, 48, 57, 92, 103
Transport, Ministry of, 88
Treasury, 23, 69; Permanent Secretary, 70
Trimmers, 35
Tugmen, 35
Tunnel-miners, 35
Turner and Newall, 73
Turners, 86, 129, 146, 153
Typists, 8, 10, 13, 24, 25, 27, 79, 116, 130,
    131, 146

Unemployment, 109 *et seq.*, 113 *et seq.*,
    118, 119, 120, 121, 122, 123, 125 n.,
    126, 127, 129 *et seq.*, 144, 145, 146,
    151, 152, 167
Unfilled vacancies, 129 *et seq.*, 146
Union International, 73
United Nations, 12
United States of America, 12 *et seq.*;
    Bureau of the Census, 12; Department
    of Labor, 12
Unskilled manual workers, 3 *et seq.*, 9, 11,
    14, 36 *et seq.*, 39, 41 *et seq.*, 49,
    96 *et seq.*, 102 *et seq.*, 109, 118, 119,
    122, 123, 127, 128, 130, 131, 132, 133,
    136, 139, 142, 143, 144, 145, 146, 147,
    148, 151, 155 *et seq.*, 167
Upholsterers, 89, 90
USSR, 11, 12

Vehicle manufacture, 21, 30, 39, 48, 130
Veterinary Officers, 68, 69, 71; inspectors,
    69
Veterinary surgeons, 17

Wages councils, 95, 100
Waiters, waitresses, 95, 122, 127, 131, 146
Warehousemen, 29
Watchmakers, 31, 136
Water supply, *see* Gas, electricity and
    water
Weavers, *see* Spinners, weavers
Wheelwrights, 87
Wicksteed, P., 2, 139, 141
Window-cleaners, 20
Wire weavers, 89
Wiremen, 87
Wood and cork industry, 39, 40, 48, 58, 84,
    102, 120, 123, 166, 167 n.
Woodworkers, 32
Woolworths, 73
Wootton, Barbara, 149
Works managers, 76, 77
Writers, 14 *et seq.*, 65

Zetterberg, H. L., 140

PUBLICATIONS OF THE
NATIONAL INSTITUTE OF ECONOMIC
AND SOCIAL RESEARCH

published by

THE CAMBRIDGE UNIVERSITY PRESS

Books published for the Institute by the Cambridge University Press are available through the ordinary booksellers. They appear in the three series below.

ECONOMIC & SOCIAL STUDIES

*I   *Studies in the National Income, 1924–1938*
Edited by A. L. BOWLEY. Reprinted with corrections, 1944. pp. 256. 15s. net.

*II   *The Burden of British Taxation*
By G. FINDLAY SHIRRAS and L. ROSTAS. 1942. pp. 140. 17s. 6d. net.

*III   *Trade Regulations and Commercial Policy of the United Kingdom*
By the RESEARCH STAFF OF THE NATIONAL INSTITUTE OF ECONOMIC AND SOCIAL RESEARCH. 1943. pp. 275. 17s. 6d. net.

*IV   *National Health Insurance: A Critical Study*
By HERMANN LEVY. 1944. pp. 356. 21s. net.

*V   *The Development of the Soviet Economic System: An Essay on the Experience of Planning in the U.S.S.R.*
By ALEXANDER BAYKOV. 1946. pp. 530. 45s. net.

*VI   *Studies in Financial Organization*
By T. BALOGH. 1948. pp. 328. 40s. net.

*VII   *Investment, Location, and Size of Plant: A Realistic Inquiry into the Structure of British and American Industries*
By P. SARGANT FLORENCE, assisted by W. BALDAMUS. 1948. pp. 230. 21s. net.

VIII   *A Statistical Analysis of Advertising Expenditure and of the Revenue of the Press*
By NICHOLAS KALDOR and RODNEY SILVERMAN. 1948. pp. 200. 25s. net.

*IX   *The Distribution of Consumer Goods*
By JAMES B. JEFFERYS, assisted by MARGARET MACCOLL and G. L. LEVETT. 1950. pp. 430. 50s. net.

*X   *Lessons of the British War Economy*
Edited by D. N. CHESTER. 1951. pp. 260. 30s. net.

*XI   *Colonial Social Accounting*
By PHYLLIS DEANE. 1953. pp. 360. 60s. net.

*XII   *Migration and Economic Growth*
By BRINLEY THOMAS. 1954. pp. 384. 50s. net.

*XIII   *Retail Trading in Britain, 1850–1950*
By JAMES B. JEFFERYS. 1954. pp. 490. 60s. net.

XIV   *British Economic Statistics*
By CHARLES CARTER and A. D. ROY. 1954. pp. 192. 30s. net.

XV   *The Structure of British Industry: A Symposium*
Edited by DUNCAN BURN. 1958. Vol. I. pp. 403. 55s. net. Vol. II. pp. 499. 55s. net.

XVI   *Concentration in British Industry*
By RICHARD EVELY and I. M. D. LITTLE. 1960. pp. 357. 63s. net.

XVII   *Studies in Company Finance*
Edited by BRIAN TEW and R. F. HENDERSON. 1959. pp. 301. 40s. net.

XVIII   *British Industrialists: Steel and Hosiery, 1850–1950*
By CHARLOTTE ERICKSON. 1959. pp. 276. 45s. net.

*At present out of print.

XIX The Antitrust Laws of the U.S.A.: A Study of Competition Enforced by Law
By A. D. NEALE. 1960. pp. 516. 50s. net.
XX A Study of United Kingdom Imports
By M. FG. SCOTT. 1963. pp. 284. 60s. net.
XXI Industrial Growth and World Trade
By ALFRED MAIZELS. 1963. pp. 586. 84s. net.
XXII The Management of the British Economy, 1945–60
By J. C. R. DOW. 1964. pp. 457. 63s. net.
XXIII The British Economy in 1975
By W. BECKERMAN AND ASSOCIATES. 1965. pp. 650. 80s. net.

OCCASIONAL PAPERS
*I The New Population Statistics
By R. R. KUCZYNSKI. 1942. pp. 31. 1s. 6d. net.
II The Population of Bristol
By H. A. SHANNON and E. GREBENIK. 1943. pp. 92. 17s. 6d. net.
*III Standards of Local Expenditure
By J. R. HICKS and U. K. HICKS. 1943. pp. 61. 4s. 6d. net.
IV War-time Pattern of Saving and Spending
By CHARLES MADGE. 1943. pp. 139. 12s. 6d. net.
*V Standardized Accountancy in Germany
By H. W. SINGER. Reprinted 1944. pp. 68. 6s. net.
*VI Ten Years of Controlled Trade in South-Eastern Europe
By M. MOMTCHILOFF. 1944. pp. 90. 12s. 6d. net.
*VII The Problem of Valuation for Rating
By J. R. HICKS, U. K. HICKS and C. E. V. LESER. 1944. pp. 90. 10s. 6d. net.
*VIII The Incidence of Local Rates in Great Britain
By J. R. HICKS and U. K. HICKS. 1945. pp. 64. 12s. 6d. net.
*IX Contributions to the Study of Oscillatory Time-Series
By M. G. KENDALL. 1946. pp. 76. 12s. 6d. net.
X A System of National Book-keeping Illustrated by the Experience of the Netherlands
By J. B. D. DERKSEN. 1946. pp. 34. 15s. net.
*XI Productivity, Prices and Distribution in Selected British Industries
By L. ROSTAS. 1948. pp. 199. 30s. net.
XII The Measurement of Colonial National Incomes: An Experiment
By PHYLLIS DEANE. 1948. pp. 173. 25s. net.
*XIII Comparative Productivity in British and American Industry
By L. ROSTAS. 1948. pp. 263. 30s. net.
*XIV The Cost of Industrial Movement
By W. F. LUTTRELL. 1952. pp. 104. 21s. net.
XV Costs in Alternative Locations: The Clothing Industry
By D. C. HAGUE and P. K. NEWMAN. 1952. pp. 73. 21s. net.
XVI Social Accounts of Local Authorities
By J. E. G. UTTING. 1953. pp. 81. 22s. 6d. net.
XVII British Post-war Migration
By JULIUS ISAAC. 1954. pp. 294. 40s. net.
*XVIII The Cost of the National Health Service in England and Wales
By BRIAN ABEL-SMITH and RICHARD M. TITMUSS. 1956. pp. 176. 27s. 6d. net.
XIX Post-war Investment, Location and Size of Plant
By P. SARGANT FLORENCE. 1962. pp. 51. 12s. 6d. net.
XX Investment and Growth Policies in British Industrial Firms
By TIBOR BARNA. 1962. pp. 71. 12s. 6d. net.
XXI Pricing and Employment in the Trade Cycle: A Study of British Manufacturing Industry, 1950–61
By R. R. NEILD. 1963. pp. 73. 15s. net.

*At present out of print.